# HELL NO!

## *The Great Heist*

# HELL NO!

## *The Great Heist*

**Steve Hanks**

Hell No! The Great Heist

ISBN: 979-8-9878999-5-3

First paperback edition February 2026

*Nearly all false doctrines taught today by Christians and cultists alike can be traced to the distortion of the meaning of Biblical words*

Hell No! The Great Heist

8

# A Preacher Kid's Wild Ride

For decades, I was the model believer. I embraced what the church taught me about eternal punishment. My daddy was a preacher. My granddaddy was a preacher.

Now when I was a little boy, my Sunday School teacher, Mrs. Collins scared the hell out of me. I remember one night I was lying in bed bawling my eyes out, scared to death I was going to go to hell. My dad rushes in: "What's wrong?"

"Daddy, I'm scared."

"About what?"

"About going to hell."

"Who told you that?"

"My Sunday School teacher…Mrs. Collins."

My preacher daddy was pissed. I don't know if he ever confronted her, but he didn't put that fear in my head. The church did.

And I believed it for decades. Never once questioned it. Never doubted.

But then the trap door opened.

Let me be crystal clear: It's way easier to ride along with 1500 years of theology. But after lots of study in the original languages, I bumped into some massive discoveries that'll leave you staring at the ceiling at 3 o'clock in the morning.

What you're about to hear challenges Christianity's most cherished doctrine. Not with liberal theology or wishful thinking. No! Emotional motivations are theological suicide. They'll throw you into a mud hole on the side of the road.

I dove in with a meticulous examination of the Hebrew and Greek. And what I found will electroshock your doctrines that need to be electroshocked.

Make no mistake: My bleeding-heart compassion that cries out "How could God ever do this" has nothing to do with what the Greek and Hebrew revealed. These discoveries come from pure linguistic analysis. They're not feel-good discoveries. although they feel good. They're not "How could God do this" motivations.

It was the Hebrew and the Greek that beat me into submission.

I followed wherever they led even when the trail led where I didn't want it to go.

These discoveries will knock you on your butt. Now I understand if your first instinct is to fight them. I did. I fought them like they were a nasty case of hives. I fought them until they backed me into a corner with no way out.

Well, it turns out that for fifty years I was sincere in my beliefs. But sincerely wrong.

So here's my challenge to you: Follow the evidence wherever it leads. Keep an open mind. **Wherever scripture leads.** And if I'm wrong, prove me wrong from the original languages. Not from what you've heard. Not from what the preacher says. Not from what your prayer group says. But from what the Hebrew and Greek says.

And if I'm right…if what I found in the original languages is actually what God said from the beginning…well, this might be the best news you've ever heard.

Let's find out together.

## STORYLINE

# Chapter 1

# The Four Fatal Cracks

Imagine standing before a magnificent 25-story theological building that has dominated the landscape of Christianity for nearly two millennia.

Its Gothic spires pierce the sky, its massive foundation stones bear the weight of countless doctrines, and millions of believers have found shelter within its walls. Seminaries have been built in its shadow. Denominations have risen and fallen defending its architecture. Wars have been fought over its blueprints.

But today...*there's a shift in the foundation.*

It starts quietly. Almost imperceptibly. Deep in the basement archives of an ancient seminary, surrounded by towers of crumbling manuscripts and the smell of centuries-old parchment, a scholar hunches over a desk lit by a single lamp. The flame flickers against stone walls that have witnessed a thousand theological debates.

He begins to examine the building's original blueprints, written in Hebrew and Greek, the uncorrupted raw truth that human traditions have suffocated for centuries. His fingers trace across the ancient text, leaving trails in the dust. He focuses a linguistic microscope on one tiny detail in the foundation: a single Hebrew phrase in Genesis 2:17. בְּיוֹם אֲכָלְךָ מִמֶּנּוּ מוֹת תָּמוּת *"In the day you eat from it, dying you shall die."*

The lamp flickers. Outside, thunder rumbles.

For 1500 years, theologians have wrestled with this puzzle: God said Adam would die '**in the day**' he ate the fruit. BUT Adam lived 930 more years.

They're unable to reconcile the timeline, so theologians faced a gut-wrenching choice: either scripture contains a contradiction, or *divine time works differently than* **human time**.

For centuries, theologians wrestled with this paradox like Jacob wrestled the angel. Desperate, sweating, refusing to let go without a blessing. They couldn't accept that God's Word contained error. And rightfully so! *That would topple everything.*

But they also couldn't explain why Adam lived 930 more years after God said he'd die **"in the day"** he ate.

The tension is unbearable. Seminary after seminary, council after council, theologians huddle in candlelit rooms, parsing Hebrew, debating meanings, searching for resolution. The very foundation of divine justice hangs in the balance. If God's first warning to humanity is wrong, or even imprecise, how could any of his words be trusted?

They needed an answer. Any answer. Even if they had to invent one. So they did.

Their solution?

**'Spiritual death.'**

*EUREKA!*

*Spiritual death!* —to justify why Adam didn't drop immediately dead right away! Or...at least why he didn't drop dead before dinner.

**CRISIS AVERTED! SCRIPTURE VINDICATED!**

*OR SO THEY THOUGHT...*

Suddenly...*the scholar freezes.* **His breath catches.**

*Wait... what IF 'b'yom' (in the day) doesn't mean 'instantly'...well, what else could it mean?*

He lunges for the Hebrew lexicon. His fingers tremble as they trace down the page. He discovers Moses had precise Hebrew words available if he meant "**immediately**" *pith'om* (פִּתְאֹם) means "**suddenly**," *maher* (מַהֵר) means "**quickly**," and *rega* (רֶגַע) means "**at once**."

**The evidence screams from the yellowed pages:** *Why didn't Moses choose any of these other Hebrew words that clearly mean* **suddenly, quickly,** *or* **at once**?

The scholar pushes back from the desk, ancient chair groaning. The answer should make every theologian pause: *If Moses had used **suddenly, quickly**, or **at once**,* there would be **NO QUESTION** that God meant *spiritual death.*

**But Moses didn't.**

Instead, Moses chooses בְּיוֹם *(b'yom)* "**in the day**."

Dust motes swirl in the lamplight as a hidden tremor stirs the ancient foundation.

> *Since there was no immediate death 'in the day,'*
> *generations of scholars have reasoned,*
> *'God must've meant **spiritual death**.'*

The scholar closes his eyes. He's troubled. Something claws at his memory, a half-remembered verse.

'In the day...' He mutters the phrase again. 'B'yom... in the day...'

His fingers drum against the ancient desk. *'Where else does scripture use this exact phrase? What am I missing?'*

Then, like a key turning in a long-locked door, another verse clicks: *'With the Lord one day is as a thousand years'* (2 Peter 3:8).

**The scholar's eyes snap open.**

He lunges for another manuscript, hands trembling. There! Psalm 90:4. **The same truth***: 'A thousand years in your sight are like a day that has just gone by.'*

His breath quickens.

If God's **'day'** equals *a thousand years...*

...and Adam dies at **930 YEARS...**

The scholar's hands shake as he pulls another ancient tome from the shelf, dust cascading like sand from a disturbed tomb.

*'I'm getting an idea...'*

His whisper echoes in the stone chamber.

The ancient walls seem to lean in as the scholar wrestles with 1500 years of certainty. The pieces of the puzzle are strewn before him, mere fragments of an ancient map.

*Suddenly, the pieces snap into place with startling clarity.*

The room seems to tilt.

**Adam lives 930 years.** *Within God's definition* of **"a day."** *Exactly as God said he would.*

*The penalty is fulfilled. PRECISELY AS GOD STATED.*

Death. That's it. **That's the penalty.**

**NOT SPIRITUAL DEATH.**

The scholar staggers back. He knocks over a stack of scrolls that cascade across the floor like spilled secrets. He stares at the discovery in awe...and **horror.**

Lightning flashes through the narrow window, illuminating his face. Part triumph. Part terror.

If centuries of this foundational assumption is wrong, then...

### The First Fatal Crack

**CRACK!**

The sound echoes through the building like a rifle shot. Deep in the foundation, a massive fissure appears. The cornerstone doctrine that

**"death entered the world immediately"** suddenly shows a hairline fracture that runs to its very core.

Workers rush to examine the damage. They find the original architectural plans scattered around the crack, covered in centuries of dust. The Hebrew text is clear: God said Adam would die **"in the day"** he ate. In other words...*within a thousand-year divine day.*

**Adam died at 930 years.**

*The penalty was carried out exactly as God said.*

**There was no IMMEDIATE DEATH.**

The theological engineers panic. "Seal the crack!" they cry. "Ignore the Hebrew! The building must stand!"

*But it's too late.*

The damage spreads upward.

### The Second Fatal Crack

**CRACK!**

Floor One buckles and sways. The massive "Eternal Punishment" wing, built entirely on the assumption that *death's penalty wasn't fulfilled that fateful afternoon*...begins to crumble.

Support beams labeled **αἰώνιος** (**aiōnios**) which architects had always claimed meant **"eternal/forever"** *suddenly reveal their true engineering specifications.*

The scholar's research tool pulls up every usage of **αἰώνιος** in the biblical blueprints:

1. Sodom and Gomorrah suffered **"αἰώνιος fire"** (**forever** fire) *but they're not still burning*

2. **"αἰώνιος times"** (**forever** times). Had a beginning, so *they can't mean infinity*

17

3.  Strong's Concordance #166 clearly defines **eternal** (*aiōnios*) as **"quality of an age."** NOT **"endless duration"**

The "Eternal Hell" department collapses in a shower of mistranslated debris. Workers flee as ceiling tiles marked "Forever and Ever" crash down. They reveal their original labels: "Ages of the Ages"—*time periods with defined beginnings and endings.*

### The Third Fatal Crack

**CRACK!**

Floor Two shudders and tilts dangerously. The entire "Salvation from Hell" complex *built entirely on the now-collapsed foundations below* begins its inevitable descent.

The scholar traces every occurrence of **σώζω (sozo)** "**saved.**"

The pattern is annihilating:

1.  Exodus 14:30: Israel **"saved"** from Egyptian army (**physical rescue**)

2.  Matthew 8:25: **"Save us!"** from drowning (**physical rescue**)

3.  Acts 27:31: **"saved"** from shipwreck (**physical rescue**)

Nowhere in scripture does "**saved**" mean "*pray a prayer to escape hell after death.*"

The word consistently means *temporal, physical deliverance from immediate danger.*

The "Sinner's Prayer" chapel crumbles. The "Accept Jesus into Your Heart" sanctuary collapses. Fifteen centuries of salvation formulas that **appear nowhere in the original construction plans** disappear in a cloud of theological dust.

### The Fourth Fatal Crack

**CRACK!**

The sound is deafening now. The entire superstructure of systematic theology begins its final, catastrophic collapse.

The scholar watches in stunned silence as department after department comes crashing down:

The "Limited Atonement" office implodes as every instance of "world" κόσμος (**kosmos**) in John's Gospel...clearly means **"world."** Never **"elect."** John 3:16 means exactly what it says:

*God so loved **THE WORLD**.*

The "Predestination" tower topples as the **"narrow gate"** that Jesus speaks of refers to discipleship IN THIS LIFE. Never **eternal destiny**.

The "Eternal Conscious Torment" wing disintegrates as **"destruction"** and **"death"** reveal their simple, literal meanings: **CESSATION.**

**CESSATION. NOT separation**.

Even the basement archives that contain centuries of hidden councils, ancient doctrines, and sealed vaults are *buried under the rubble of* **original-language evidence**.

### The Aftermath

When the dust settles, the scholar stands in the ruins of fifteen centuries of Christian theology. *But something remarkable has happened in the clearing away of all the rubble.*

There, gleaming in the sunlight, stands a simple, beautiful structure that was there all along. *The original blueprint* written in Hebrew and Greek.

It reveals something profound: God said Adam would die **"in the day"** he ate the forbidden fruit.

*For centuries, theologians assumed this meant **immediate death**.*
*So when Adam didn't drop dead instantly,*
*they offered **"spiritual death"** to explain the discrepancy.*

19

But the Hebrew word בְּיוֹם ("b'yom") simply means **"in the day,"** and with God, **one day** is as *a thousand years*. Adam lived 930 years and died *exactly within God's day*. Just as God promised.

**The penalty was carried out PRECISELY as God said it would.**

All it took to uncover this truth was the courage to examine **one small Hebrew word**.

ONE word.

FOUR fatal cracks.

The collapse of a theological empire built on sinking sand...

...and out from the rubble, **a startling realization emerges**: What if we've built elaborate theological systems on mistranslated foundations?

What if God's actual plan, revealed in the original languages, is more beautiful, more hopeful, and more worthy of the God revealed in Jesus Christ than we ever dared imagine?

The foundation was faulty.

*The blueprint was never the problem.*

What follows in this book is NOT *destruction*. It's **RESTORATION**. We don't tear down God's truth; we clear away centuries of *human additions* to reveal the original design.

**Welcome to the archaeological dig of the millennium!**

Let's uncover what's been buried under 1500 years of theological debris and *rediscover the gospel that's better than we ever dared imagine.*

### *The Original Sin of Mistranslation*

*Nearly all false doctrines taught today*
*by Christians and cultists alike can be traced to the*
*distortion of the meaning of Biblical words*

20

## Chapter 2

# The Theater of Illusions

Now that we've watched a magnificent theological building collapse from one faulty Hebrew word, let me show you something even more disturbing. Let's examine **HOW the illusion was constructed**.

For centuries, Christians have been watching an elaborate theological magic show. They've *mistaken the tricks for reality.*

My friend Johnny at the Magic Castle in Hollywood tells me about mentalists whose mind-reading acts defy explanation. Some audience members become convinced the performer possesses genuine psychic powers. When Johnny explains it's skilled technique and psychology, they get upset. They **want** it to be supernatural.

Now imagine this particular mind-reading show has been running for centuries. Generations are taught that the performer **actually possesses supernatural psychic abilities**. Then someone discovers the simple psychological techniques that were there all along. The whole thing was an elaborate demonstration that became literalized through **centuries of misunderstanding**.

### The Theological Magic Show

For centuries, Christians have been watching a theological magic show. A doctrine so horrifying, so monstrous, so contradictory to the word of God revealed in Jesus that **it requires ELABORATE explanations and TORTURED justifications**.

Yet generation after generation, believers have nodded along like I did, afraid to look too closely at the mechanisms behind the illusion.

The doctrine?

**Eternal conscious torment**—the belief that *God will maintain a cosmic torture chamber where the **vast majority of humanity** will suffer unimaginable agony without end or purpose.*

### *But…what if this foundational belief is a complete fabrication?*

What if your entire view of God's plan is based on a map where someone mistranslated "north" as "south" 1,500 years ago, and everybody's been walking the wrong direction ever since?

What if everything you believe about judgment and eternity is the result of a 1,500-year-long game of telephone. Where good people kept passing along bad translations until nobody remembers what the original words actually meant?

*This book is gonna blow your freaking mind.* It did mine. **So buckle up.**

Let's go back to Genesis. Yep, all the way back to the **beginning** to follow God's redemptive purpose as it unfolds throughout scripture. *No theological hand-me-downs.* No reading later ideas back into the text. *We'll just let the Bible speak for itself.*

Let's go back to the original script. What God actually said about sin and death before theologians got their grubby little hands on it. I'm kidding, c'mon, we're gonna have some fun. Alright, here we go.

### Good Scholars, Bad Sources

Imagine doctors for decades treated depression by inserting ice picks through eye sockets to scramble the frontal lobe. Nobel Prize-winning physicians destroyed healthy brain tissue, convinced they were curing mental illness. These **lobotomies** weren't performed by quacks. *They were mainstream medicine.* Brilliant doctors; catastrophically wrong treatment.

This is precisely what happened with Christian doctrine. Well-meaning theologians built elaborate systems on **mistranslated foundations**, turning Jesus' simple gospel into *something he never preached.*

The result?

*A complete lobotomization of the good news that leaves people more confused than a blind lesbian in a fish market.*

This confusion reaches peak absurdity with Christianity's marred concept of **'being saved.'**

When people approached Jesus asking what they needed to do to **be saved** or to **inherit eternal life**, his answers were *remarkably straightforward and practical; candid and simple.*

"Love God and love your neighbor as yourself."

"Sell your possessions, give to the poor, and follow me."

"Repent and believe the good news of the kingdom."

And when Jesus told Nicodemus he must be "born again" in John chapter 3 when Nicodemus expressed confusion, *Jesus was astonished*: "You are Israel's teacher and *do not understand these things?*" (John 3:3, 7, 10)

Jesus expected a teacher of the Law to recognize this concept from the Old Testament scriptures where it refers to **spiritual renewal** and **covenant restoration**. Not *escaping hell or securing heavenly real estate.*

Simple and direct. Focused on **transformed living** and **right relationships** in the **present**. Not primarily about *escaping future torture.*

But over the centuries, we've turned this into an *impossibly complex theological menu* where you have to order *exactly the right combination of beliefs* with *precisely the right wording or* **face eternal damnation.**

We've morphed Jesus' straightforward teaching about **entering God's kingdom** into an *elaborate system of escaping God's* **eternal torture chamber**.

That's not just a minor misunderstanding. It's a **COMPLETE INVERSION** of what Jesus taught.

### The Twist Ending

This isn't some theological debate club bullshit. If God's plan was always to restore everyone...and not torture billions forever...then everything you've

23

been taught is backwards. Like what God's really, like how we tell people about him, whether we write off "lost" people, what we're hoping for after death. The whole playbook gets torched.

Consider these questions:

What if the penalty for sin described in Genesis was **physical death** within a divine timeframe. *Not eternal torment?*

I repeat: PHYSICAL DEATH...*within a timeframe. NOT eternal torment.*

What if the blood of Christ addresses **physical corruption** rather than *satisfying a requirement for eternal punishment?* Well buddy boy, keep your pickup in park, because scripture will prove to you over the next few pages that the blood of Jesus addresses **physical corruption**.

There's lots more to tell you, but I'm not sure you can handle it. (Yes, you can, I *know* you can. *You can do this!*)

- What if God's unconditional covenant with Abraham reveals his ultimate intention for ALL humanity? Every human ever born!

- What if the **fusion of evil** with human nature at the Fall is a fusion so thorough, so wicked, so vile, so poisonous, yet *temporary*, and destined for **separation** at the *final restoration?* (Wait'll you hear what the *final restoration* is... If you don't have a hernia, you soon will.)

I'd better say that again (minus the hernia). After all, we all need a little repetition in our lives. You never tire of your spouse's whisper, "I love you," right?

*What if **the fusion of evil** with human nature at the fall is temporary, destined for **surgical separation** at the final restoration!*

Can you imagine...if this is true...that God's plan is **infinitely more glorious** than anything we ever dreamed?

*What if the fusion of evil—when evil has become so fused with the human heart that the two are forever and inextricably bonded together is temporary, destined to be **surgically extracted** at **the judgment seat of Christ**, where God himself performs the ultimate operation to **rip to shreds** what no earthly power could ever remove?*

Matthew 3:12 shows exactly how this works. *'His winnowing fork is in his hand... the chaff he will burn with unquenchable fire.'* In winnowing, the fire doesn't destroy the wheat. It burns away the chaff attached to it. Jesus isn't burning billions of people forever. No. He's separating the corruption FROM people and **completely destroys the corruption while PRESERVING THE PERSON.**

The implications are mind-blowingly profound. If we've misunderstood the very nature of the problem Christ came to solve, we may have **completely botched** the nature of his solution.

I knew a pastor. Let's call him Pastor Pablum, who spent twenty years preaching about hell and eternal torment. Every sermon included warnings about the eternal consequences of rejecting Christ. His ministry was driven by the desperate urgency to rescue souls from never-ending punishment.

One day, while he prepared yet another sermon on divine judgment, Pastor Pablum decides to research the original Greek words translated as **"eternal"** and **"forever"** in his English Bible.

*What he discovers shakes him to his core.*

The Greek word **aiōnios**, typically translated as **"eternal,"** actually refers to *an age, or period of time*. NOT necessarily *endless duration*. The phrase *eis tous aiónas tón aiónón*, rendered as **"forever and ever,"** literally means **"unto the ages of the ages."**

Uh-oh! Code red in the seminary!

*What if **aiōnios**, typically translated as "eternal," actually refers to **an age or period of time**. A beginning and an end. NOT an endless duration.*

25

"My God," he whispers, "I've been mistranslating scripture for two decades."

Pastor Pablum spends the next three years excavating biblical languages, early church writings, and the historical development of the doctrine of hell. He also discovers that many early Christians, including some of the most respected church fathers, believed in the eventual restoration of all things, not eternal torment.

From that day forward, Pastor Pablum became Pastor Epiphany, though his congregation started calling him Pastor "Lightbulb."

### Tradition

This journey down Hebrew/Greek Demolition Lane will challenge deeply held traditions. For many readers, the concept of **eternal punishment** has been presented as a fundamental Christian doctrine. I don't take this challenge lightly, and I'm not dismissing the serious theological work of those who've defended traditional views.

*But tradition isn't infallible.*

Throughout church history, Christians have been called to *test all things against scripture.* (1 Thessalonians 5:21). The Reformation was built on the willingness to challenge traditions that had accumulated over centuries when they contradicted the clear teaching of scripture.

I encourage you to read this book with an open mind. **Compare these ideas to scripture. NOT tradition.** Do not accept my words blindly. (Only a fool would do that.) Instead, study, and test everything I say with the word of God.

*Fact check everything I say.* But NOT with parroted talking points, but by a thorough word study of **each and every one of the Hebrew and Greek words** that I present to you. My aim is to encourage a renewed understanding of God's redemptive plan *without weakening faith in the Bible.* **The word of God remains constant**.

ONLY OUR INTERPRETATIONS IMPROVE.

## The Cure That's Killing You

Imagine you've been diagnosed with terminal cancer. For years, you've undergone excruciating treatments based on this diagnosis: radiation, chemotherapy, experimental drugs with terrible side effects. Then one day, a new doctor reviews your case and makes a shocking discovery: you never had cancer at all. You had parasites that are easily treated without those torturous interventions. How would you feel about all the suffering you endured based on a mistaken diagnosis?

This is the situation many Christians find themselves in. They've been told they have a spiritual disease (**inherited sin**). This disease requires extreme measures (**believing exactly the right things to escape eternal torture**). Their entire spiritual lives have been mutilated by theological malpractice.

But what if the malpractice ends today? What if the actual human condition described in Genesis is quite different, and God's remedy is more simple, effective, and beautiful than we've been told to believe?

## The Precipice

*The case for complete restoration* presented in this book *isn't built on philosophical preferences or emotional desires*. Sure, the idea that God will ultimately restore all things is both *philosophically satisfying* and *emotionally appealing*. Who wouldn't want that?

But emotions and preferences are a dangerous foundation upon which to base your understanding. God forbid we base our beliefs on our human opinions and emotional preferences. But THIS case is built on **careful examination of scripture**. We begin with Genesis and follow the unfolding revelation of God's redemptive purpose.

We'll explore:

1. The true nature of **the death penalty** pronounced in Genesis

2. The meaning of God's **unconditional covenant** with Abraham

3. The significance of Christ's **"pure blood"** in addressing the corruption of death

4. The **fusion of evil** with human nature and *God's ultimate plan to separate the two*

At each step, *we'll allow scripture to interpret scripture*; we'll **examine original contexts and meanings** rather than imposing later theological frameworks on the text. That's right. *We'll let the bible speak for itself* instead of we the people telling the bible what it should say.

> *We let the bible speak for itself*
> *instead of we the people telling the bible what it should say*

### Flight 447

An air traffic controller clears Flight 447 to "descend to flight level 250" (25,000 feet). Static on the radio makes it sound like "flight level 150" (15,000 feet). The pilot descends exactly as he thinks he heard, straight into a mountain range. Black box recovery reveals the truth: the instruction was correct, the reception was garbled, 287 people died following orders they thought they understood perfectly. The command was clear. The hearing was compromised. The crash was preventable.

The Christian doctrine of **eternal conscious torment** is like that garbled radio transmission. The original command, God's justice, divine judgment, and redemptive purpose is perfect. But centuries of static interference from Latin mistranslations have caused theologians to hear something completely different, leading billions straight into theological disaster that could have been avoided by simply checking the original signal.

And so centuries of misreading the "radio transmission" of Hebrew and Greek texts have produced something bitter and harsh that drives people away from the God who actually wants to heal and restore them. *Even against their will.*

*WHOA, wait a minute, Steve, whaaat did you just say?! Steve, did you really just say God restores them EVEN AGAINST THEIR WILL?*

Yes, I did say **"even against their will."** We'll discover that *God's redemption is so thorough* and *so ingrained in his plan of redemption* that **there's NO WAY man's stubborn rebellion and sniveling petulance can mess it up.**

*Welp, shit just got real.* But let's not get ahead of ourselves.

### Buckle Up

The journey ahead requires us to set aside some deeply ingrained assumptions and approach familiar texts with fresh eyes. That can be disorienting, even unsettling. When ideas that have shaped our understanding of faith are questioned, *it's natural to feel defensive or anxious.*

I ask only that you consider the evidence presented. Test it against scripture. Remain open to the possibility that God's redemptive plan may be more **beautiful** than traditional theology has ever dared to imagine.

If the case presented in these pages aligns more closely with the original meaning of scripture than the traditional understanding of eternal punishment, then embracing it does not **abandon** orthodoxy. *It returns to it.*

In the chapters that follow, we'll build the case step by step, we'll examine the biblical evidence and its implications. We'll address common objections and explore the practical significance of this understanding of how God views us. I invite you to join me on this journey of discovery as we seek to understand more fully the height, depth, and breadth of God's redemptive love.

Let's begin at the beginning with the nature of the penalty pronounced in the Garden and its implications for our understanding of liberation from the corruption of this temporary world.

Buckle up, because this is gonna be one helluva ride.

No pun intended.

Actually, pun totally intended.

## Chapter 3

# The Divine Heist

MESOPOTAMIA. 2000 BC. SUNSET.

Blood soaks into sand. Split animal carcasses form a grotesque pathway. This is covenant-making. Ancient Mesopotamia's version of signing your life away. Literally. Both parties walk between the butchered animals. They declare: "May this happen to me if I break our deal." It's a death oath. No lawyers. No loopholes. Just blood and consequences.

Abraham stands before the carnage, knowing what comes next. He's supposed to walk through this death corridor with God. They both take responsibility for keeping the promise. His hands shake. One wrong move, one broken promise, and humanity's future dies in this blood-soaked sand.

But then—

WHAM.

Abraham drops to the ground like he's been gob-smacked with a sledgehammer.

> *As the sun was setting, Abram fell into a deep sleep*
> *[tardema], and a thick and dreadful darkness came over him.*

This isn't sleep. This is God when he hits the override button on human consciousness.

The same move he pulls on Adam before he creates Eve.

The same move he pulled on Saul to protect David.

Every time **tardema** appears in scripture, it's God saying: "Humans out of the pool. I'm doing something too important to let you anywhere near it."

31

And humanity's collective response: 'Thanks for the vote of confidence, God. Really feeling the trust here. Nothing says "I believe in you" like divine chloroform.'

CUT TO: Abraham's unconscious body. The blood path awaits.

Then—smoke and fire. A blazing torch. God's presence moves between the carcasses.

Alone.

He walks both sides.

He takes all responsibility.

The most revolutionary legal document in human history gets signed while the human party is knocked out cold.

FADE TO BLACK.

This is how God makes sure humanity can't fuck up his plan. He literally knocks out the human representative and handles everything himself. But this isn't just a one-time trick God pulls on Abraham.

### The Pattern

That word TARDEMA (תַּרְדֵּמָה) isn't ordinary sleep.

It appears only a handful of times in scripture.

Every single occurrence describes a divinely-induced supernatural unconsciousness where God performs sovereign acts without human participation.

- **Adam's tardema** when God created Eve (Genesis 2:21). Adam can't participate in or influence the creation of his covenant partner. Thank God for that. If it was left up to Adam, he'd have designed Eve and she'd have looked like a platypus. And you think for one minute if Adam was in charge of Eve's creation, he'd have come up with sex? Hell no. He'd have designed her with a built-in fishing rod holder and a beer tap. God knew what he was doing when he knocked Adam out cold.

- **Abraham's tardema** during the covenant ceremony (Genesis 15:12). Abraham can't participate in or affect the covenant terms

- **Saul's tardema** when David takes the spear (1 Samuel 26:12). Divine unconsciousness prevents interference with God's plan

The pattern is crystal clear: Tardema is GOD'S METHOD to ensure that certain foundational, covenantal acts remain ENTIRELY WITHIN God's own sovereignty.

God uses TARDEMA to exclude human cooperation. Like when he handles eternal benefits we'd inevitably screw up. And he's right. We've tried our darndest to add eternal conscious torment to the menu for 1500 years.

On the other hand, he DOES use if…then (obey gets blessings, disobey gets curses) when you need to learn not to touch the stove.

Tardema is forever.

If…then is for next Tuesday.

He uses tardema when he must eliminate ANY HUMAN INTERFERENCE.

It's like God looks at humanity's track record. Adam eats the fruit, Cain kills Abel, everybody drowns except Noah, and God says, 'Yeah, I'm gonna need you unconscious for this next part.'

### God Walks Alone

The pattern screams from the page when we examine what actually happens in Genesis 15: "When the sun had set and darkness had fallen, a smoking firepot with a blazing torch appears and passes between the pieces."

GOD ALONE walks between the animal pieces. What about Abraham? God divinely paralyzes him. God forbids him from participating, observing, or influencing the ceremony.

GOD shoulders responsibility for both sides of the covenant.

This isn't a mutual agreement where both parties assume obligations.

No.

This is a unilateral covenant where God alone bears all the responsibility for fulfillment.

Abraham CAN'T break the contract EVEN IF HE TRIES.

Why?

Because God knocks him the fuck out! "Stay out of my way, Abraham!"

## The Surgery

Imagine you need life-saving surgery, but the procedure is so delicate that even the slightest movement is fatal. The surgeon doesn't ask you to hold very still and promise not to move. Instead, he puts you under anesthesia; thus he ensures you're completely unconscious throughout the entire operation.

Why? Because the success of the surgery is too important to risk human interference. Your life depends on the surgeon's skill. NOT on your cooperation.

That's exactly what God does with Abraham.

The covenant is too important. The eternal destiny of all humanity hangs in the balance, so God makes sure Abraham cannot sabotage it. That's why God puts him into divine anesthesia.

## ALL Means ALL

Now here's where this gets really exciting. While Abraham is unconscious, unable to negotiate terms or limit scope, what exactly does God promise?

Genesis 12:3: "ALL families of the earth shall be blessed through you."

Genesis 18:18: "ALL nations of the earth shall be blessed through him."

Genesis 22:18: "In your offspring ALL nations of the earth shall be blessed."

Abraham can't wake up and say: "Whoa, hold on a minute God, this seems a little broad. How about just the good families? Or maybe just the ones who pray the right prayer?"

Nope. God knocks Abraham out. "STFU Humanity. Stay out of my way!"

God determines the scope of his redemption all by himself that includes:

ALL families.

ALL nations.

And since the covenant's fulfillment depends entirely on God's faithfulness (Abraham snores like a grizzly bear with sleep apnea during the ceremony), then God's covenant cannot be undone by human rebellion, NOR DOES IT REQUIRE HUMAN ACCEPTANCE.

Jesus tells this same story. Workers hired at dawn agreed on a denarius for the day. At 5 PM, one hour before quitting, the owner hires more workers and pays them the same full day's wage. The early workers lose their minds: "We worked twelve hours in blazing heat! They worked one hour! And you pay them the same?!" The owner's response: "I'm paying you exactly what we agreed. Are you envious because I am generous?" (Matthew 20:1-16)

That's God's covenant with Abraham. Some get in early. Some get in late. Everyone gets the full inheritance.

Catch that? There ain't no "accept Jesus into your heart." No "make Jesus Lord of your life." No raising your hand while every head is bowed. No walking the aisle. No signing the card. God's plan for redemption doesn't need your permission, your decision, or your cooperation. Abraham doesn't accept the covenant. He's knocked out cold. And neither does humanity get to vote on God's redemption plan. God demands NOTHING from us. No acceptance needed. No decision required. No prayer to pray.

## You Can't Break It

Here's the legal principle that destroys every limited restoration doctrine: Abraham can't break a covenant he has nothing to do with.

Think about it:

- He didn't negotiate the terms (he was snoring)

- He didn't agree to conditions (he was knocked out)

- He didn't make promises he could later break (he was drooling on his pillow)

- He didn't limit the scope (God determines "all families" while Abraham is knocked out cold)

What's the only way this covenant can fail?

IF GOD HIMSELF BREAKS IT.

And since God "cannot deny himself" (2 Timothy 2:13), the covenant's success is ABSOLUTELY GUARANTEED.

Think of it like this: The money's in the bank whether you believe it or not. But if you trust it's there, you sleep better at night. Does your disbelief change the fact that it's there? Not at all.

Trust affects WHEN individuals personally experience what's already provided. Not WHETHER it was provided.

Abraham's trust allows him to personally experience covenant benefits in his lifetime. His relationship with God, a sense of purpose, glimpses of the promise. BUT the ultimate fulfillment (blessing all nations through his descendant) never depends on HUMANITY'S TRUST.

It depends ONLY on God's faithfulness to his word.

### The Comedy

Now we get to the truly hilarious part.

Picture this scene: God carefully designs the most important covenant in human history. He deliberately knocks Abraham out to prevent human meddling. He personally handles every detail to ensure the promise can't be sabotaged, limited, or lawyered. This isn't a prenup. It's a promise. God's not an insurance adjuster looking for reasons to deny your claim.

Fast-forward two and a half millennia. Theologians discover this sleeping-man covenant and think to themselves: "You know what this unconditional covenant needs?

"CONDITIONS!"

### The Insanity

A patient wakes from life-saving surgery and criticizes the surgeon: "Next time keep me awake so I can help!" The medical team runs an updated diagnosis: "The patient just developed brain damage."

This is pretty much what traditional theology does with the Abrahamic covenant. God uses divine anesthesia to prevent human interference, then theologians spend the next 1500 years to add back the human interference that God explicitly prevents.

You've got to wonder what those committee meetings looked like.

Committee Member 1: "So God made an unconditional promise to bless all families of earth while Abraham was unconscious and couldn't interfere..."

Committee Member 2: "Right. Clearly, what God meant was that it's conditional on human performance and limited to people who pray the right prayer."

Committee Member 1: "But... Abraham was asleep. God specifically prevented human input."

Committee Member 2: "Exactly! Which is why we need to add human input back in."

[pause]

Committee Member 3: "Should we maybe... you know... trust that God knows what he was doing when he put Abraham to sleep?"

Committee Members 1 & 2: "HERETIC!"

Committee Member 3: "Guys, I think I'm hearing God say 'Boys, grab your ears firmly with both hands and pull your heads outta your ass.'"

## Botch-Proof

The tardema pattern repeats:

Adam's tardema: Couldn't influence Eve's creation. Wakes up. She's there. Done deal.

Abraham's tardema: Couldn't influence the covenant. Wakes up. It's signed. All families blessed.

The pattern teaches us that God's most fundamental covenantal works happen while God makes humans INCAPABLE OF INTERFERENCE.

That's right. God renders man INCAPABLE of mucking it up.

So why would we expect God's ultimate fulfillment of the Abrahamic covenant to suddenly [TA-DAA] require human cooperation?!

If God makes Abraham UNCONSCIOUS that prevents him from accepting the promise, why does God suddenly need humanity to ACCEPT the promise for him to fulfil it?

The theological bomb: God doesn't just make Abraham unconscious. He makes him unconscious specifically to prevent the "accept/reject" decision.

And if acceptance wasn't needed then, it's not needed now.

If God removes Abraham's ability to accept the covenant, then why the does God require human acceptance to fulfill it today?

If Abraham couldn't accept it. God knocks him out to prevent it. Why the Sam Hill hell must WE accept it?

## Christ Seals It

Paul makes the connection explicit in Galatians 3:16: "The promises were made to Abraham and to his offspring." Not offsprings (plural), but one: Christ. Jesus is the "seed" of Abraham through whom all families of earth will be blessed. And since the original covenant is unconditional. Abraham is asleep during its establishment. It's fulfillment in Christ must also be unconditional.

This is why Paul writes with such confidence: "As one trespass led to condemnation for ALL men, so one act of righteousness leads to justification and life for ALL men" (Romans 5:18).

The scope of Christ's redemptive work matches the scope of the original covenant: universal, unconditional, and guaranteed by God's faithfulness alone—I repeat—GOD'S FAITHFULNESS ALONE.

Not yours. Not mine. Not anyone's.

Here's the theological nuclear bomb: Galatians 3:8 says God "preaches the gospel beforehand to Abraham, saying, 'In you shall ALL the nations be blessed.'" And that blessing comes through πίστις (*pistis*), means "faithfulness." But here's the kicker: that *pistis* (faithfulness) isn't OUR faithfulness. It's GOD's.

Think about it: Abraham is unconscious when God makes this promise. Did Abraham demonstrate his faithfulness while knocked out cold? Hell no! God demonstrates HIS faithfulness by making promises that depend on NOTHING from humanity.

Paul says ALL nations get blessed through GOD's faithfulness to his promise. The same promise he makes while Abraham slept. Whether individuals trust God's faithfulness in this life and get an advance on their inheritance or wait until the final judgment when God's faithfulness overwhelms their resistance. Either way, EVERYONE gets what God promises.

Why? Because the blessing depends on GOD's πίστις [HIS faithfulness]. NOT ours.

Your faithfulness to enjoy Abe's covenant don't mean shit to God.

## God's Faithfulness Is Our Guarantee

Paul already settles this in Romans 3:3-4: "What if some were unfaithful? Will their unfaithfulness nullify God's faithfulness? Not at all!"

Get this through your thick theological skull: If eternity with God depends on human faithfulness, billions are screwed. We can't even stay faithful to a diet for two weeks.

Human faithfulness is about as reliable as a chocolate teapot. As steady as a one-legged cat trying to bury turds on a frozen pond. Thank God the covenant depends on HIS faithfulness, because ours isn't worth the paper a sinner's prayer is written on.

God's faithfulness is our guarantee. Not OUR faithfulness. OUR faithfulness don't mean jack. Our faithfulness? Pshhh! It's like a drunk toddler promising to perform brain surgery. Like a compulsive liar swearing to tell the truth. Like asking a meth addict to guard the pharmacy. Hell, our faithfulness is like depending on gas station sushi for fine dining.

And thank God for that. Because the "sinner's prayer" theology says YOUR faithfulness saves you. Say the right words, believe the right things, don't lose your salvation. But God retorts, "Shut up, bitch! MY FAITHFULNESS is what grants you foreverness with me!" as he playfully rubs shit on your face (Malachi 2:3). Okay, I might've made up that last part. That's on me.

God's faithfulness is our guarantee. Our guarantee is based upon God's faithfulness. Not our faithfulness. If salvation depends on you saying a prayer and meaning it forever, hell is standing room only.

The fulfillment of God's covenant promises DEPENDS NOT ON UNIVERSAL HUMAN TRUST. It depends on GOD'S unilateral faithfulness.

This isn't wishful thinking. It's the clear trajectory established by God's unconditional promises...to whom? To Abraham.

I don't know about you, but this makes me happier than a shark in a fish tank full of tubby ladies riding the cotton mouse. (Husbands, ask your wives to explain that to you.)

## The Crime

God says: "All families blessed."

Tradition adds: "BUT...TERMS AND CONDITIONS APPLY."

This violates Proverbs 30:6: "Do not add to his words, or he will rebuke you and prove you a liar."

God makes an unconditional covenant with universal scope while Abraham is divinely unconscious. BUT MAN ADDS CONDITIONS.

Why'd God make it unconditional? To prevent human additions and limitations. But centuries of well-meaning, but low-IQ theologians have committed this exact crime.

It's like the patient who sues the anesthesiologist for malpractice: "Doctor, you didn't let me hold the scalpel during surgery! I demand a do-over!"

## "Let Go of Me, God!"

God puts Abraham to sleep because HUMANITY'S ETERNAL DESTINY MUST NOT RISK HUMAN SABOTAGE! It's like you take a chainsaw away from a five-year-old at the petting zoo.

God's love is so savage, so bulldogged, so hell-bent on winning that HE MUSCLES HUMANITY COMPLETELY OUT OF THE EQUATION for the covenant that ensures eternity with him. It's like God rips the car keys from a drunk driver. That's not a violation of human dignity. It's the ultimate expression of divine love.

## Tuesday's Consequences

You might think, "Yeah, but Steve, what about 'obey and you'll be blessed; disobey, and you'll be cursed'?" Great question. I've wondered the same thing myself.

41

Here's the key distinction:

Earthly blessings require OUR cooperation.

Eternal restoration does NOT require our cooperation.

The temporal benefits (health, prosperity, earthly success) depend on our choices.

But the eternal benefits—global redemption—we can't stop God's eternal benefits NO MATTER HOW HARD WE TRY! (And brother, we've given it our best shot for 1500 years!)

Let me show you exactly how this works throughout scripture:

### Sometimes Yes, Sometimes No

God gives the blueprint, but Noah has to swing the hammer. No ark, no survival. His sweat, his obedience, his choice.

Fast-forward to a teenage girl in Nazareth. The angel appears with an impossible proposal. Mary can say no. God won't force her womb. She has to consent to carry the Messiah. Her body, her willingness, her courageous "yes."

Or the blind man who cries out as Jesus passes. Jesus doesn't heal everyone that walks by. This man must reach out for what Jesus offers: individual healing demands individual action.

These are temporal blessings. They require your cooperation.

But watch what happens when God handles eternal matters.

The universe explodes into existence from nothing. God doesn't form a committee. He speaks, and galaxies ignite. No human input requested or required.

God puts Adam under anesthesia. Adam lies unconscious in Eden while God performs the first surgery. He creates Eve from his rib. Adam doesn't get to offer suggestions about his wife's design. He wakes up to a fait accompli. God fashions his exquisite partner while he sleeps. By the way, Adam's first words when he woke up and saw Eve: "Whoa! You'd better stand back girl; there's no telling how big this thing'll get." [ba-dum-CHING]

But I digress.

And here's the granddaddy of them all: Abraham prepares for the most important ceremony in human history, and God knocks him out cold. While Abraham's unconscious, God walks between the pieces alone. He takes full responsibility for blessing all families of earth. Abraham can't mess it up because he is asleep. It's impossible to thwart God's plan when God knocks you out cold.

How about this one: Jesus steps into human flesh. He doesn't ask humanity's permission. The word becomes flesh. Not through human consensus, but through divine initiative. No human permission. God fulfils the eternal covenant while we still argue about the details.

Here's one of my favorites: At Calvary, soldiers hammer nails while religious leaders mock. Humanity commits cosmic murder, completely oblivious that they're witnessing massive redemption. The cross accomplishes salvation while humans are so flummoxed that they don't know baby shit from butterscotch.

Three days later, in a tomb outside Jerusalem, death meets its match. God raises Jesus. He never consults a human. He doesn't ask permission. He doesn't wait for our agreement.

God conquers death while humanity sits around with their thumbs up their collective asses, writing out four steps to salvation, reciting sinner's prayers, and hoping God grades their paperwork with a passing score.

This is eternal restoration. God doesn't require our cooperation. Why? Because God knows we'd eff it up. We've proved him right, too, haven't we? We've busted our asses trying to ADD CONDITIONS to an UNCONDITIONAL contract for 1,500 years. For 1,500 years we've hammered conditions into an unconditional contract like we're nailing amendments to God's front door. We've twisted ourselves into theological pretzels trying to ADD CONDITIONS to an UNCONDITIONAL contract.

The pattern screams from every page: YES, God requires your participation for earthly blessings! But NO, he excludes you completely from eternal ones. Not because he doesn't love you, but because he loves you too much to let you turn your salvation into a five-year-old's shop experiment with daddy's power saws.

The pattern is unmistakable: God requires human cooperation for temporal, earthly benefits, but his most crucial eternal works happen through divine initiative alone.

### Sweet Dreams

Abraham's tardema isn't just the most important nap in biblical history. It is God's love letter to all humanity, written in the language of divine sovereignty and sealed with the guarantee of unconditional faithfulness.

When Abraham falls into that supernatural sleep, God ensures that every family of earth eventually wakes up to the reality of his love.

The sleeping man couldn't sabotage God's plan.

The awakened world can't escape his love.

Sweet dreams, Abraham. Thanks to your divinely-induced unconsciousness, the whole world gets to wake up to the most beautiful surprise in the universe: we're all invited to the wedding feast, and God himself guarantees our attendance.

The contract was signed while you slept.

The party is planned for when everyone wakes up.

Chapter 4

# The Reckoning

Now that we've seen God's unconditional promise to restore all families of the earth through Abraham, we can examine *what actually happened in Eden*. The penalty God pronounced for sin has been **completely mislabeled** for centuries by theological tradition. *This mislabeling* has led to treatments **FAR WORSE than the original condition**.

## The Wrong Bottle

Imagine you walk into your local pharmacy to pick up a prescription. The pharmacist hands you a bottle with a label that says: "Take one pill a day for 7 days." You follow the instructions. After a week, not only has your condition not improved, but you've developed devastating new symptoms.

You go back to your doctor. He examines the medication and makes a shocking discovery: The pills in the bottle don't match what's on the label. You've been taking the wrong medication because somebody mislabeled the bottle.

"No wonder you feel worse," your doctor says. "These aren't heart pills. They're fertility drugs. You came in for chest pain. I tried to help you have triplets."

This is our story. We have swallowed the wrong theological medicine on Genesis's death penalty for 1500 years. We have worked from a mislabeled theological bottle. The medication inside (**eternal conscious torment**) doesn't match the label on the bottle (**the death penalty described in Genesis**). And this mislabeled theology hasn't just failed to address our spiritual condition. It's made things worse and bastardized our understanding of God's plan and purpose.

45

Now that we've established the unconditional nature of the Abrahamic covenant, let's rewind even further and look back at what the hell happened in the Garden of Eden.

### "In The Day..."

Let's start with the actual text. In Genesis 2:17, God warns Adam:

> *"But of the tree of the knowledge of good and evil you shall not eat, for **in the day** that you eat of it you shall surely die."*

### THE MILLION-DOLLAR QUESTION:

*Did Adam die the day he ate the fruit?*

Traditional theological answers something like this: "Well, he didn't die physically that day, *so he must have died spiritually*. Physical death came later as a consequence of spiritual death."

You've heard this a million times, haven't you? But is that what the text really says? Or are we in violation of Proverbs 30:6: *'Do not add to his words, or he will rebuke you and prove you a liar.'*

Adding words to scripture is *like trying to improve the Mona Lisa with a crayon.* It might seem like a good idea at the time, but you just messed up a masterpiece.

Did God warn about '**spiritual death**'?

*Does Genesis even mention **spiritual death** anywhere?*

Hell No! (Whee! The title of this book again!)

This "**spiritual death**" idea got tacked on later by theologians who saw that Adam didn't drop dead the minute he took a bite of the forbidden fruit. So they invented a whole new concept—**spiritual death**—it's nowhere in the original text!

## B'yom

So if Adam didn't die that day, and '**spiritual death**' is nowhere in the text, what the hell's really going on here?

Let's look at the numbers: God designs Adam to live forever. Did you know the human body regenerates? Most cells replace themselves every 7-10 years. You are not the same physical person you were a decade ago. So why do we die? Oh but wait…here's a strange coincidence: nobody in recorded history has ever lived past 1,000 years. You ever notice that? Methuselah hit 969. Adam hit 930. Both of them came in at just under the 1,000-year milestone. Coincidence? Hmmm…let's examine what God really says.

## The Hebrew

The phrase "**in the day**" is the Hebrew expression "**b'yom**" (בְּיוֹם).

Here's the critical question:

*If God meant that Adam would die instantly, why didn't he just say that?* Why didn't he say "**instantly**"? He could have. God could have used "**pith'om**" (פִּתְאֹם), which means "suddenly" or "instantly."

*But did he?* **No, he didn't.** He chose "**b'yom**," a term that deserves closer examination.

Check out Numbers 6:9: "If any man die very suddenly [*pith'om*]…" Moses describes a drop-dead-on-the-spot death. No warning, no countdown, just *bam*. You're done. Instant. Immediate.

So if Moses meant "Adam dropped dead the instant he ate the fruit," he had the perfect word choice ready to go. He could've written:

> *…for in eating of it, you shall **pith'om** die*
> *(you shall **SUDDENLY** die).*

But he didn't write that, did he! Nope. Moses chose the word *b'yom* "in the day," meaning within a timeframe. What is that timeframe? One thousand years.

Different word. Different meaning.

### Bitch Slap

Ah, but wait. There's another translation disaster hiding in plain sight. The Hebrew phrase "dying you shall die" is **mōt tāmūt** (מוֹת תָּמוּת) in Genesis 2:17. This construction (infinitive absolute + imperfect verb) …don't worry about all that grammar shit, it's just to show how smart I am. But it emphasizes **CERTAINTY of future occurrence**, not **TIMING of the occurrence**.

I'll say that again: it's the CERTAINTY of a **future** occurrence; not the TIMING of the occurrence.

Think of it like this: If I say "If you keep smoking, you will die," I'm not saying you'll drop dead the instant you light the cigarette. I'm saying death becomes your certain future.

Or if I say "You will definitely get fired if you keep showing up drunk," I'm not saying you'll be fired the instant you walk in drunk. I'm saying it's absolutely certain to happen in the future.

That's exactly what God says to Adam. The Hebrew construction means "You will most certainly die." It does NOT say "You will **immediately** die."

God promised inevitable **future** death. He did NOT threaten instant execution.

See the difference? Can you see how this destroys the entire "spiritual death" invention? Theologians created that concept because they thought God meant immediate death. I get it. I believed it for decades. But the Hebrew grammar shows God emphasized **certainty**. Not **immediacy**.

Combined with "b'yom" (within God's 1,000-year day), the Hebrew is crystal clear: Adam would absolutely, certainly, definitely die within God's 1,000-year timeframe.

Which he did. At 930 years old.

Traditional theology builds eternal damnation on misunderstanding Hebrew verb tenses. When people reject rigorous study and replace it with secondhand religious interpretations, they create a monumental barrier to what God actually says. When you reject the original language, you miss that God describes the absolute CERTAINTY of death. NOT how QUICKLY it happens.

No wonder Augustine gets it wrong. He was reading Latin translations of Greek translations of Hebrew verb constructions. That's like playing "Telephone" through three languages with grammar rules that don't exist in Latin.

So when we combine the verb construction that emphasizes **certainty** with the timeframe of **'b'yom,'** the picture is crystal clear: God tells Adam he will **absolutely certainly die within his divine timeframe.**

*God does NOT tell Adam that he drops dead instantly!*

### God's Clock

Now that we've nailed down both the certainty AND the timeframe, let's understand how God's clock actually works. It's like when a parent tells their child "we'll leave after dinner" and the child expects to leave right after dessert. He doesn't realize the family's "after dinner" includes cleanup, coffee, and conversation. The child hears correctly but misunderstands the timeframe.

Similarly, when God says "in the day," he operates on a different clock than we do.

Psalm 90:4 and 2 Peter 3:8 tell us that "with the Lord one day is as a thousand years, and a thousand years as one day." This isn't poetry. It's God's timepiece. But here's the knockout punch: Psalm 90 defines God's timeframe AND the death penalty in the same breath. The same psalm that defines God's "day" as a thousand years also describes him commanding people to "return to dust." The exact penalty pronounced in Genesis.

And who wrote Psalm 90? Moses. The same Moses who wrote the Genesis death penalty. Same author. Same timeframe. Same dust.

Preach it, Grandpa Moses!

According to the death penalty pronounce by God, Adam lives 930 years and returns to dust. **Exactly within God's definition of "a day."**

This isn't coincidence. It's confirmation. The death penalty is carried out precisely as God says it will be...*within his divine timeframe*...exactly as the psalmist (in this case, Moses) describes.

### The Evidence

Adam dies within God's "day" of 1,000 years. At 930 years old. The Hebrew verb construction **guarantees it will happen (mōt tāmūt = CERTAINTY)**, and **b'yom** tells us **WHEN**. The "when" is **within God's timeframe**.

*The penalty is carried out exactly as God says it will be, within the divine timeframe he specifies.*

### Everyone Dies

Adam and Eve didn't die within a 24-hour human day, but *they definitely died within **the thousand years that God calls "a day"**.*

The problem isn't with God's statement.

*The problem is that we insist on interpreting it through our limited human timeframe.*

### Dust to Dust

Genesis 3:19 makes the death penalty crystal clear:

> *By the sweat of your face you shall eat bread, till you return to the ground, for out of it you were taken; for you are dust, and **to dust you shall return**.*

There it is. The clear explanation of the death penalty that Adam experiences at 930 years. Exactly within God's definition of "a day." It's **physical death**. The body breaks down and returns to the elements from which it was formed. Nothing more, nothing less.

This is reinforced throughout scripture. Ecclesiastes 12:7 describes death as the time when *"the dust returns to the earth as it was, and the spirit returns to God who gave it."*

The consistent biblical picture is of **physical death** as *the consequence of sin.* Theologians must've paid somebody to help them bungle these verses.

### Life in Prison

Picture a school principal that deals with a student who gets caught throwing spitballs in class. The original school handbook, written by the superintendent, clearly states the punishment: detention for one afternoon. But over the years, someone mistranslates the handbook into a different language, and when they translate it back, "detention for one afternoon" somehow turns into "detention PLUS expulsion, banishment from all future education, and painful electric shocks for life."

The current principal, who relies on this mistranslated version, announces the extreme punishment to the student's parents.

The parents pull out the original handbook. "Wait a minute! The superintendent clearly writes 'detention for one afternoon.' Where does all this extra punishment come from?"

The principal, genuinely confused, looks at his mistranslated copy. "But this version says..."

"That's not what the original says!" the parents insist. "Somebody added all that extra punishment through bad translation!"

We would immediately recognize this as a translation error, not the superintendent's intent. Yet this is precisely what happens with our understanding of sin's penalty. God clearly states the punishment in Genesis— **physical death within a divine timeframe**—but through *mistranslation* and *theological additions*, we have somehow accepted "physical death PLUS eternal conscious torment." Even though the original Hebrew NEVER mentions it. Here comes that pesky Proverbs 30:6 violation again. They added to God's words and now, by golly, they're getting proved to be a liar.

## Faceplants

If physical death within a divine timeframe (1,000 years) is the penalty for sin, this raises a devastating question:

*Why would additional punishment be necessary?*

*"Whoa, that's a helluva great question, Steve!"* Yes, it is! I'll repeat it: **Why would additional punishment be necessary?**

Seriously, this is a theological train wreck looking for a wall to crash into.

> *If physical death within a divine timeframe*
> *is the penalty for sin...*
> ***Why is additional punishment necessary?***

Do you have an answer? No. You don't! You can't answer the question. **Why is additional punishment necessary** if 'physical death' is the ***ultimate punishment*** as God declares in Genesis 3:19?

If God's stated penalty for sin is physical death—return to dust—and that penalty has been carried out for every human being who ever lived, **why is additional punishment necessary**? Where in the original covenant with Adam did God mention anything about **eternal torment after death**?

*He didn't! Did he? Hell fuckin' NO!*

**This concept is NOWHERE in Genesis!**

It's like you discover that the fine for a parking ticket is $25, and that fine has already been paid. So why does somebody else insist you also owe $50,000 and life in prison?

The biblical penalty for sin is DEATH ITSELF. **The cessation of physical life and return to dust**. *Not eternal conscious torment.*

I'll say that again: The biblical penalty for sin is **death itself**. The cessation of physical life and return to dust. *Not eternal conscious torment.*

One more time for the nosebleed section:

*The biblical penalty for sin is **death itself**. The cessation of physical life and return to dust. NOT eternal conscious torment*

OMG this flips theology on its head. **If death itself is the penalty**, then the penalty is already served…*and so the solution isn't to escape some post-mortem torture chamber.*

**Well then, you can go ahead and excommunicate me now and beat the rush!**

What IS the solution?

**The SOLUTION is to overcome death through RESURRECTION.**

Imagine a courtroom where a judge pronounces sentence on a convicted criminal: "For your crime, you are sentenced to five years in prison." The bailiff then adds, "And after that, you'll have to pay a $50,000 fine and perform 2,000 hours of community service."

Everyone recognizes the bailiff has lost his mind. The bailiff has no authority to add to the judge's sentence. Only the judge can pronounce sentence, and he clearly states exactly what the punishment is.

God's the judge. We're the dimwitted bailiff. *We've added punishments that the Judge never pronounced.*

In Genesis, God, the ultimate Judge clearly pronounces the sentence for sin: **PHYSICAL DEATH—RETURN TO DUST.**

*God didn't add eternal torture. MAN DID.*

Who gave men the authority to add to God's clearly stated sentence?

Certainly not God. He says *exactly* what the punishment is.

Nothing more.

Nothing less.

Look, I get it. You say, "Well, there goes the seminary curriculum!" Yep. Poof! Gone. Like a flea fart in the wind.

Because what we've done here is NOT some **theological malpractice** or *denominational fantasy*. We've simply let the Hebrew text speak for itself, without 1500 years of Christian commentary, church tradition, or English translation filters that contaminate God's word.

No Christian systematic theology. GONE.

No Greek philosophy. GOODBYE.

No Latin mistranslations. GET THE FUCK OUTA HERE.

Just the original Hebrew words that God actually speaks in Genesis *b'yom* (in the day). NOT *pith'om* (immediately).

And **physical death**. *Return to dust.*

Not **spiritual death** plus *eternal torment*.

If this kicks over your theological apple cart, well then ooops, my bad. Deal with it. The raw truth. As for me, I'd rather follow the simple, yet terse warning in Proverbs 30: 6 **do not to add God's words** than to twist scripture to fit centuries of man-made doctrine. I'd rather let God be true even if it makes every theologian a bullshitter.

This isn't about being comfortable.

This is about **accuracy**.

The Judge pronounces one sentence: *physical death within his timeframe.*

That sentence is carried out for every human who's ever lived.

*Case closed.*

If theologians want to add eternal conscious torment to God's clearly stated penalty, they can explain that to him when they see him.

As for me, I'll stick with what God actually says.

Nothing more.

Nothing less.

# Chapter 5

# Bad Blood

We've established that the penalty for sin is physical death within God's timeframe. **Not infinite wide-awake torture**. But this raises a critical question: *HOW does sin actually lead to death?* What's the genuine mechanism that turns Adam's rebellion into YOUR death sentence? And here's the million-dollar question: What does Christ actually DO to fix this death sentence we inherited?

Here's where to look for your answer: It's in understanding **what happened to our human blood when Adam sinned**.

### The Poison

Leviticus 17:11 gives us a vital clue: *"For the life of the flesh is in the blood."*

When Adam sinned, **something nasty happened to his blood**. *It got corrupted*. This corruption passes down through all generations. It causes the *gradual deterioration* of the human body until it eventually **returns to dust**.

It's like a *genetic mutation* that causes **progressive physical decline**.

The soul that sins shall surely die because the soul that sins *corrupts its blood,* and corrupted blood is the *only* way humans die. This corrupted blood is the real "hereditary sin." Not some **mystical guilt** that passes down. No, it's the **actual physical corruption** that leads inescapably to **death**.

### The Spring

Imagine a small mountain town with one water source. It's a spring that feeds the entire community. One day, someone contaminates the spring with a substance that doesn't make people immediately sick but gradually damages their cellular structure that leads to premature death.

Everyone who drinks the water is affected. Not because they personally contaminated the spring, but because they drink water from the same contaminated source. Children born in the town aren't guilty of contaminating the spring, and yet they suffer because the water they drink comes from that same source.

This is how Adam's sin affects humanity. When he introduces corruption into human nature, that **corruption** passes down through the generations. **Not as guilt**, but as *a physical condition that leads to DEATH*.

We don't inherit Adam's guilt…that's what preachers tell you.

Instead we inherit corrupted blood that **leads to our OWN death**.

Now it makes perfect sense why Jesus had to be *conceived by divine birth*. With God's **incorruptible** blood that coursed through his veins. And here's what's will gut-punch you: The blood of a baby never commingles with the mother's blood during pregnancy because of the placental barrier. This means Jesus is born with **uncorrupted blood**. Free from Adam's corrupted blood…AND Joseph's corrupted blood. No human blood allowed!

## The Cure

Imagine a hospital where everyone suffers from a rare blood disease. This blood disease gradually breaks down the body until death inescapably occurs.

**No one ever has survived it.**

Then to everyone's shock, a donor arrives with a unique blood type that's completely free of the disease. Not only that, but his blood contains properties that counters the disease's effects.

When transfused into patients, this remarkable blood **reverses the damage**.

*This is what Christ's blood does for humanity.* We all suffer from the **corrupted blood** that we inherited from Adam, a blood condition that leads *inevitably to death*. However, Christ's pure, **uncorrupted blood** provides the **transfusion** that reverses this corruption and **restores life**.

### The Transfusion

Here's what's so fantabulous about this: If *physical death* is the penalty for sin…and this death is because of *corrupted blood*…then **Christ's sacrifice ALONE. His PURE blood. Addresses the BLOOD problem.**

*He didn't pay off some cosmic ledger to satisfy God's honor or wrath…*

He gave us **uncorrupted blood** that reverses the corruption that leads to **PHYSICAL DEATH**.

1 Corinthians 15:26 identifies **death** as "the last enemy to be destroyed."

Death itself is the enemy THAT GETS DESTROYED. **Not some kind of HUMAN post-mortem punishment.**

*And Christ's resurrection is the victory over this last and final enemy.* This is why Paul focuses so intensely on resurrection in 1 Corinthians 15. The entire Christian hope centers *not on escaping hell* but on **conquering the nasty enemy of DEATH through resurrection**.

As Paul says, "For as in Adam all die (**physically**), so also in Christ shall *ALL be made alive* (**physically**)" (1 Corinthians 15:22).

### Misdiagnosis

A doctor diagnoses a patient with an exotic, incurable disease that requires expensive, painful treatments that the best they can do is delay death. For years, the patient endures these treatments, drains his savings and suffers terribly.

But then one day, a specialist reviews his case. He discovers he never had that disease at all. He has a completely different condition, one that's entirely curable with a simple procedure. For fuck's sake all that suffering and expense was a total waste.

Listen, the traditional doctrine of sin and salvation is like that **misdiagnosis**. It claims we suffer from **'spiritual death that requires endless punishment'** that requires the divine treatment of **'someone to suffer eternal punishment in our place.'**

But a careful reading of Genesis reveals we actually suffer from **physical death**. Physical death due to corrupted blood. And at precisely 3:00 PM on Wednesday afternoon, April 5, in the year 30, **Christ's pure blood conquers that physical death**!

Just like Adam's physical death wasn't immediate, neither is resurrected life immediate. Both run their course in due time. Traditional theology distorts this simple truth when they insert concepts that are nowhere to be found in the original text. The distortion begins when they misunderstand **"in the day you shall die"** that requires *immediate death*, which leads to the invention of **"spiritual death"** as an explanation. It's like a helpful but misguided auto-correct that keeps changing "duck" to something completely inappropriate. (If you need me to explain that, then you should get out of the house more often.)

But I digress.

Once spiritual death is established, it's easy to extend this 'spiritual death' to **'infinite spiritual death,'** and eventually to **'eternal conscious torment with excruciating pain for trillions of years.'** But this entire theological framework collapses when we return to what Genesis actually says.

The death penalty pronounced in Genesis is **physical death** within God's timeframe. *That penalty has been carried out for every human who has ever lived.* **No additional punishment is necessary** to satisfy divine justice regarding the original sin. Why? Because—

**Christ's pure blood...**

**...provides the solution...**

**...to the corruption...**

**...that causes death...**

**...that makes our resurrection possible.**

God's justice is satisfied. Not by **endless punishment**...

...but by the *victory of life over death.*

But here's what makes this so revolutionary: This corrupted blood isn't just a side effect of sin. It's the EXECUTION METHOD. God doesn't kill you. *Your corrupted blood is a masterful executioner.* And it's not punishment. *It's consequences.* If you eat a spoonful of arsenic, you die. It's not punishment. It's consequences.

The death penalty isn't some external punishment God slaps you in the face with. It is the natural consequence of the corruption the fruit of the tree of knowledge of good and evil injects into Adam's very life force...his blood.

Now we can see why Christ's solution is so perfectly designed.

Okay, pause. Take a breath. Because what I'm about to say next is going to sound insane.

You might want to sit down for this one. When I first saw this in the Hebrew, I sat there staring at my Bible for twenty minutes.

I thought, "No way. God couldn't have... did He?"

But the more I dug, the more undeniable it became.

Here's the divine paradox that'll drop you to your knees: Adam's corruption isn't Plan B. **It is the NECESSARY PRELUDE to Plan A.**

Without corrupted blood, we'd never need pure blood. Without Adam's poison, we'd never receive Christ's cure.

God didn't scramble to fix Adam's mistake.

And here's the proof: God doesn't say "IF you eat of it, you shall surely die." He says "WHEN you eat of it, you shall surely die." Not IF. WHEN. God already knew Adam would eat **because God NEEDED Adam to eat.**

Why? Because God creates perfect. But perfect isn't the same as incorruptible. A perfect heart CAN sin. An incorruptible heart CANNOT. And here's the kicker: **God cannot sin. Therefore God cannot CREATE the fusion of evil with human nature. Only man can do that. God needed man to do something even God couldn't do. GO ROGUE. Corrupt the system. Fuse evil with nature.**

Once evil is fused, God can extract it. And extraction produces what creation alone never could: a nature that isn't just innocent. It's INCAPABLE of sin. Forever.

Adam's fall opens the door to something impossibly, incomprehensibly, unimaginably better...

...not just innocence restored, but corruption replaced with incorruptible blood.

Not just Eden regained, but a nature that CANNOT ever again sin rather than merely HASN'T sinned.

Adam gave us corrupted blood that kills.

Christ gives us pure blood that resurrects.

The poison had to come first to make way for the cure that leaves us better than if we'd never been poisoned at all.

**THE DROP KICK:**

**God cannot sin.** Therefore God cannot CREATE corruption

**Only man can fuse evil with nature.** God needed man to go rogue

**Extraction requires fusion.** God can't remove what was never there

**Perfect does not equal incorruptible.** *Can* sin vs. *cannot* sin

**WHEN...not IF**...sin was a necessary prelude to Plan A

*God needed man to do something*
*God couldn't do—sin.*

Hell No! The Great Heist

# Chapter 6

# The Cure

Now that we've stripped away the religious horseshit about sin's penalty, we can grab ahold of what Christ *actually came to solve.*

His work doesn't satisfy cosmic ledgers. It provides **the ONE THING** that reverses Adam's blood corruption. That is: [drum roll, please]—

**Pure, brand new, spanking clean UNCORRUPTED BLOOD.**
*Untainted blood to override the death sentence that courses through our veins.*

But before we dive into this revolutionary understanding, I need to address the theological seizure that we just detonated.

### Brace Yourself

If you're sharpening your denominational pitchforks and screaming "HERETIC!" because I demolished your eternal torture chamber, take a deep breath. First of all, I'm NOT a bleeding-heart liberal who **waters down the gospel** or turns God into a cosmic teddy bear. I see you clutching your systematic theology books like a security blanket ready to pounce with your predictable questions: "But what about sacrifice?! What about God's wrath?! What about justice?!"

*Relax.*

*It's gonna be okay.*

Because I'm about to show you what REALLY happened. Not the theological fairy tale that Miss Poppins your Sunday school teacher spoon-fed you, but the actual mechanism behind **sin, death,** and **redemption** that's been right there. Hiding in plain sight all along. And watch this—it makes God's

61

justice MORE perfect, Christ's sacrifice MORE powerful, and the gospel MORE good news than your wildest theological dreams.

So drop your torches and your "Sinners in the Hands of an Angry God" sermons for just a few minutes, because when you finish this chapter, you'll discover that the REAL story is *far more glorious* than anything your skeptical tainted heart could ever conjure up.

## The Master Key

Imagine being locked in an ancient mansion with hundreds of rooms, each secured by a different ornate lock. For generations, people have tried to pick these locks using elaborate tools and complex techniques, but with limited success. The process is painful, time-consuming, and often damages the locks.

Then one day, someone magically discovers a master key right under their noses. A simple key that effortlessly opens every door in the mansion. All the elaborate lock-picking methods instantly become unnecessary.

For centuries, theologians have complicated Christ's work with elaborate theories, like he satisfies God's wrath, pays our debt, and fulfills divine justice.

*Oh, but what if Christ's solution is so much simpler than all their theories?* What if, when we understand *the real problem* Genesis identifies, Christ's solution is **perfectly tailored** to the *actual issue* we face. **Elegant, straightforward,** and **devastatingly effective.**

Now that we've established what the original death penalty actually is: *physical death…within God's timeframe of 1,000 years…***that results from corrupted blood**…well then, now we can **PROPERLY** understand what Christ's redemptive work addresses. And let me tell you **it makes theologians reach for the antacids**. It crushes traditional atonement theories, yet it *preserves the **biblical truth*** of Christ's sacrifice.

## Blood IS Life

Now here's where this gets wild, so let's start with a revelation that will delightfully scramble your theological brain circuits: **Your blood** doesn't just *carry your life.*

Your blood **IS** your life. Alright, I can already see I'm gonna have to say this a bunch of times.

The Hebrew equates the two, life and blood. How? **Life equals blood**. Bear with me here for a quick Hebrew lesson, because I know you don't know what the hell I'm about to say. הַדָּם **הוּא** הַנֶּפֶשׁ (ha-dam **HU** ha-nefesh) is Hebrew, translated into English is, "the blood, it [is] the life; the soul."

Look at the Hebrew word I magnified, like a magnifying glass: הוּא (HU). (I blew it up for you to make it easy for you to see.) This word **HU** is the key. It's the Hebrew word for "is…it is." This word creates an unbreakable equation: blood = life = soul. They're not three separate things. They're one thing viewed from three angles. This word HU means blood IS life IS soul. Not similar. Not connected. Identical. This word binds blood, life, and soul together so tight you can't pry them apart with a crowbar. They're one substance.

Genesis 9:4 states it plainly: "You shall not eat flesh **with its life**—that is—**its BLOOD**." Notice it doesn't say the life "contains" the blood. No. It doesn't say the life "carries" the blood. No. It says the life IS the blood. This is radically profound, so don't gloss over this like you scroll through social media.

Deuteronomy 12:23 removes all doubt: **"The blood IS the life."**

Not contains.

*Not carries.*

**Not represents.**

**IS.**

This isn't metaphor or poetry. The Hebrew word "הוּא" (**HU**) means "**it is**."

Like saying 'they're the **exact same thing**.' This Hebrew word HU doesn't just connect blood and life and soul. It makes them identical. Three words for the same thing.

Your blood **IS** your life.

Leviticus 17:11 hammers this home: "For the life of the flesh is in the blood...and I have given it for you on the altar...to make atonement for your souls...for it is **THE BLOOD** that makes atonement **BY THE LIFE**."

Notice it says *the blood makes atonement* '**BY** the life'...it doesn't say *the blood makes atonement* '**FOR** the life.'

It says **BY** the life. It doesn't say **FOR** the life.

**BY** = the mechanism through which atonement works.

**FOR** = would mean substitution or exchange.

HUGE difference!

The blood doesn't atone **FOR** the soul (as if they're separate things being treated). The blood atones **BY** the soul because **blood IS soul**.

And here's where it gets even more explosive: The Hebrew word for "**life**" here is **nephesh** (נֶפֶשׁ) nephesh is also translated as "**soul**." Brace yourself, because here it comes...

The blood atones **BY** the soul because the blood **IS** the soul.

**They are the same thing—that do the same work.** Your soul, your life force—the animating principle of your physical existence: your soul doesn't just *reside* in your blood...

**Your soul IS your blood.**

((GULP!...)) **Whaaat?!?** *Steve, did you just say...?*

Yes!!! You heard me! I said exactly what I said: Your soul **IS** your blood.

I know your brain wants neat categories. Blood here, soul there, life in another drawer. But Hebrew doesn't work that way. It's like if you try to separate wetness from water. They're different aspects of the same thing. Your blood carries your life, your life includes your personality, your personality feels emotions. It's all YOU.

*And scripture pounds this home over and over.*

Three different passages (Genesis 9:4, Leviticus 17:11, Deuteronomy 12:23) all tell us the same revolutionary truth. scripture is consistent:

**Blood equals life.**

*Life equals soul.*

**BLOOD EQUALS SOUL.**

**This absolutely obliterates** whatever you thought you knew about sin's corruption, because when Adam's blood got corrupted, *his SOUL—his life itself*—became corrupted.

This isn't about guilt that passes down. Get that out of your thinking. *It's INFINITELY crueler and harsher than guilt that gets passed down.* It's about corrupted blood. A CORRUPTED SOUL that passes down from generation to generation.

We don't inherit Adam's guilt. That'd be a walk in the park. No... *we inherit his corrupted blood* that results in our OWN corrupted soul, which leads to our own physical death. The death sentence that God pronounced in the garden.

**This SOUL corruption**—*this biological-spiritual aberration*—is what Adam passes down from generation to generation.

It's not some mystical, spiritual '**guilt**' that gets passed down.

No.

It's **ACTUAL CORRUPTED LIFE ITSELF**.

We didn't inherit Adam's guilt. **We inherited his corrupted SOUL-BLOOD.**

You are NOT guilty of **Adam's sin**.

*It's worse than that. Way worse than that.*

You got infected with **Adam's corruption**.

65

**Big difference.**

But wait, there's more. Since blood is soul...

*...then Christ's blood is Christ's soul...*

... and so Christ's blood transfusion into you and into me is literally God's SOUL TRANSFUSION into us! Much better idea, don't you think?

## Genetic Code

Imagine a genetic research laboratory working with pristine human DNA sequences. One day, a single viral strand accidentally splices into the genetic code, inserting itself between the existing sequences. The viral DNA doesn't replace the human DNA. It fuses with it at the molecular level. It becomes part of the genetic blueprint itself.

So now every cell that reproduces carries both **the original human code** AND **the viral corruption**, inseparably woven together. Children inherit this hybrid genetic structure. Not by choice, but **by biological necessity**.

Note that the corruption doesn't kill immediately. Just like it didn't kill Adam and Eve immediately. However, it programs the cellular breakdown that ensures death *within God's divine timeframe. **One thousand years**.*

For generations, doctors have treated the symptoms of this cellular breakdown. The aging, the deterioration, the inevitable mortality, but no one can address the root cause: ***the corrupted genetic code itself.***

*The viral splice is so thoroughly integrated that if you tried to remove it, you would DESTROY THE ENTIRE DNA STRUCTURE.*

But hold on a minute...Voila! *A breakthrough occurs.* A geneticist discovers completely pure, *uncorrupted DNA from an **untainted** source.* This isn't just treatment for the symptoms. **It's a REPLACEMENT** for the corrupted blueprint itself.

Anyone who receives this pure genetic code *stops the deterioration* and rebuilds from the cellular level up.

## Soul Transfusion

Hang in there, bros and hoes, because here's what happened that fateful afternoon when Adam ate the forbidden fruit.

**His blood got corrupted.**

And now…here's what makes theologians consider a career in real estate: Since blood IS life—**blood IS soul**—this means **Adam's very SOUL became corrupted.**

But not 'soul' like your literal mind imagines; some ghostly spirit floating around independently. In Hebrew thought, Adam's soul-blood-life-personality-emotions **ALL become corrupted as ONE integrated reality.**

*When his blood got corrupted,* **his entire being got corrupted.** *His emotions twisted. His desires warped.* **His personality permanently bent toward evil.**

This isn't some mystical 'guilt' that transfers. I wish it was as sweet-sounding and harmless churchy sounding as that. But no, it's way worse: It's **ACTUAL CORRUPTED LIFE ITSELF.**

We don't inherit Adam's guilt. **We inherit his corrupted SOUL-BLOOD…LIFE, PERSONALITY…EMOTIONS.** A 100% integrated reality that IS us.

You're not guilty of Adam's sin. No. Like I said, it's way the hell worse!

You are infected with the **totality of Adam's corruption.**

*Massive difference.*

Not Adam's *guilt* spreads. No.

**Adam's DEATH spreads.**

Death—through *corrupted blood.*

Death—through **corrupted SOUL.**

Blood IS soul—one unified reality, not two separate things.

**Same with Christ's!** *Christ's blood IS Christ's soul.*

**The blood transfusion Christ offers is literally a SOUL TRANSFUSION.**

(Read that again. S-l-o-w-l-y.)

This isn't metaphor. This isn't hoodoo voodoo. This is what the Hebrew text *actually says* when you don't force it through Greek categories; when you let it speak as God's truth.

So Christ transfuses His pure soul into our corrupted souls. Got it.

But this raises an exciting question: What was this perfect sacrifice supposed to carry out? For centuries, Christians have assumed they know the answer. Most say something like: "Jesus died to save us from eternal punishment" or "He satisfied God's wrath against sin."

*But what if we've been guessing...when we didn't need to?*

What if God actually gave us a detailed blueprint that clearly outlines exactly what the Messiah is supposed to carry out? What if, instead of relying on theological speculation, we simply read the divine specifications?

Fortunately, we don't have to guess.

God gives us the exact specifications in one of the most overlooked passages in scripture.

## Chapter 7

# The Magnificent Six

So you're sure why Jesus died? You think it's to escape hell? Think again.

God tells us his EXACT specifications for his mission on earth. SIX precise objectives the Messiah accomplishes, and not ONE of them is "save people from eternal torture." Not one.

That's right. God literally records his blueprint in Daniel 9:24, and traditional theology ignores it for 1500 years. But then, BAM! In one fell swoop God's blueprint demolishes their **cosmic torture chamber**.

Let's look at Daniel 9:24, which outlines six specific objectives the Messiah accomplishes. Three he already has, three more to come:

> *Seventy weeks are decreed about your people and your holy city, to finish the transgression, to put an end to sin, and to atone for iniquity, to bring in everlasting righteousness, to seal both vision and prophet, and to anoint a most holy place.*

Look at this list.

1. Finish transgression

2. Put an end to sin

3. Atone for iniquity

4. Bring in everlasting righteousness

5. Seal both vision and prophet

6. Anoint a most holy place

Where's 'saving souls from hell'? Where's 'rescuing people from eternal torment'?

IT AIN'T THERE.

The Son of God comes to earth, God declares his mission statement, and whadya know, eternal conscious torment is nowhere to be found in the list. In fact, eternal conscious torment doesn't even make honorable mention. You'd think it would at least crack the top six!

These six objectives center on **ending sin itself and its consequences** (which we've established primarily is **physical death**). They do *NOT* focus on *satisfying some divine requirement for eternal punishment.*

But here's the cool part: **every single one of these objectives is about RESTORATION and COMPLETION.** *NOT on PUNISHMENT and SEPARATION.* This perfectly aligns with what we've discovered about God's ultimate plan.

So how exactly does Christ accomplish these objectives? How does he actually end sin and its effects?

The answer is in understanding how **Christ's pure blood** *directly addresses each of these six objectives*. Rather than satisfying divine wrath or paying cosmic debts, Christ's blood accomplishes something far more practical and profound:

**Christ's blood** doesn't appease anger—it repairs DNA. **Christ's blood** doesn't pay debts. It purifies contamination. **Christ's blood** doesn't satisfy justice. It restores what's broken. Because at the end of the day, the question isn't "How do we satisfy God's wrath?" The question is "What fixes humanity?" And the answer, every single time: **Christ's blood.**

When 1 John 1:7 tells us that "the blood of Jesus his son cleanses us from all sin," it's NOT using a *metaphor*. **The blood of Christ LITERALLY cleanses our corrupted blood.**

*It reverses the biological corruption that Adam introduced.*

70

## Factory Recall

Imagine an automobile manufacturing defect that affects millions of vehicles. The defect causes a critical component to gradually deteriorate until the vehicle eventually breaks down completely. The manufacturer issues a recall, offering to replace the defective component with a properly functioning one.

This repair doesn't just compensate owners for having a defective vehicle; it actually fixes the problem at its source. After the repair, the vehicle functions as originally designed.

*This understanding transforms how we view liberation from the corruption of this temporary world.* It's not primarily a **legal transaction** where Jesus takes our punishment. **It's a *BIOLOGICAL RESTORATION* where his pure blood cleanses *our corrupted blood*** and thus frees us from the *internal corruption* that leads to DEATH.

It's like the difference between paying someone's medical bills versus actually curing their radiation sickness.

Hebrews 9:22 tells us that "without the shedding of blood there is no forgiveness of sins." This makes perfect sense when we understand that sin corrupts blood, and only pure blood can cleanse that corruption.

Get a firm grip on that phrase: **FORGIVENESS OF SINS** and brace yourself for a massive punch in the gut, because here's where traditional theology gets taken to the emergency room for translation trauma.

[CUT TO THE LOCAL TV STATION] 'And now for tonight's theological weather report, it looks like we'll have more of the same traditional interpretation with partly cloudy understanding and...'

*[Intern rushes in with paper]*

'Wait, I'm sorry folks, we're getting breaking news from our Greek language desk. It appears there's been a MASSIVE mistranslation error discovered in Hebrews 9:22.'

'Holy shit. We've been reading 'forgiveness of sins' for 1500 years when the Greek actually says 'JUBILEE.''

'Our biblical language correspondent is telling me that the Greek word 'forgiveness' **ἄφεσις (aphesis)** commonly translated as '**FORGIVENESS OF SINS**' in the ESV is the EXACT same word used in the Septuagint for the "**Year of Jubilee**" in Leviticus 25:10 '**ἔτος ἀφέσεως**' (**YEAR OF RELEASE/JUBILEE**).'

'Folks, that's like reading '**detention**' and you think it says '**execution**.' That's like reading '**surgery**' and you think it says '**torture**.''

'Ladies and gentlemen, **aphesis** doesn't mean *pardon guilt*—it means **complete liberation, total release, restoration to original condition**. In the YEAR OF JUBILEE, slaves are freed, debts are cancelled, and property is returned to its original owners. Everything is restored to how it is supposed to be!'

'Notice this Jubilee reset everything is for **everyone** every 50 years. No qualifications, no prerequisites, no prayer to pray. You didn't have to "accept" Jubilee. You just get it.'

'So folks, breaking news tonight: Hebrews 9:22 actually reads: Without the shedding of blood there is no **JUBILEE**.'

*That's what the word FORGIVENESS OF SINS means!*

'Oh, and get this. At the Last Supper, Jesus says his blood is shed "for the FORGIVENESS (**aphesis**) OF SINS" (Matthew 26:28). Same word. **JUBILEE**. Jesus himself declares the ultimate Jubilee, the total liberation for everyone.' No exceptions.

'But wait, it gets uglier for traditional theology. Our Greek language correspondent just discovered something that'll make every seminary dean consider smoking weed: There IS no Greek word for 'forgiveness' as English speakers understand it. None. Not one word that means 'pardon guilt so you don't go to hell.'

'I repeat: The Greek language has NO word that means what your pastor taught you 'forgiveness' means. No word for 'judicial acquittal.' No word for 'God declaring you legally innocent.' Zero.

'Every single Greek word your Bible translates as 'forgiveness' actually means **liberation from bondage, release from slavery, cancellation of debt, or...JUBILEE!**

'The Greeks had *aphesis* (release), *charizomai* (gracious debt cancellation), and *apoluo* (setting free). What they DIDN'T have? A word for 'God pardons your guilt so you avoid eternal torture.'

'Augustine needed that word to exist. It doesn't. Never did. The entire penal substitution framework is built on a **mistranslation** that turns LIBERATION into PARDON and JUBILEE into ACQUITTAL.'

'This has been a special report. We now return you to your regularly scheduled theological demolition. We'll continue following this story as it develops. Back to you in the studio.'

This makes perfect sense when we understand that sin corrupts blood, and only pure blood brings complete **JUBILEE**. Total liberation from that corruption.

But if this hasn't detonated your theological brain, what I'm about to say will. When Jesus says *'Father, forgive them'* from the cross, he doesn't just ask for a pardon. He says ἄφες. JUBILEE language. **He proclaims complete liberation for HIS OWN EXECUTIONERS.**

Think about that. The Roman soldiers who hammer nails through his hands. Jesus secures their JUBILEE. The Jewish leaders who orchestrate his death. JUBILEE. The mob that screams 'Crucify him!.' JUBILEE.

Not "don't punish them," but "ERADICATE FROM THEIR HEARTS COMPLETELY the corruption that drives them to execute me."

The cross wasn't just payment for sin. It was the proclamation of universal JUBILEE. *Even for those driving in the nails.* If Jesus proclaims **Jubilee** for his own murderers without them asking to be set free, without their belief in

God, without their permission, without them even knowing they needed it, then who the hell do you think you are to think that **ANY HUMAN CAN ESCAPE HIS UNBRIDLED DETERMINATION TO SET THEM FREE!**

I told you at the beginning of this book: I won't attack your beliefs. I'll reveal **better** ones. God's plan really IS wildly better!

## The Ring

A young man had been kidnapped as a child and sold into slavery in a distant land. For twenty years, he labored under cruel masters, his identity forgotten, his name changed, his heritage erased. The chains around his wrists had worn grooves so deep they seemed part of his very bones.

He has no memory of his true family. As far as he knows, he has always been a slave.

Meanwhile, his father never stops searching. He spends his fortune hiring investigators, following every lead, never giving up hope. Finally, after two decades, he finds his son.

But here's the plot twist: the son doesn't recognize his father. He has no idea he even *has* a father. When this stranger approaches him and claims to be family, the slave shakes his head. "You must be mistaken. I'm nobody. I've always been nobody."

But the father doesn't just come with words. He arrives with legal documents that declare the debt paid in full, the slavery contract void, and the chains unlawful. He brings new clothes to replace the slave rags, a signet ring to restore the family name, and deed papers that show that his son was heir to the entire estate.

As the chains fall away and the father gently places the family ring on his son's finger, twenty years of stolen memories came flooding back. The son looks into those familiar eyes and whispers, "You didn't just forgive me... you brought me **home**."

74

"That's what fathers do," came the gentle reply. "You were never really a slave. You were always my son. I just came to remind you who you've always been."

THIS IS JUBILEE mistranslated as forgiveness of sins.

This is the story of the prodigal son. **This is jubilee.** *Not just to pardon the slave* but to **awaken the son.** Not just to *forgive the debt* but to **restore the memory.** Not just to *remove the guilt* but to **destroy the lie that you were ever anything less than beloved.**

God's blood-bought jubilee doesn't merely forgive what you've done like we think of in the English meaning of the word. No! It's an entirely foreign concept to our natural mind. FORGIVENESS. It's not merely forgiveness. It's complete and total restoration. *Even for his executioners.*

## The Exodus

A skeptical friend once challenged me: "Steve, that father story sounds like a Hallmark movie. Come on, has God ever actually done anything like that, or are you just making stuff up to sell books?"

I chuckled and cracked open my Bible. "Hold my beer and watch this."

Picture an entire nation born into slavery in Egypt. For 400 years, they labor under cruel taskmasters, their true identity forgotten, their heritage buried under the weight of bondage. They cry out in desperation, not even knowing if anyone is listening.

But their father had never stopped watching. He hears their cries and remembers his covenant with Abraham, the promise he'd made generations before they were even born.

God doesn't just send a message of comfort. He doesn't just say, "I forgive you for all the times you've complained about your slavery."

Instead, he arrives with supernatural legal documents: ten devastating plagues that declare Egypt's slavery contract null and void. He brings treasures to replace their rags, gold and silver from the Egyptians, and deed papers to an entire Promised Land that is rightfully theirs.

But here's the most beautiful part: *As they walk out of Egypt, free for the first time in centuries, God reveals their true identity.* **"Israel is My firstborn son,"** he declares to Pharaoh.

They weren't just escaped slaves. They were **God's children** who had been stolen and *needed to remember who they'd always been.*

The Exodus wasn't about forgiveness. It was about **JUBILEE**.

## *The Exodus wasn't about forgiveness. It was about jubilee.*

"Without remission of blood there is no forgiveness of sins" (Hebrews 9:22). No, no, NO, a thousand times NO. That's a shitty translation. Here's the real deal: *"Without remission of blood there is no JUBILEE!"*

Christ's blood—his Jubilee—is **complete liberation**, **total restoration**, and the **revelation of their true identity** as *the covenant people of God.*

And if God performs this kind of blood-bought **JUBILEE** for an entire nation in history, and if he performs this kind of blood-bought **JUBILEE** for his EXECUTIONERS, what makes you think he won't perform this kind of blood-bought **JUBILEE for ALL creation**?

This isn't just a beautiful story.

It's God's proven pattern.

*Jubilee doesn't just forgive the crime—*
*Jubilee breaks the chains, burns the prison,*
*and restores you to the throne you were born to occupy.*

Look, I know this challenges everything you've been taught, so in the words of Joan Rivers, "Can we talk?!" Listen, when you get back to what scripture ACTUALLY says instead of what theologians CLAIM it says, *God's plan is so much more amazing than the fairy tale they've peddled.*

And you ain't seen nothin' yet!

You see when we strip away the theological additions and return to what scripture actually says, God's plan is **infinitely more beautiful, more perfect, and more humane than anything theology could dream up.**

*The truth really IS better than the man-made doctrines!*

But this raises the ultimate question: What is the final destination of Christ's blood-bought jubilee?

If his pure blood cleanses our corrupted blood and brings complete liberation, *where is all this restoration heading?*

**The answer is the most fantabulous outcome imaginable.** One that makes *every theological argument* **worth fighting** and *every translation error* **worth correcting.**

Because Christ's work doesn't just cleanse.

*It culminates in something that will take your breath away.*

## Chapter 8

# The Last Enemy

Picture a master architect who designs the most magnificent city ever imagined. For years, construction goes according to his detailed plans: beautiful buildings, flowing gardens, and perfect infrastructure. But then a catastrophic earthquake strikes. It leaves the entire city in ruins.

Insurance adjusters survey the devastation and shake their heads. "Total loss," they declare. "We'll cut you a check for the damages and you can build something else somewhere else."

But the architect pulls out his original blueprints and smiles. "You don't understand. This isn't about cutting losses or building something different. This city is my forever dream. Every foundation, every beam, every detail is planned for permanence. I'll not abandon the design. I'll **restore** it."

"But the cost..." the adjusters protest.

"Already paid for," the architect replies, as he points to a line item in his budget labeled 'Restoration Fund: Fully Allocated.'

"This is part of the plan. Every broken stone will be rebuilt. Every damaged foundation will be restored. When I'm finished, this city won't just be repaired. It'll be more glorious than the original."

**This is resurrection.** Not Plan B because Plan A failed. Not damage control because sin won the day, but the architect's **original intention** is fulfilled *exactly as designed*. Everything broken is made new, everything corrupted is restored, everything lost is found again.

Paul calls death "the last enemy to be destroyed" because the architect never intended for his city to stay in ruins.

*If death is the penalty for sin, **then RESURRECTION is the solution**.* This is why Paul places such emphasis on the resurrection in 1 Corinthians 15. It's not an afterthought or a bonus feature of salvation. No. **IT'S THE ENTIRE POINT!**

> *For as in Adam **ALL** die, so also in Christ shall **ALL** be made alive.* (1 Corinthians 15:22)

## The Antidote

Christ conquers death itself. Not your Christian death if you believe hard enough. DEATH. Period. Hindu death. Atheist death. Satanist death. Death ITSELF gets destroyed, and death doesn't check your theology first. You think death asks if you're Christian before it kills you? No? So why does your resurrection need your permission?

Imagine a deadly poison that contaminates the entire planet's water supply. Every human being who drinks water is affected, and there's no escape. Everyone is slowly dying from this poison. Then a brilliant scientist develops an antidote so powerful that a single drop can purify an entire lake. The antidote is distributed. It gradually works its way through the water systems of the world.

The scope of the poison's effect is universal. It affects everyone. Wouldn't it make sense that the antidote's effect would be equally universal? **If the poison reached all,** *why wouldn't the antidote?*

Notice the parallel structure and the use of the word "**ALL**" in both clauses of 1 Corinthians 15:22. The scope of those who die in Adam is the same as the scope of those who will be made alive in Christ—**EVERYONE!**

It's like a legal contract where Clause A says "all parties affected by the accident" and Clause B says "all parties receiving compensation." You can't claim different groups of people. It's the same "all" in both clauses.

This is why Paul calls death "the **LAST** enemy to be destroyed" (1 Corinthians 15:26). **Death itself is the enemy**—the *last* enemy—*not some unending permanent ongoing punishment after death.*

*And Christ's victory over death through resurrection is the solution.*

## Rome's Device

The method of Christ's death takes on new significance in this framework. Consider what actually happened on the cross. While crucifixion was designed by Romans as the most horrific form of execution, **God used this brutal method to accomplish his redemptive purposes.**

The nail wounds in his hands and feet cause bleeding, and most significantly, when the soldier pierces his side with a spear, "at once there came out blood and water" (John 19:34). This wasn't coincidence. It was God ensuring that Christ's pure blood is completely given for humanity.

Jesus doesn't just die; **he sheds his blood completely**. The spear thrust into his side confirms his death and also confirms that his life—**carried in his blood**—has been fully poured out. As John carefully records, "blood and water" flowed from his side (John 19:34), demonstrating that Christ's pure blood had been completely given for humanity's cleansing.

God takes Rome's instrument of death and makes it the instrument of life.

## The Spear

The biblical emphasis isn't on how much blood was shed, but on whose blood it was and what it accomplished. Christ's blood was effective not because of the method of extraction, but **because it was PURE, UNCORRUPTED blood that could cleanse *what Adam's corruption had polluted*.**

The spear thrust confirmed what the cross had already accomplished. Christ had given his life completely. The "blood and water" that flowed weren't about maximizing quantity but about **confirming the completeness of his sacrifice**.

## ALL Equals ALL

Here's where this gets devastating for traditional theology. If Christ's blood provides the solution to Adam's corrupted blood, and if **ALL** humanity shares in that corruption, then the scope of Christ's redemptive work MUST BE AT LEAST AS UNIVERSAL as the problem it addresses.

Think about it. Would a competent doctor create a cure that only works for some people with the disease? Of course not! Does God do less? But that's an emotional tug at the heart strings kind of a reason. Romans 5:18-19 confirms this with mathematical precision:

"Therefore, as one trespass led to condemnation for **all** men, so one act of righteousness leads to justification and life for **all** men. For as by the one man's disobedience the many were made sinners, so by the one man's obedience the many will be made righteous." BOOM! Not emotional. *Mathematical precision.*

Paul couldn't be more clear if he used a megaphone. Same "all." Same "many." Same scope. It's not even subtle. *"Whoa, but hold on a minute, Speedy Gonzalez Steve…"*

Yeah, yeah, yeah, I know what you're thinking, so before you start with your *"but 'many' doesn't mean 'all'"* theatrics, let's castrate that bull right now: In Greek, **"THE** many" (οἱ πολλοί hoi polloi) with the definite article **"THE"** means **"THE** totality. The whole infected group. It's not "some people" or "a bunch of folks." It's the whole damn crowd.

Also, when Paul says "THE many" fell through Adam, he means every single human. You agree with that, right? Of course you do, because you believe Adam's sin affects everyone. Now here's where this gets fun: Paul uses the EXACT same Greek construction…THE many…for Christ's work. Same Greek phrase. Same verse. Same Paul.

You can't admit "THE many" means "everyone" when talking about Adam, then suddenly claim it means "only believers" when talking about Christ. That's not translation. That's theological gymnastics.

If ALL fell through ONE man's sin, then ALL are made righteous through ONE man's obedience. You can't change the math halfway through the equation.

ALL = ALL, or Paul needs a new calculator.

Imagine a symphony building toward a triumphant finale. The music progresses through dissonance and tension. Every note points toward resolution.

But just before the climax, some in the audience insist the symphony ends with the tension unresolved. They claim the composer intended most of the discordant notes to remain forever discordant. Only a select few finding harmony. Absurd. No skilled composer introduces tension without resolution.

Similarly, God doesn't introduce resurrection only to leave most of humanity permanently unresolved in death. The narrative builds toward complete resolution. Death destroyed, not merely conquered for a select few.

Good news! Your loved ones aren't damned to sniffing sulfur, eating worms, and drinking piss water! Christ's pure blood transforms everything. It's not about escaping punishment; it's about being washed clean FROM THE CORRUPTED BLOOD ITSELF.

It's not about satisfying God's desire to punish; it's about *satisfying God's desire to restore life*. It's not about paying the price of eternal torment; it's about *paying the price of death so that resurrection of brand-new bodies follows*. And most importantly, it suggests a scope of redemption that extends as far as the problem it addresses *to all humanity who are affected by Adam's corruption*.

A locksmith spends years developing elaborate tools and techniques to open an ancient, complex lock.

One day, a child discovers that the lock can be opened simply by pushing on a hidden panel. No elaborate tools or painful sacrifices required. The solution is elegant, simple, and accessible to all.

Traditional theology makes Christ's redemptive work seem like that elaborate lock-picking system: *complex, difficult to understand*, and **based on human cooperation**. But when we acknowledge the **real** problem (**corrupt**

**blood is death**) and Christ's solution (**pure blood is resurrection**), the magnificence of God's plan is *better than our wildest dreams.*

Traditional theology focuses on "saving souls from hell." Biblical theology focuses on "**saving bodies from physical death BY THE BLOOD OF CHRIST.**" I'll say that again, it's a doozy:

*Traditional theology focuses on "save souls from hell," but biblical theology focuses on*
*save bodies from **physical death BY THE BLOOD OF CHRIST***

The first view accepts *the permanence of death* **yet offers escape routes to heaven**; the second view **challenges death itself as THE ENEMY GOD DESTROYS.**

If the penalty for sin is physical death within God's timeframe…and if **Christ's pure blood provides the solution to the corruption that causes death**…then the ultimate outcome is **resurrection of dead bodies**: *a resurrection that is as widespread as death itself.*

Adam ate the fruit and didn't die that day. Panic. Theologians invented spiritual death to cover the gap. Spiritual death spawned original sin. Original sin spawned eternal torment. The whole nightmare is built on one mistranslated word. B'yom meant "within a thousand years." Adam died at 930. God's word was precise. Ours wasn't.

And what comes next is even more brilliant. In the next chapter, we explore the fusion of evil with human nature…and God's ultimate plan to **separate the two**. This will complete our understanding of **God's ultimate redemption.**

## Chapter 9

# The Extraction

Physical death is the sentence for Adam's sin. Christ served it. Done. Finished. Finito.

BUT there's something else *terribly wrong with us*. Something more massively horrible than the penalty of physical death. Are you ready for this? **It's the fusion of evil WITH OUR HUMAN NATURE.**

Hear me out as you flex your sphincter so tight you can't drive a wet watermelon seed up it with a sledgehammer. When Adam and Eve ate the forbidden fruit, the clock for their physical death begins to tick. Tick-tock, tick-tock. And this countdown is a good thing, because our physical death that's meant to kill us…instead opens the floodgates to physical life without end.

So as I mentioned, a momentous horrendous curse worse than physical death is on the horizon. It's the diabolical progeny of the evil that fuses itself with our hearts. Listen, evil didn't just influence Adam and Eve externally or temporarily. No, it's more horrific than that. **Evil fused itself with our very nature**—*so thoroughly integrated*—that to separate one from the other is **impossible** *without the physical destruction of the person.*

Stay with me here, because **God's solution is more radical than you can imagine:** This complete eradication of evil from the heart of man (again, thanks to the sacrifice of the Lamb of God) this eradication only happens *in a certain location*, **at a future moment in time**, under divine circumstances. What might that time, circumstance, and location be…?

[PULL BACK THE CURTAINS TO REVEAL…]

**GOD'S ULTIMATE OPERATING ROOM: The Judgment Seat of Christ**

It's beautiful! Take a deep breath and follow me. Imagine a master chef who prepares a delicate soufflé. He carefully whips egg whites into a cloud-like froth, then gently folds in rich chocolate and other ingredients. Once baked, the components completely **BOND**: *the eggs, chocolate, and other elements fuse into a single new creation.*

Now imagine someone asks the chef to remove just the egg whites from the finished soufflé.

**It's impossible. He has to destroy the whole soufflé.** He cannot separate the ingredients without an *annihilation of the entire dish.*

**This is precisely the predicament** God is faced with when the evil in the garden bonds itself to human nature. When Adam and Eve ate the forbidden fruit, evil didn't just *influence* them. No, it's much worse. **Evil FUSED itself with their nature.** *Evil so thoroughly integrated with them* that to separate one from the other is **IMPOSSIBLE…**unless you destroy the whole person. I'll say it again:

*Evil fuses itself with man's very nature*
*so thoroughly integrated that to separate one from the other is*
*IMPOSSIBLE without UTTER DESTRUCTION OF THE PERSON*

We've established that *physical death within God's timeframe* is the original penalty for sin, and that **Christ's pure blood** provides the solution to the corruption of death. But the monumental challenge is to surgically separate the evil that has burrowed itself so deeply into our hearts that **the two are INSEPARABLE.**

And as I mentioned, this is the **nasty, bitch-ass piece** to this theological puzzle. That is, *the fusion of evil with human nature so thoroughly integrates that they BECAME ONE AND THE SAME.* You can't tell them apart.

### The Burrowing

When God warns Adam not to eat from the tree of the knowledge of good and evil, *what exactly is at stake?* Traditional interpretations focus on **the acquisition of moral knowledge**. As if Adam and Eve were *previously moral* *imbeciles* who couldn't distinguish right from wrong. But c'mon! Adam named millions of varied species, every bug, bird, beast, and begonia across the entire planet. And he recalls every name without notes. Adam was Elon Musk on steroids. Listen, Adam already knows how wrong it is to disobey God. *He doesn't need to eat the fruit to learn that disobedience is wrong!*

So what is really at stake when God warns about the tree of the knowledge of good and evil?

### The Hostile Takeover

Consider two ladies discuss a tragic event like the loss a loved one. The first lady has studied grief extensively in books. She knows the five stages of grief, understands the neurological processes involved, and can articulate the emotional journey with precision.

The second lady just lost her husband of fifty years.

Which lady truly "knows" grief?

This distinction helps us understand what happened in Eden. The Hebrew word for "**knowledge**" (**yada/ידע**) gives us a clue. This isn't just intellectual knowledge; it's **experiential, intimate knowledge**. The same word used when Genesis tells us "Adam **knew** his wife Eve" (Genesis 4:1).

When Adam and Eve eat the forbidden fruit, evil doesn't just influence them externally…no.

**Evil invades and colonizes their DNA.**

It's like a hostile virus *rewrites the source code of human nature itself.*

This wasn't about Adam learning, or even studying what evil is. **It's about evil *welds itself* into his very DNA** and *metastasizes* **through his entire being** until it is *inextricably woven* **into the fabric of what it means to be human.**

Evil doesn't just corrupt them. **Evil performs a HOSTILE TAKEOVER.** Evil installs itself as *the operating system* that runs every human heart from that moment forward. The fusion is so complete, **so fundamentally**

**transformative**, that to separate good from evil is **like trying to remove the heat from fire without extinguishing the flame**. I'll say that again:

> *To try to remove evil from man's heart is to*
> *try to remove heat from the fire*
> *without extinguishing the flame*

Evil doesn't just attach to human nature ring around the collar. **It *merges at the molecular level*.** It is **inseparable from our identity. Evil rewrites our essence** so thoroughly that *the corruption* and *the person* no longer exist independently. I repeat: the corruption and the person CAN NO LONGER EXIST INDEPENDENTLY.

**This is the MONUMENTAL SURGICAL CHALLENGE that God faces.**

### The Cancer That Thinks It's You

A gardener notices a beautiful flower overtaken by an invasive vine. She tries to remove the vine but discovers their roots are completely intertwined. Tear out one, kill both. The only solution: extract both together, separate them carefully, and replant the flower with clean roots.

Jesus uses the metaphor of *wheat and tares* in Matthew 13:24-30. When the servants discover weeds (**tares**) growing among the wheat, they ask if they should pull them up. The master refuses, saying:

> *"No, lest in gathering the weeds **you root up the wheat along with them**."*

You've heard the wheat and tares are evil and good people. Nope. This parable isn't just about the coexistence of good and evil people. **It's about the coexistence of good and evil WITHIN EACH HUMAN HEART.** (More about this in a moment.)

Now then, pay attention, because here's where the '**blood IS soul**' revelation destroys your traditional brain. Remember **blood IS soul**. Well, since evil fused with our **soul-blood** since Adam, *the wheat and tares* represent

88

the **pure** and the **corrupted** elements within each person's soul, so intertwined at the molecular level that *to separate them destroys the person.*

Since **blood IS soul**, and evil has fused with our **soul-blood**, the wheat and tares represent **pure** and **corrupted** elements **fused together** within each person. So intertwined at the molecular level that to separate them obliterates the man.

The roots of the wheat and tares *are so intertwined that you CANNOT REMOVE ONE without TOTAL DESTRUCTION OF THE OTHER.*

You inquire, *"But Steve, I thought wheat and tares was about good people and bad people."* Well, hold on, let's slow this speeding bullet train. If this parable was about separation of *good people* and *evil people*, then we have a serious problem. God says this about the wheat and tares, 'if you remove the tares, you'll also destroy the wheat.' You've heard the wheat and the tares are evil and good people, right? Throughout history, God demonstrates his willingness to separate righteous people from wicked people. He does exactly that during Noah's flood, doesn't he? The flood destroys the wicked but preserves *the righteous.* That's a separation of good and bad people, isn't it?

He does it again with the angel of death in Egypt that kills the firstborn while it passes over the homes of those with blood on their doorposts. And Pharoah's army in the Red Sea. So why does Jesus suddenly say "don't separate good people from bad people" if God did the same *people-separation* in Noah's day, Egypt, and Pharoah's army?

**The pattern is clear:** God has no problem to destroy the wicked people and preserving the righteous people. And yet he forbids the separation of the wheat and the tares because the **separation also destroys the wheat**. Does this make sense to you now? *The easiest way for you to understand is to imagine how impossible it is to destroy the wet without destroying the water.* You can't separate one without the other. It's impossible. It crashes the laws of physics.

Now we can get a better idea what divine judgment is. It's not divvying up people into heaven and hell. It's about the separation of the corruption within the heart—the TARES from the WHEAT. *This surgical separation only happens at the final judgment, where God at long last has the opportunity, the tools, and the setting to surgically rip out of our hearts what has molecularly bonded itself to us since Eden.*

## The Promise

Only God himself can extricate this evil that fuses itself into our DNA. And remember, it depends NOTHING upon our cooperation; it has nothing to do with whether we agree to the deal or not. Remember Abraham's **tardema**? Anesthesia? God performs the surgery while we're **tardema**; while we're knocked out, anesthetized. God puts Abraham to sleep lest Abe puts his two cents in: "Hey God, you should demand mankind to 'accept you into their heart.'"

To which God replies, "Abe, cut the bullshit. Here's the deal: **I put you to sleep.**" *Why, God?* "Because you humans are such control freaks. You'll try to hold the scalpel during your own heart surgery. Your pride and arrogance insists on 'works.' Your pride and arrogance, which equates to self-flagellation puts a demand on others that even you yourself cannot fulfill. You'll even demand people to 'accept Jesus into their heart' lest they burn in sulfur and dog shit. You'll turn my unconditional covenant into a 'works' requirement. So Abe, follow my recipe: It's called **'Shut the Fucupcakes.' Leave me alone! Get out of my way! Let me do the surgery! Let me operate!**"

Then anesthesia hits. Abraham's out cold.

Now fast forward 2,000 years to another divine surgery. This one's at Calvary. Remember when Jesus said 'Father, forgive them' from the cross? Follow me closely here, because you're about to see man-made theology that's as messed up as a football bat. What did Jesus really say?

Remember that aphes [forgiveness] means JUBILEE. Complete liberation, regardless of whether we agree to it or not. He demands NOTHING from you. (We do. We demand 'ya gotta believe it or burn like hell.')

Here's what Jesus absolutely, certainly, unequivocally, and without their consent ensures for his violent and decrepit executioners:

*He doesn't merely ask for their pardon.* He guarantees that one day, **the very evil that drives them to hammer nails through his hands...the vile wickedness that drives them to execute the King of the Jews...the Messiah RIPS THAT SHIT OUT OF THEIR HEARTS.**

*THAT'S **aphes**. That's **JUBILEE**. That's "Father... **FORGIVE** them."*

The Roman soldiers were clueless, but **Jesus proclaims their future surgery**—*the glorious day when the corruption that drives them to crucify God...that same God* **one day surgically extracts that hatred from their hearts**. The mob that screams, 'Crucify him!' has no idea **that the man they are murdering is simultaneously SECURING THEIR COMPLETE RESTORATION.**

"Father forgive them" is not a mere forgiveness like we know of in English, like 'you were a bitch, but I forgive you.' No! **God's forgiveness is a surgical removal of the evil EVEN FOR THOSE DRIVING THE NAILS INTO HIS HANDS AND FEET.**

And this proclamation isn't just for the crucifixion crowd. God, through his prophets, extends this same guarantee to ALL humanity.

The prophet Ezekiel promises:

> *I will give you a new heart and put a new spirit in you; I will remove from you your heart of stone and give you a heart of flesh.* (Ezekiel 36:26)

And in Jeremiah 31:33, God promises:

> *I will put my law in their minds and write it on their hearts.*

This isn't flowery verbiage. These are surgical promises. They're God's guarantee that he will literally remove the corrupted heart that has tormented humanity since Eden and replace it with one that actually works right.

But here's what makes this surgery unlike any earthly procedure: **it requires the complete death of the patient.** Not near-death. Not mostly dead. *Completely, utterly dead.* **ABSOLUTE TARDEMA!** Because the fusion of

91

evil with human nature is so thorough, so molecularly complete, that only death can create the environment suitable for the extraction.

## Your Stone Heart

You have someone in mind.

You might not admit it out loud. But there's a face. A name. Maybe someone who hurt you. Maybe someone who hurt someone you love. Maybe someone you've never met. Just a face from a headline, a trial, a story that made your blood run hot.

You know who they are.

And somewhere deep in your chest, there's a voice that whispers: *Good. Let them burn. Let them burn forever.*

Sit with that for a moment.

Picture them burning. Skin blackening. Lungs filling with fire. Screaming. Clawing. Begging for death that never comes.

A thousand years pass. The fire doesn't cool. The screaming doesn't stop.

A million years. A billion. The stars burn out and still—*still*—they writhe in agony.

Worlds without end.

If that doesn't crack something inside you...

If you can hold that image in your mind and feel nothing...

If that voice in your chest still whispers *good*...

A heart that can contemplate eternal conscious torment—for *anyone*—and remain unmoved?

That heart is stone.

And then God looks at *you*—the one who would celebrate his children burning, who would call unending agony *justice*, who would watch the flames and feel satisfaction—

And he says, "Get on the table."

Because your heart is stone too.

And he will cut it out. And He will replace it with flesh.

Not because you deserve it. You don't.

But the surgeon doesn't operate based on what you deserve.

He operates because it's *who he is.*

Let me show you exactly why this divine surgery can't happen while you're still breathing.

## Chapter 10

# Flatline

Imagine a patient with a rare condition where a malignant tumor has completely infiltrated his heart. The cancer cells have so thoroughly intertwined with the healthy cardiac tissue that no surgeon can separate them. Any attempt to remove the cancer destroys the heart itself.

The only solution is a complete heart transplant. To remove the *entire hybrid heart* and **replace it with a brand new healthy one**. But such a procedure is beyond current medical capabilities.

Remember Ezekiel and Jeremiah from the last chapter? Those aren't flowery metaphors about a "new heart." They're God's literal promise to perform divine heart surgery. To RIP OUT the heart that's been fused with evil and replace it with one that actually works. This operation is beyond human capability. *But not beyond divine intervention.*

**Here's what makes this surgery so remarkable:** The trauma of extraction attacks the corrupted heart itself. The evil that fused with human nature *violently resists its own destruction.* But the person receives the gift of a pure, new heart *without feeling the agony of separation.* It's not the individual that screams. **It's the evil that "screams." It's the EVIL THAT SCREAMS as God destroys that evil.** The individual feels pure incomprehensible peace as God liberates him from what has tormented him since Adam's fall.

### The Separation

This heart transplant...**this separation of evil from human nature**...*is precisely what complete restoration is all about.* It's not just about forgiving sins or escaping punishment. **IT'S MUCH MORE FRICKING UNBELIEVABLE THAN THAT**. *It's a fundamental transformation of human* *nature*. It's a **permanent purge of the evil** that fused itself with your heart, like rust that penetrates so deeply into metal that the two are chemically bonded.

But here's the thing: this separation can't happen in this life. It can't. The fusion is too complete; **too thorough. It can only happen through DEATH and RESURRECTION.**

Romans 6:7 tells us that "anyone who has died has been set free from sin." The Greek here (δεδικαίωται dedikaiōtai) is legal language. It means "acquitted, justified, released." Death acts as the judge's gavel. DEATH declares you officially free from sin's jurisdiction. But don't confuse the **paperwork** with the **procedure**.

Hebrews 9:27 says, "It is appointed for man to die once, and after that comes **judgment**." That word "**judgment**" κρίσις (krisis) doesn't mean "sentenced to torture." It means SEPARATION. The root meaning is "to distinguish, *to separate one thing from another*." Think of a surgeon who makes an incision. He separates healthy tissue from diseased tissue.

Death gives you the legal paperwork. You're officially released from sin's claim on you.

Judgment (krisis) is the operating room where God at long last SEPARATES the corruption from your heart.

Death is legal freedom. **Judgment** is actual liberation.

Death is the legal release. **Judgment** is the surgical procedure.

Here's what makes this separation so remarkable: The violence of extraction *happens to the corrupted nature itself*. NOT TO YOU. The evil that fused with human hearts *fights desperately against its own destruction* like a parasite as it's being torn from its host.

*But the person, that's YOU, experiences peace. Not trauma.*

It's the **EVIL** that writhes and screams in terror as God annihilates it, while the individual receives the gift of their original, uncorrupted nature and their peace is restored.

The biblical imagery of "weeping and gnashing of teeth" *describes EVIL'S death throes*—**not human suffering**—*the violent crushing of what has tormented humanity since the garden.*

This is why Paul says in Romans 8:23 that we "groan inwardly as we wait eagerly for our adoption as sons, **the redemption of our bodies**." The final solution to sin isn't just forgiveness…

*…it's the complete redemption of our bodies through DEATH and RESURRECTION…***bodies with hearts finally freed from evil's nasty, filthy corruption.**

**God's plan is to completely, utterly, permanently RIP THE FUCKING EVIL OUT OF MAN'S HEART**…and then…EVIL'S WICKED REIGN **is OVER…!!! It's OVER!**

Now then, I want you to think about something: if evil's reign is truly over, God CANNOT leave ANY capacity for sin still inside us. Is that true? Not even a molecule. Not even a remote possibility the size of a pubic hair. *"Wait Steve, you're saying God removes our ABILITY to sin? Doesn't that destroy free will?"*

Good question. Wrong worry. Here's why:

### Sin-Proof

Listen, if God didn't completely and permanently rip out *the capacity to commit evil* from us…if he didn't utterly and entirely *stamp out the ability to sin* completely and permanently out of our heart, then there's a one hundred percent chance that at some time in the future, out of billions of people who still have the ability to sin across endless time, somebody eventually will screw up. Even a microscopic probability becomes mathematical certainty when you multiply it by infinity.

One cosmic 'oops' across endless time and we're back to square one.

Thus, this transformation goes so much deeper than temporary forgiveness. It's the surgical removal of the evil that has fused itself with the human heart like cream stirred into coffee.

Now, to extract something that's completely fused SHOULD destroy both substances. The coffee AND the cream. The person AND the evil.

But here's where divine surgery becomes miraculous, and I need you to FEEL this, not just understand it:

When God rips the evil out of our hearts, it's the corruption itself that experiences the violence of separation. The corruption fights desperately against its own annihilation.

We, you and I, experience liberation. Not trauma.

The evil viscerally and violently screams as God destroys the corruption that poisoned us since Adam. We feel the incredible relief of our heart that is finally restored to its original purity.

*It's not our heart that gets ripped apart.* No way. It's the alien invader that hijacked our heart that God crushes, annihilates, and destroys.

We don't lose part of ourselves. The evil is an invader. It's not us. The invader gets destroyed. God destroys the evil intruder. WE RECOVER OUR TRUE SELVES for the first time since the garden.

### You Must Die to Get Your Wings

Consider the transformation of a caterpillar into a butterfly. The caterpillar doesn't simply grow wings and fly away. Instead, inside the chrysalis, the caterpillar's body completely dissolves into a soup of cells. From this apparent destruction, the butterfly's body forms…new, beautiful, and capable of flight.

The caterpillar must **dissolve into a soup of cells** for the butterfly to emerge. *The transformation is total. Every cell rebuilt from scratch.* Yet there's **continuity of identity**. The butterfly is the same organism as the caterpillar, despite the complete transformation.

This is one of nature's most vivid pictures of death and resurrection. *The old must be completely broken down so the new can emerge.* This is what happens in **divine heart surgery**. *Our sin-fused nature undergoes **complete dissolution through death*** so that our purified nature emerges through resurrection.

The death doesn't destroy the person. It destroys what CORRUPTS the person.

That's so good I'll say it again:

> *The death doesn't destroy the person.*
> *It destroys what's corrupting the person.*

Here's what makes this metamorphosis so beautifully merciful: The violent dissolution affects the corrupted hybrid nature, the sin-fused cells that have poisoned human identity since Adam. They fight desperately against their own destruction, like diseased tissue resists healthy regeneration.

**But the person experiences transformation. NOT DESTRUCTION.**

*It's the corruption, the evil that gets liquefied and dissolved,* while our human heart gets completely rebuilt from pure, uncorrupted source material; that is, from God's own heart. How? By his life. What's his life? His blood. What's the blood? It's God's soul, his heart, his emotions.

Just as the butterfly emerges more beautiful than the caterpillar ever was, redeemed humanity emerges more glorious than Adam before the fall, not because the person was destroyed, but *because everything that destroys Adam (and us) finally gets eliminated through divine metamorphosis.*

Now here's where this gets absolutely mind-blowing:

> *Not just freedom from the DESIRE to sin...*
> *freedom from the CAPACITY to sin.*

The final state of humanity isn't only freedom from the ability to sin. God takes it even further: **HE REMOVES OUR ABILITY TO SIN.**

After the final resurrection and the separation of evil from human nature, **we won't even have the machinery to generate sinful desires**.

The machinery for sin is COMPLETELY GONE.

The sin-generating equipment. **Completely extracted**.

*It's IMPOSSIBLE to sin!*

The machinery itself—gone. Poof! Like smoke in a hurricane. Thank you, Jesus!

**But wait…here's the cruise missile that blows up all the questions you have to what I just said:**

### Can God Sin?

If the omnipotent Creator of the universe **CANNOT** lie (Hebrews 6:18)

…and we know he can't.

Or be tempted by evil (James 1:13) …

…and we know he can't.

*Not because he **chooses** not to do so…*

…but because **it's literally IMPOSSIBLE for him to do so**.

Well then how in the Sam Hill hell will WE have the ability to sin if God himself can't?!?

God doesn't have "freedom to sin but chooses not to."

No.

God does not even have the ABILITY to sin!

And our Creator conforms us into HIS EXACT IMAGE!

When Romans 8:29 says we're "predestined to be conformed to the image of his Son," it means **the same kind of nature**. One where sin isn't just undesirable. **It's IMPOSSIBLE.**

## Smoke in a Hurricane

This concept is so foreign to traditional thought that it requires multiple analogies to break through our theological brain cramps.

Remember the **blood IS soul** revelation from Chapter 6, right? Alright then, when corrupted **soul-blood** gets replaced with pure **soul-blood**, you don't just get new desires. **You get an entirely new operating system.** *The corruption that generates evil impulses is gone at the source.* It's not about **choosing differently**; *it's about the evil-generating machinery completely blown to smithereens!*

Imagine a person whose addiction-generating brain chemistry is completely removed and replaced with neurochemistry that's physically incapable of experiencing addiction. They don't "choose not to crave drugs." **The brain machinery that generates those drug-cravings is GONE.**

It's like asking someone to grow gills after their lungs have been surgically perfected for air-breathing. They can't "choose" to develop gills; they don't have the biological equipment. Or picture a car with its engine completely removed. It can't "choose not to drive." It has no driving capacity whatsoever.

That's exactly what happens to us. In eternity, we won't think, "Gosh, I'd love to commit adultery, but I just can't." No! We'll have **ZERO capacity for anything contrary** to God's perfect life, peace, happiness, and joy that he's planned for us since the beginning (Isaiah 64:4 and 1 Corinthians 2:9):

> *Eye hath not seen, neither ear heard, nor has entered into the heart of man the things which God has in store for him.*

Isaiah says it. Paul confirms it. God promises it.

Here's the reality: The violent removal of our capacity for evil is the annihilation of the corrupted nature itself. It's NOT the annihilation of US. When God surgically extracts the sin-generating machinery from our hearts, the evil equipment gets destroyed—ripped out, incinerated, obliterated—while we're finally FREE. Free to be fully human. Free as God originally designed us. Free with NO DESIRE TO SIN. Not even a flicker. Not even a whisper. Gone.

We scream, not in agony, but with joy unspeakable and full of glory.

However…**THE CORRUPTION SCREAMS BLOODY MURDER AS IT DIES.**

We scream from the mountaintop, "Hallelujah" as we feel inexplicable peace that passes all understanding. The joy unspeakable and full of glory. The complete liberation.

We never again feel the dreaded enemy of fear. We now live in a world without end with none of the internal war that has raged in us since Adam.

We don't lose our freedom…

…we gain it for the first time since the garden.

## Chapter 11

# The Appointment

Have you ever wished, or prayed for God to take away your nasty desires for…hell, you name it: lust, worry, fear, unforgiveness…laziness, overeating, drugs, alcohol…anything else? The weaknesses we ALL have. Well, I have good news! *During God's ultimate heart surgery, the divine fire of God **burns away the corrupted nature that generates** those evils that plague us.*

Traditional theology says *"God will burn you."*

God says, "I will burn **the heart that torments you**."

God's not our enemy who's gonna singe our hairy butts. He's our **surgeon** that removes what torments us. Who wouldn't want the wicked temptations that torture us to be burned away?

That's not restricted freedom; it's EXPANDED freedom. It's the freedom to be *fully human as God intended…***WITHOUT THE CORRUPTION that fuses itself to our hearts**.

Traditional theology makes God the threat. Scripture's theology makes **the corrupted heart** the threat…and **God the solution**.

People that read this can think of their own struggles with lust, worry, fear, etc. and realize "YES! I want those tormenting thoughts OUT OF ME!"

Traditional view: **"God will burn me!"**

Scriptural view: **"God will burn what's tormented me!"**

Here's what makes this surgery so merciful: At the judgment, the divine fire *burns the corrupted nature itself.*

And let me tell you that evil doesn't go down without a fight. The evil that generates those tormenting desires fights viciously against its destruction. At the final judgment, God kicks ass while YOU experience **liberation**. **NOT INCINERATION**. It's the evil corruption that writhes in pain in the fires of God as he crucifies it. Meanwhile you feel the incredible relief of freedom from the behaviors you hate.

The "burning fires" is God as he destroys the evil machinery that was installed, like a computer virus, in your heart. You are the spectator as your tormentor finally get what it deserves while you recover your original, pure, and undefiled nature. Actually you're not a spectator, because you're knocked out cold like Abraham during the covenant ceremony.

### The Scope

The scope of this ultimate heart surgery is given to ALL men. Just as ALL humanity has experienced the fusion of evil with human nature through Adam, so ALL humanity experiences *the **separation of evil from human nature** through Christ.*

This is stated in passages like 1 Corinthians 15:22-28:

> *For as in Adam ALL die, so in Christ ALL will be made alive... Then the end will come, when he has DESTROYED all dominion, authority and power... The last enemy to be destroyed is DEATH... so that God may be ALL in ALL.*

Notice the final state: "...so that God may be all in all." *This suggests a* **comprehensive restoration** *where God's presence fully permeates* **EVERYTHING** *and* **EVERYONE**.

Here's what makes this universal surgery so magnificent. (Yes, you heard me right: UNIVERSAL SURGERY.) The violent destruction affects all God's enemies: dominion, authority, power, and finally death itself. **Notice it doesn't destroy THE PEOPLE who have been forever enslaved by these forces**. When Paul says Christ will "destroy all dominion, authority and power," *it's the corrupt systems and evil forces that experience God's annihilation.* NOT the humans! **Humans experience liberation from what has plagued them since the fall.**

The corruption fights like a gladiator against its massive extinction. But on the flip side, countless people feel the relief of *freedom from what has controlled and tormented them forever*. It's not humanity that gets destroyed. *It's everything that **destroys humanity** that gets destroyed.*

Now that we've established the problem…*evil fused with human hearts,* and the necessity of divine surgery, **where exactly does this ultimate operation take place? BRACE YOURSELVES…**

Scripture gives us a precise place. Remember where? And when?

**THE JUDGMENT SEAT OF CHRIST.**

Paul writes in 2 Corinthians 5:10: "For we must all appear before the **judgment seat of Christ,** so that each one may RECEIVE what is due for what he has done in the body, whether good or evil."

Hold up. Wait a minute. That word "**receive.**" What a lousy translation. The Greek word for "receive" is **κομίζω (komizō)** and it doesn't mean "get what's coming to you." That's what preachers tell you, isn't that right? "You'll RECEIVE a spanking, you'll RECEIVE a whip-lashing, and you'll RECEIVE eternal conscious torment. Well, that's NOT what it means.

RECEIVE (the Greek word *komizō*) means **"recover what was stolen from you."** RECOVER WHAT WAS STOLEN FROM YOU. It's the same word as when *someone RECOVERS stolen property* or *RECLAIMS something that was rightfully theirs all along*. Well now, how much different is that from what we were taught!

This is why studying scripture in the original languages matters. **Mistranslations create false doctrines.**

Let's re-read 2 Corinthians 5:10:

> *For we must all appear before the judgment seat of Christ, so that each one may **RECOVER (not receive) … RECOVER***

*(NOT receive) ... RECOVER what rightfully belongs to us...AFTER our divine surgery.*

RECOVER what rightfully belongs to us. Not RECEIVE punishment of thirty lashes and an STD.

## The Rap Sheet

So, what does this action of "**RECOVER**" look like at the judgment? Think of a patient who arrives at a world-renowned medical center for a complex surgery. The medical team has the complete chart. Every injury, every malfunction, everything that's gone wrong with his body. But they don't review this chart **to PUNISH him for being sick.** *They prepare for the most sophisticated surgical procedure ever attempted:* the complete separation of a life-threatening parasite that's fused itself to his vital organs.

This is what happens at the judgment. God reviews everything we've done "in the body." Not to condemn us, but to **SURGICALLY EXTRACT EVERY TRACE OF THE EVIL CONTAMINANT THAT FUSED ITSELF INTO OUR HEARTS THROUGH ADAM'S DISOBEDIENCE.**

Here's how God precisely targets this surgery. Alright, here we go. The violent extraction affects *the parasitic contamination itself.* In other words the evil that has fed off our human nature since Adam. NOTE: **The evil fights viciously against its own removal**, like a cancer resists chemotherapy or a virus struggles against its imminent destruction from the antibiotics. But you and I experience healing. Not harm. Not a whipping with Dad's belt. No, we feel inexplicable peace.

*But the evil...? Oh fuck! The evil feels painful agony.* **The vile contamination thrashes about in agony** as it gets separated from our hearts that it has corrupted, while we feel the incredible relief of finally having our life-threatening infection *completely eradicated.* God's surgical precision ensures that **ONLY the alien corruption** gets destroyed. **NOT you and me.** *God preserves our original, pure human nature and fully restores us to perfect health.*

106

## The Evil Feels the Burn

Malachi 3:2-3 describes God as one who "sits as a refiner and purifier of silver." The Hebrew word מְצָרֵף (*metzaref*) meaning "refiner" or "smelter." It's someone who uses fire to separate precious metal from worthless dross with surgical precision. It doesn't mean punisher. Not tormenter. Not the guy running a guillotine.

Now listen to me: **The refiner doesn't DESTROY the silver. He PURIFIES it.** *The fire eliminates what doesn't belong while it preserves what's valuable.* The silver emerges more beautiful than it was before the contamination occurred. Did you catch that? *More beautiful than before!* That means more beautiful than Adam in the garden. More perfect than Adam, and the best part: **incapable of sin.**

Traditional theology has turned God's judgment into a cosmic courtroom where an angry judge sentences criminals. But when we examine the Greek and Hebrew, we discover that's complete bullshit mythology. The judgement ain't punishment! **It's a surgical suite where the Great Physician performs…performs what? THE ULTIMATE HEALING.**

Here's the progression:

1. **The Diagnosis**: Evil is fused with human nature (Romans 7:17-20). CHECK! Happened with Adam.

2. **The Prognosis**: No earthly power can separate them (Mark 10:27). CHECK! Like trying to separate heat from fire, or wet from water.

3. **The Treatment plan**: Divine heart surgery (Ezekiel 36:26). We get a heart of flesh. Our heart of stone is thrown into the lake of fire. CHECK!

4. **The Surgical suite**: The judgment (2 Corinthians 5:10). God's operating room. CHECK!

5. **The Procedure**: Fire separates the corruption from the person (1 Corinthians 3:13-15). CHECK! It's a refiner's fire; not a fiery furnace.

6. **The Recovery**: Each person receives back (*komizomai*) their *original, uncorrupted nature*. CHECK! God rips out the cancer. He does NOT punish us for the cancer.

7. **The Result**: Hearts capable of life forever and ever without any hindrance from fused evil. CHECK, CHECK, AND **CHECKMATE**!

### Not One Left Behind

Here's what makes God's plan even more extraordinary: **This surgeon, God himself, has never lost a patient**. Romans 5:18 tells us the scope of Christ's surgical success: "Therefore, as one trespass led to condemnation for **ALL MEN**, *so one act of righteousness leads to justification and life for* **ALL MEN**."

The Greek word for "**all**" is πάντας (pantas). It means **every single one**, without exception. No loopholes. No fine print. Nobody falling through the cracks in eternal conscious torment on a technicality. Pantas—Pronounced PAHN-tahs—ALL. "All" means "No exceptions! Nobody's left behind."

Here's the hermeneutical rule: When the SAME WORD appears TWICE in the SAME SENTENCE in a PARALLEL STRUCTURE, it MUST mean the SAME THING both times. Did you get that? If you didn't, read it again.

You can't say "all means everyone" in the first half, then suddenly switch to "all means only some believers" in the second half. That's not interpretation. *That's theological musical chairs.*

But here's the promise: **Every patient makes a full recovery**.

Not one is lost.

Not even one remains contaminated.

The Great Physician's skill is **absolute**, his tools are **perfect**, and *his power and his love ensure that he will never rest until every trace of the alien contamination is obliterated, annihilated, and thrown into the lake of fire.*

## The Parasite

When the surgery is complete and God extracts your evil, what remains? **All that remains is YOU…as God originally designed you to be**…*free from the alien influence…the parasite that* **distorted your nature since the Fall**.

Here's the earth-shattering revelation:

*The fire doesn't destroy the person.*
*It destroys what corrupts the person.*

Dayum that's great news! This is why Paul writes with such confidence in 1 Corinthians 15:26: "The last enemy to be destroyed is death."

People don't suffer death without end after they die. **The corruption DOES suffer death without end. THE CORRUPTION suffers a furious and catastrophic obliteration into non-existence**. Death means "non-existence." Death gets destroyed. Not you.

This is great news! The evil that holds humans captive suffers the most furious, dreadful, and excruciating death. And then what happens? God casts that evil that's destroyed mankind for 6,000 years into the lake of fire for permanent and **total destruction**.

Here's what complete surgical success looks like: The violent extraction is over. The corruption fights so desperately against its own annihilation. God completely eliminates it, smashes it, and casts it into the abyss for total and complete destruction.

Now don't freak out when I tell you there's a shitload of screaming involved. The question is not WHETHER there's screaming. The question is WHO is screaming?

Who screams? What screams?

The screams and thrashes are **the alien parasite**. That evil monster that has devoured human nature since Adam. The screams don't come from the person being liberated. *They come from the alien evil as God destroys it.*

Now then, the surgery is complete. What emerges is humanity as God intended. Pure, free, and can finally live *without **THE INTERNAL SABOTEUR** that has poisoned every person, every choice, and tormented every man, woman, and child since the beginning of time.*

God restores people to their true perfection. When? How? **After their tormentor is permanently shredded**. Now then, when God tears the evil out of all men's hearts…voluntarily for some, involuntarily for others… (**it's an unconditional covenant**…remember?) So let me ask you: after the evil gets ripped out of our hearts, then WHO rejects Jesus? Take as much time as you need. If you need help in your answer, the answer is—NOBODY! **NOBODY! IT'S IMPOSSIBLE** to reject God's love. WHY?

BECAUSE GOD ERADICATES THEIR REJECTION MECHANISM!!!

## *It's impossible to reject Jesus AFTER God eradicates their rejection mechanism*

I'll bet you've NEVER heard that before. I sure never did. Not until God removed the blinders that kept the Hebrew and the Greek hidden from me. When we understand the judgment as God's **divine operating room** *it transforms how we see God as our father*. Instead of *fearful dread for that day*, we **ANTICIPATE** it. **It's the day of our complete liberation.**

Instead of *fear of the fire*, we look forward to the fire as **our final purification** that *frees us to live with hearts no longer torn apart by evil.*

*The judgment isn't God's torture chamber.* **It's God's HEALING CENTER.** And every member of the human race eventually finds themselves on that surgical table, where the Great Physician performs the miracle that *no earthly power could ever accomplish*: **the complete eradication of evil from human nature.**

That's not terrifying. That's liberating. **It's the best news EVER!**

When you understand what actually happens at the judgment, you realize that everyone—*absolutely everyone, without exception,* has an appointment with **the greatest surgeon ever: THE CREATOR OF THE UNIVERSE.**

Hell No! The Great Heist

*And his success rate is 100%.*

Here's why that table is open to everyone: If b'yom had meant "instantly" ...if Adam had dropped dead the moment he bit the fruit then maybe you'd need a password to get on the table. Maybe you'd have to "accept Jesus into your heart" to qualify for surgery. But b'yom didn't mean instantly. It meant within a thousand years. Adam died at 930. Physical death. And what passed to every human wasn't guilt. It was corrupted blood. It's the corrupted blood that causes man to do evil. The corrupted blood caused a corrupt heart. You know, the one that is desperately evil?

You didn't sign up for corrupted blood. You were born with it. And since everyone has the same disease, everyone gets the same surgery. No passwords required. No acceptance speeches. God doesn't ask permission. He rips the evil out of every soul who ever drew breath because every soul whoever drew breath inherited the corruption that only his scalpel can remove.

On a personal note, I've always felt I'd be okay on judgment day. *But there was always in the back of my mind a teensy-weensy bit of trepidation.*

But NOW...*now I'm looking forward to that day!* **That's the day EVIL gets ripped out of my heart!**

**The old me: FEARFUL** I looked at judgment as the cosmic courtroom where I hope God goes easy on me.

**The new me: JOYFUL.** The judgment is the divine operating room where **God frees me from all that has ever held me back.**

**The old me: FEARFUL.** "Please God, don't let me be condemned."

**The new me: JOYFUL. "FINALLY!** Let's go, God, **rip this fucking evil OUT of me!"**

This revelation liberates all of us from the nagging, tormenting, demented fear of judgment day. Even the most confident of believers harbor a haunted whisper of "what if I'm not good enough?" If you've never had that thought I'm gonna call you, "Liar, liar, pants of fire." (Of course the fire that is a purifying fire.)

111

**This revelation destroys our fear forever**, and replaces it with the *most excited anticipation*:

> *I have an appointment with the Greatest Surgeon*
> *who created me, and his success rate is 100%!*

Ladies and gentlemen, in just a few pages we have demolished the most cataclysmic event in human history and turned it into the most eagerly awaited love-fest we could ever imagine. Like when Mom and Dad tucked you in bed on Christmas Eve. "Santa's coming, Santa's coming!" you whispered.

Whether you had that family warmth or not, God's our true father, and he has prepared something infinitely more wonderful than any earthly Christmas morning.

We've gone from "Please God, don't let judgment day come" to "Come quickly, Lord Jesus. Bring it on!"

And remember—

*The fire doesn't destroy the person.*
*It destroys what corrupts the person.*

## Chapter 12

# Eli, Eli

What if Jesus' torture on the cross wasn't just to pay for your and my sins, **but it was also to exhibit the violent eradication of evil?**

Hold onto your britches bitches, because this land mine's about to annihilate 1,500 years of Augustine's fucked up translations. What am I talking about? Well, for centuries, Christians focused on Christ's *substitutionary death*. He died the death we deserved. And boy oh boy, it's true.

BUT WAIT...WHAT IF there's more to it than that? What if there's *another hidden layer to his suffering* that **we completely missed**? What if the agony of the man Christ Jesus...what if his agony was the **wickedness**, the **evilness**, the **atrocity** of OUR hearts?

Ladies and gentlemen, this'll make you shake in your boots and weep with gratitude: Jesus didn't only die *instead* of us. There's more, MUCH more: his death **shows the PROCESS** *the evil in our hearts goes through* when *the evil that's* **MOLECULARLY FUSED** into our hearts **gets surgically extricated... and violently ripped utterly out of our hearts**.

This isn't a movie fantasy. This is incredible insight *you've never before heard!* So let's let the bible explain itself. Let's let the bible show us the horrible terror that Jesus morphed into that fateful day when the son of God became "**Jesus-As-Evil.**"

I'm not sure you can handle this, but let's give it a whirl!

---

## The Tumor on the Cross

Christ didn't carry our sin. No, that's Sunday-School-lame-pablum. **He BECAME our sin.** He didn't carry our evil like a bucket of water. He BECAME our evil! Christ became the cancer…

…and then what happens? **We watch God BRUTALLY DESTROY that cancer.** Christ didn't just bear our corruption. He BECAME our corruption.

And then comes the unthinkable: **He experiences corruption's utter annihilation.**

He showed us what happens when God destroys evil: Evil **screams**, evil **fights**, and then it **dies**.

The evil screams were God's screams as **he BECAME our disease**. He shows us in 3D living color the horrific death as evil dies: violently, brutally, viciously.

Scripture consistently presents Christ not just as our substitute, but as our *first through the fire.* Remember that phrase: FIRST THROUGH THE FIRE. Jesus experiences complete and utter destruction of his body…yes, DESTRUCTION of his body as God destroys 'him-as-sin' with his furious fiery flames of destruction. Jesus goes first so that we know what to expect when our turn comes.

Jesus didn't have surgery to remove a tumor. *Jesus WAS the tumor!* **Jesus BECAME the tumor.** He—Jesus the tumor. God utterly destroys his one and only son. Why? Because that's how God destroyed OUR sin.

That's why the "ME" in "Why have you forsaken ME?" is so gut-wrenching. It's not that Christ **carries** sin like a sack of potatoes. No, he screams throughout God's utter destruction of him. It's **Christ-AS-sin** that suffers the full-fledged terror that OUR sin experiences when God utterly destroys OUR sin…when God the father annihilates it…when he tears it limb by limb away from our hearts.

Jesus BECAME our sin. He doesn't merely take it away.

Jesus BECOMES our sin that God destroyed.

Jesus himself experiences **the full annihilation.**

What pain do we experience? NOTHING!

We get **FULL LIBERATION!**

When do we get our full liberation? We get our FULL liberation at the judgment, remember? Oh shizzle, this is gettin' good! I'll come back to this in a minute.

Isaiah 53:4-5 gives us the dangerous revelation: "Surely he took up **our pain** and bore **our suffering**...by the ripping and twisting of his flesh...we are healed."

Notice the progression: Christ experiences the **flesh-ripping process** that produces...what? **Our total healing!**

Notice Isaiah doesn't say 'by his wounds we are forgiven.' He says 'by his wounds we are רָפָא (rapha)...HEALED.' That's surgical language. That's the language of a physician that removes a disease. It's not a judge who declares a pardon. God doesn't just change our legal status. He surgically extracts the corruption that's fused to our hearts.

Hebrews 2:10 makes it even more clear: "In bringing many sons to glory, it was fitting that God...should make the PIONEER (ἀρχηγός ar-KAY-goss) of their salvation **PERFECT** through what he **SUFFERED**."

"**Perfect**" here (τελειόω) doesn't mean morally flawless. Christ was already sinless. It means "brought to completion."

"**Suffered**" (παθημάτων - pathēmatōn) doesn't just mean "felt pain." As bad as that was, it's way the hell worse. It means **he felt every millisecond of evil's violent destruction.** What happened to him is what happens to our evil as it gets ripped to shreds. In other words, when **CHRIST-AS-EVIL** gets ripped to shreds. God ripped **Christ-as-evil** to shreds until there was nothing left. Why? Because CHRIST IS THE EVIL. God once and for all destroyed the evil that has been in our hearts since forever.

And finally, Christ is the **pioneer**—the one who goes first that creates the path. The word **"pioneer"** (ἀρχηγός **ar-KAY-goss**) literally means **"one who leads the way by going first."** Christ doesn't just die for us only. He **was crushed in THE DEATH PROCESS** *that the evil in our heart undergoes.*

I warn you this is grotesque. But let's continue.

### Two Surgeries

Before we examine the parallels, we must clarify a crucial distinction that traditional theology has confused: "If Christ paid for our sins, *why is any purification process necessary?*"

Because **PENALTY PAYMENT** and **CORRUPTION REMOVAL** are two distinct aspects of redemption.

Here's what I promised a few minutes ago...

### The Bill Is Settled

Christ died for our sins. Yes. *His physical death handles the death penalty imposed on us in Genesis.* We all die within God's thousand-year timeframe. **Christ takes that hit.** Debt paid. BOOM! We get a brand-new body. If all they did was kill him, that'd be bad enough. But here's what'll wreck you: **The evil that's molecularly fused with our heart since Adam is STILL THERE.**

*"Wait, what Steve? Even though Jesus died for us...you're saying that after we die we STILL have that corruption in our hearts?!?"*

YES. Christ's death doesn't magically extract the parasite from your chest. Christ paid your death penalty. Most definitely. We get brand new bodies.

**But look at yourself.** You still fuck up your marriage, you can't stop scrolling porn, you still have that voice that says 'God doesn't really love you.' **The parasite didn't vanish** when Christ died. It's still in there, feeding off you, tormenting you until 'the last day' when GOD SURGICALLY RIPS THAT MONSTER OUT OF YOUR HEART.

Judgment day isn't about punishment. In other words, *you don't get tortured* for having cancer any more than you get tortured for having a mental illness.

The Judgment is about HEALING your lousy fucked-up deceptive corrupt heart. *The cancer that torments you since birth finally gets ripped out, shredded, destroyed, and thrown into the lake of fire for its final destruction.*

Where and when? *At the judgment seat of Christ!*

You think you'll miss your evil heart?

Hell No! You'll weep with relief when he rips it out of your chest.

Why isn't it an immediate extraction of the evil from your heart? Well let me ask you, what's God's pattern for purification? When Israel left Egypt, were they *instantly* ready for the Promised Land? No. They had 400 years of slave mentality beaten into their DNA. The wilderness wasn't punishment. *It was detox.* **God had to burn the Egypt out of them** before they could handle the freedom.

Same with us. Christ pays our death penalty. Done! Completed! As soon as we die, ta-daa! He gives us a new body. But wait…*the corruption that's in our heart still needs to be surgically removed.*

Someone can pay for your cancer surgery, but you still need the actual operation. Paul confirms this in 1 Corinthians 3:13-15. Each person's work gets *tested by fire.* **The corruption burns** while the person emerges *"as through fire."* Paul's fire imagery in 1 Corinthians 3 describes exactly how the surgical removal works.

"Tested" (δοκιμάζω dokimazō) doh-kee-MAH-zoh doesn't mean pass/fail examination. It's the word for assaying metals. It's fire revealing what's pure gold and what's worthless dross. The fire doesn't judge the metal; it reveals what was always there. The impurities burn away; the gold remains. Same person, minus the shit.

Not punishment. It's PURIFICATION. It's an ugly process for the evil. *The evil screams as the fire burns.*

117

You don't scream. You get LIBERATED. **You emerge free.**

Our panic arises when we think purification means suffering. *It doesn't.* Purification means **liberation**.

*The **CORRUPTION** suffers destruction* while you and I experience **the unimaginable relief of finally being freed** from the poison that's putrefied our hearts since Adam.

## Fusion Takes Time

If you're like me, you wonder why God doesn't instantly rip the evil out. I'll answer that question with a question: If God could snap his fingers to remove the evil from our hearts, why didn't he do it for Adam in the garden?

**It's because evil didn't merely land on you like a fly on your sandwich. It FUSED WITH YOU.** Evil isn't layered on top like dirt we can wash off. It has BECOME our hearts. When Jesus BECOMES evil, *the host and parasite are now one organism.*

You can't snap away cream that's been stirred into coffee. *Fusion requires surgical separation.*

**Surgery…even God's divine surgery…takes time.**

*"But God can zap us instantly clean if he wants to!"*

That's a fair assessment. So then why didn't he? Why didn't God just snap his fingers and zap Adam instantly clean?

Because God's surgical love requires **process**, not *shortcuts*. **Careful process**, not *instant zapping*.

## The Preview

This is where this gets nasty, and heads all over the world explode. Jesus **felt** on the cross what your **evil feels** on the operating table. *"Wait Steve, WHAT did you just say?!?"*

Listen to me…do everything in your power to grasp this: JESUS FELT WHAT OUR EVIL FEELS when God burns **our evil** *out of our hearts*.

How could this be? **How could Jesus feel what our evil will feel?** *"Good question. How does Jesus feel what OUR EVIL will feel?"* It's because **JESUS BECAME OUR EVIL.** I've already told you this.

Whew, it'll wreck you for a New York minute. When we examine Christ's crucifixion alongside the **"weeping and gnashing of teeth,"** the parallels are shocking. Both describe **the violent death of CORRUPTION.**

They do *NOT* describe OUR suffering at the Judgment Seat. It's the **corruption** that screams in agony. NOT us.

Alright, hold your beer. This shit's about to get WILD: Jesus BECOMES the wicked vile corruption. he BECOMES the vile criminal, the wickedness, the slimy serpent…and thus HE experiences **the full brunt of the horrific agony of the death of evil**. *He felt…he experienced…he suffered the agonizing, violent, visceral, gut-wrenching agony that evil will feel on that day when that nasty ogre gets ripped apart from our human flesh and thrown into the lake of fire.*

The *"weeping and gnashing"* **describes the violent death throes of EVIL ITSELF as it's ripped to shreds.**

The **CORRUPTION** screams as it dies.

That's why Jesus screamed his guts out that fateful dark Wednesday afternoon at 3:00 PM on April 5, 30. We're going deeper. You'd better get ready.

### Legion's Scream

Rewind two years to a graveyard on the eastern shore of Galilee.

Jesus gives his disciples a live demonstration, a prophetic preview of exactly what happens to him at the cross.

Remember the Gerasene demoniac? When Jesus approaches Legion, screams came through the man's mouth: "What have you to do with me, Jesus, Son of the Most High God? I beg you, **do not torment me!**" (Mark 5:7)

Note the words: "Do not TORMENT me!" Evil screams a visceral scream, "DO NOT TORMENT ME!"

Notice: The MAN doesn't scream. LEGION does. The evil possessing him is terrified of its coming destruction.

Fast forward two years later to the cross. (2 Corinthians 5:21). Jesus' pure soul-blood has literally BECOME the corruption that was Legion.

**JESUS BECAME LEGION.**

When Jesus screams "My God, My God, why have you forsaken me?" **It's the same scream Legion screamed two years earlier.**

Follow me closely: Legion screamed that terrified panic-filled death scream as Jesus destroys that ogre. At the cross, Jesus BECOMES the ogre that he destroyed two years earlier…and he screams the identical terror-filled screams. **Same terror. Same death throes. Same evil as it experiences annihilation.**

Only this time, **Christ BECOMES the evil that is destroyed.**

Christ who becomes sin screams the same Legion's scream. When the screaming stops…when sin is finally dead…peace returns.

The Gerasene man sits peacefully after Legion leaves… clothed and in his right mind.

Christ rose peacefully after sin's destruction. He greets Mary in the garden with gentle words: 'Woman, why are you crying?'

We sit peacefully like the Gerasene man after God destroys our tormentor.

**But there's more to what Jesus screamed…**

## Chapter 13

# The Scream

We just watched Legion shriek in terror as Jesus destroyed him. We just watched Jesus BECOME Legion at the cross and scream the same death scream.

But here's what'll wreck your Sunday afternoon picnic: Even while screaming evil's death throes, Jesus was preaching.

Every Jewish child memorized Psalm 22. They could recite it in their sleep. So when Jesus screams "My God, my God, why have you forsaken me?" …every Jew watching knows exactly where he points.

This isn't a random cry of despair. This is the Son of God. **Even while he feels sin's annihilation**, he directs everyone to a specific scripture: one that starts with **abandonment** and ends with **universal restoration for all mankind**.

Think about this. While Jesus has literally BECOME the sin that God destroys…while Jesus experiences the full violence of evil's death throes…he manages to preach one more sermon. Not with explanation but with a reference every Hebrew heart recognizes.

> *ALL the ends of the earth will remember and turn to the Lord,*
> *and ALL families of nations will bow before him (Psalm 22:27).*

Jesus was pointing them to a psalm about *temporary suffering* that leads to *universal restoration*. While he experiences evil's death throes, he directs everyone to scripture that promises *ALL families will bow*.

Even in agony, Jesus preaches complete restoration. Matthew and Mark specifically preserve his words: "Eli, Eli, lama sabachthani?"— "My God, My God, why have you forsaken me?"

Traditional theology struggles to explain this cry. If Christ is God, how can God forsake God? Various theories attempt to resolve the paradox, but *what if we've missed the obvious explanation*? Here it comes…

**Christ BECAME the SIN that SCREAMED in terror.**

*Christ BECAME the SIN that SCREAMED in TERROR!*

*Same scream…*

*…same physical body…*

*…same destruction.*

The point is Christ doesn't have sin *attached to him*. No. You MUST hear me: at that moment **HE IS THE EVIL THAT ENTERED ADAM THAT BECAME THE EVIL PASSED DOWN TO YOU AND ME.**

There's a magnificently big difference between *carrying a disease* and **BEING the disease**.

Christ isn't **infected** with sin. He **BECOMES** the **infection**.

The screaming mouth? Christ's mouth.

The screaming entity? Christ-as-sin.

Not *two things in relationship*. **One thing** experiences *total destruction*.

This is why the "ME" in "Why have you forsaken ME?" is so profound.

The ME isn't Christ carrying sin.

The ME is **CHRIST-AS-SIN**.

One entity: Christ-as-sin. The **abandonment and annihilation** happens to Christ because HE BECOMES THE SIN THAT GOD DESTROYED ON THE CROSS…. the sacrificial lamb.

My God, get ahold of this theological warhead. When sin entered Adam, *Adam stayed Adam*. Just corrupted. When sin entered you and me, *we stayed you and me*. Just infected. We didn't BECOME sin. We didn't BECOME evil itself. The sin, the evil attached itself to us.

**But Christ?** He BECAME the evil that attached itself to us. The same evil he cast out of the Gerasene man. Legion. You think you've had it rough. He had it **BAD BEYOND ALL COMPREHENSION**! He BECAME sin. In 2 Corinthians 5:21, notice it doesn't say he "carried" our sin or "bore" our sin like luggage.

NO. "God **MADE** him…*who had no sin*…TO BE SIN."

**GOD MADE JESUS TO BE SIN. We just have it. He BECAME IT.**

Not *to have* it. Not *to hold* it. Not *to carry* it. **TO BECOME IT.**

Yes, GOD **made him to be sin** (rather than Christ sinning) …

…and yet *his blood remained pure*.

*He is sin with sinless blood.*

The eternal Son who had unbroken fellowship with the father for all eternity BECOMES what the father annihilates. But get this. It's important. *His blood **stays uncorrupted**. Why? Because **he never personally sinned**.*

### Jesus Screams Bloody Murder

Then…it happens. The scream that echoes through the eons of man's history. The sinless blood that carries all of humanity's sin feels the father's fury…and sin screams: 'My God, my God, why have you forsaken me?' *He's not seeking answers.* **He's shrieking in terror as its annihilation begins.**

*This wasn't Christ seeking information from the father.*

**This is sin as it experiences its own destruction. For God to exterminate sin…God must exterminate Jesus.**

For the first time in eternal existence, the son experiences absolute abandonment. *Not because he carried sin*, but because **he IS sin**.

123

The father turns away from his own son because God makes his own son (who is the word made flesh…and thus is God himself) to BECOME what holiness cannot touch.

*That's why Jesus' screams are literally evil's screams.* He BECAME LEGION. For three hours that fateful afternoon, the sky turned black, the earth convulsed, and God made him to be all the evil that ever was and ever shall be.

He isn't a person who carries evil who happens to scream. **He IS the evil that screams!** *He experienced every ounce of evil's violent and excruciating destruction.* Yes, the man…his body…got killed. Because ALL of him…ALL OF HIM…except for his blood…was EVIL.

You and I never *became* sin. Only Christ *became* sin *by divine decree*. Not by personal failure.

And when the lamb of God, who LITERALLY BECAME EVIL…screams, "My God, my God, why have you forsaken me?" the terror that pours out of his lungs…**THAT TERROR is OUR SIN as it experiences the annihilation, the destruction, the obliteration into non-existence.**

**Jesus became our sin. Therefore, God DESTROYS his own son**. But remember, his blood remained pure. But here's what makes this cosmically horrifying: Christ isn't just "the son of God" like some lesser being. **Christ IS God** (John 1:1, 14). So when the father annihilates Christ-as-sin, God destroys **part of himself**. God destroys that aspect of himself—the word made flesh— the part of God that he himself made to become sin (2 Corinthians 5:21).

**God…killed God…to kill sin.**

Can we pause here for a moment… The love of God takes my breath away. Christ wasn't experiencing personal purification. **He became sin itself** (2 Corinthians 5:21). He *temporarily bore* **the concentrated evil** that had irreparably fused itself with human nature.

## God Screams

But here's what the Greek reveals that will make you weep with gratitude: When Hebrews 2:10 says Christ was made perfect through what he "suffered," that word is παθημάτων (pathēmatōn).

This doesn't mean he "felt pain."

It means **"UNDERWENT THE COMPLETE PROCESS OF THE DESTRUCTION OF SIN."**

Let this shatter your heart and rebuild it. The eternal son who exists in perfect bliss with the father…and since he's the word, he IS the father as he BECOMES the corruption that destroys all of humanity.

Jesus **experiences** (the Greek word **"pathēmatōn"**) *the complete painful horrific extraction.* My God, what the hell is going on here?! Let me give you the complete picture.

Evil screams in terror when it's about to die. Jesus, like the One Ring dissolving in Mount Doom, screams as he's locked in the throes of death.

The parasite thrashes and rips flesh as it's torn from its host.

The parasite is Jesus, the spotless lamb of God.

Sin viscerally shrieks through the lamb's own mouth.

Jesus IS the corruption. God, the word made flesh, IS the corruption. God himself claws and writhes against his own extraction, fighting with superhuman fury.

The father recoils from his own word made flesh. God's face turns in holy revulsion AGAINST HIMSELF. His word made flesh has BECOME the wicked, vile, cursed evil that God swore in Genesis he would destroy.

When God cursed the serpent in Genesis 3:15, he promised to crush its head. Four thousand years later God cursing his own word made flesh. He curses himself. I know. It's tough to comprehend.

125

Four thousand years after God curses the serpent in the garden, God himself—**the word made flesh**—transforms into the serpent in the garden.

God keeps his promise.

The crushing begins.

"My God, My God, why have you forsaken me?" The journey from becoming sin…to experiencing sin's annihilation.

Jesus pioneered the path. He underwent every second of the extraction so we would know exactly what happens to our evil on the operating table in the operating room, the judgment seat of Christ.

The evil screams. Not us.

The corruption writhes in agony. Not us.

The parasite experiences obliteration. Not us.

Christ becomes the evil that experiences its own death so we could experience evil's death without permanent death ourselves.

If Jesus became sin, why didn't he burn forever in eternal conscious torment?

Because God made his word with a flesh body to become sin…but his blood never became sin.

GOD HUNG ON THE CROSS THAT DAY.

Thank you, Jesus, for bearing what was never yours to bear.

For becoming what you never were.

For dying the death that wasn't yours.

So we could live the life that you promised to Abraham.

## Chapter 14

# The Setup

Christ showed us what happens when God rips the evil out of our hearts. It screams, it fights, it dies. Now it's time to see what happens to US when it's OUR turn.

Our destiny is not about who gets to go to heaven and who goes to hell. It's about God that performs **the ultimate heart surgery**...*when he rips the evil out of our hearts. God rips that all-encompassing evil that has fused itself to our human nature...that evil that causes misery, heartache, and pain, and has since the day the doctor slapped our behinds.*

Judgment Day is NOT about **eternal punishment**. No, no, NO! It's about **COMPLETE RESTORATION**. I'll bet you never heard THAT before. Complete restoration. The final judgement is when God at long last addresses the root cause of all human suffering: **The fusion of evil with human nature.**

This aligns perfectly with what we've already proven: **if physical death** within God's timeframe is the *original penalty for sin*, and **that penalty has BEEN CARRIED OUT ALREADY for all who have died**, then Judgment Day...it's NOT about punishment. Why not? Because **we've ALREADY suffered the punishment.**

Judgement Day is about **RESTORATION**.

You've got to make sure you get this. Judgment Day is NOT about imposing ADDITIONAL PENALTIES. We've already suffered the ultimate penalty; the one that God laid out for Adam in the garden. The penalty was physical death, and then you return to dust. Nothing more, nothing less. So if judgment isn't a trial to pile on penalties for you because of what an asshole you've been your whole life, or you didn't say the prayer just right...what is it?

Judgment day is the surgical theater for ULTIMATE RESTORATION. The ultimate restoration that God promised to Abraham. His promise that all families of the earth shall be blessed. Well how can all families of the earth be blessed when we're a bunch of mongrified dead-to-God zombies that lie, cheat, steal, and eat too many doughnuts? How's God going to fix this? He has the answer, and it's different than ours. He rips away the evil that made us such assholes to begin with.

### The Refiner's Fire

This'll drive it home for you. Think of a metalsmith who purifies gold. Intense heat separates impurities but doesn't destroy the precious metal. The fire appears destructive, but the fire actually liberates the gold from what corrupts it.

The biblical imagery of **FIRE** associated with **JUDGMENT** scares the living shit out of the most hardened of hearts. But the fire takes on *new meaning* in this framework. Fire doesn't represent torment. **Fire is God's purification**.

As 1 Corinthians 3:13-15 says:

> *Their work will be shown for what it is, because the day will bring it to light. It will be revealed with fire, and the fire will* **TEST the quality of each person's work**. *If what has been built survives, the builder will receive a reward. If it is burned up,* **the builder will suffer loss BUT YET WILL BE SAVED even though only as one escaping through the flames**.

Did you catch that? Look at this: *even the person whose work is* **completely burned up** *is still* **saved** "as one escaping through the flames." The flames don't destroy the person. They consume what is **impure**. The flames burn out the contamination but **PRESERVE THE PERSON**.

We've already seen that word "**TEST**" is δοκιμάζω (dokimazō). It's the word for *assaying metals*. Fire doesn't destroy the metal. *The fire burns out the shit to reveal what was always there*. The fire burns the impurities away. All that remains is pure gold. Pshhh…and we thought all this time that it meant the fire destroys the person. We're such scriptural dimwits. And wait until you get to the lake of fire in chapter 19. You'll look forward to diving in and swimming laps. I kid you not.

But I digress.

## *The fire consumes what is impure but* **preserves the person**

This is consistent with Malachi 3:2-3, which describes God as "like a refiner's fire" who "will sit as a refiner and purifier of silver. He will **purify** the Levites and **refine** them like gold and silver."

### The Master Silversmith

The old silversmith sits before his furnace; his eyes locked on the crucible that contains raw silver ore. His weathered hands adjust the flames with practiced precision. Twelve hundred degrees, no more, no less. He knows that too little heat will leave the impurities trapped forever; too much will destroy what he treasures most.

He cannot leave. Not for a moment. Not for food, not for rest, not even to stretch his aching back. One degree too hot for too long and decades of precious silver will be ruined forever. One moment of inattention and everything he loves about this metal is lost.

As the silver melts, ugly dross bubbles to the surface like poison that's drawn from a wound. The silversmith carefully skims it away, layer after layer of contamination that seem permanently fused with the precious metal. His eyes burn from the heat, his body screams for relief, but he cannot, he will not abandon his post. This silver is irreplaceable. *This silver is everything.*

The furnace roars. More impurities rise. More careful removal. Hours pass like an eternity. His assistant asks, "How much longer? How will you know when it's finished?"

The silversmith doesn't dare look away to answer. Every second of attention could mean the difference between restoration and ruin.

Then, after what seems like forever, he sets down his tools and leans forward over the crucible. A slow smile spreads across his exhausted face.

"Now," he whispers. "It's ready now."

"But how do you know?" asks his assistant.

The silversmith steps back, tears of relief mix with satisfaction. *"Because I can see myself in it."* Isn't that just like our God? After all the fire, after the dross has screamed its way into oblivion, God leans over what's left of you and he whispers:

*"I can see myself in you now."* Just as Malachi promised: "He will sit as a refiner and purifier of silver."

**Here's the divine precision of God's fire:** The intense heat blasts away the impurities. The corruption writhes and burns as it gets separated from the precious metal of human nature. But the person experiences purification. Not incineration. It's the evil that screams in the flames as it dies, while the person feels the relief of finally being free from what has contaminated his heart since Adam. *The refiner's fire doesn't torture the silver. It liberates the silver from what corrupts its magnificent purity.*

God's fire is the same. It burns away the dross **while it preserves and purifies what he originally created to be priceless.**

Who did he originally create to be priceless? YOU!

### The Cure. The Surgery. The Resurrection.

**When we combine all three elements we've explored:** the true nature of the death penalty, Christ's pure blood as the solution to corrupted blood, and God's promise to **separate evil from human nature,** *we get a comprehensive picture of **God's ultimate redemption**…*and it's NOT infinite conscious torment.

It's not about some people escaping punishment while others suffer infinitely. Are you kidding me? It's about the COMPLETE RESTORATION of ALL humanity through three supernaturally divine works: overcome physical death through resurrection… cleanse corrupted blood through Christ's pure blood… and separate evil from human nature through divine heart surgery.

This perfectly harmonizes with the *unconditional nature of the Abrahamic covenant* that we explored earlier. God's promise to Abraham: bless all families of the earth through Abraham. This is how it finds **its ultimate fulfillment**. Not in *some* people escaping punishment while *others suffer infinitely*, but in the **COMPLETE RESTORATION** of **all humanity** toward God's original covenant with Abraham.

As Paul says in Romans 11:32 (you're not going to believe what this says): "God has **bound** everyone over to disobedience so that he may have mercy on them all." This verse demolishes every 'free will' objection to complete restoration. Whaaat? God has bound everyone to disobedience? Like WTF God! Explain that to me please, Lord. "Alright, I will" he says.

Listen to this: The Greek word for "**bound**" is συνέκλεισεν. (soon-EK-lay-sen) It's literally "imprisoned, shut up together, enclosed on all sides." God didn't passively "allow" humans to. He actively, on purpose, and with intention **LOCKED** all of us inside it. Why does God **LOCK** everyone inside disobedience? Read the purpose clause: "SO THAT he may have mercy on them all." If this doesn't make you drop out of seminary and ask for a refund I don't know what will.

Ladies and gentlemen, this wasn't Plan B. *This was the setup.* Alrighty, stay with me here. Let's break this down:

Who binds? GOD. God binds. Not you. Not Adam. Not "human nature." God is the one who does the locking up. The binding. **On purpose.**

Why does he do it? Check the Greek. Romans 11:32, "God has bound everyone over to disobedience **SO THAT** he may have mercy on them all." That little word "**hina**" (ἵνα) means "**so that.**" It's a PURPOSE clause. God binds everyone to (get ready for it) disobedience **SO THAT** he can show mercy. And here's the kicker: How can God lock man in disobedience and then damn him for being disobedient? Hmmm? He can't. He doesn't. He won't. I repeat: *This ain't Plan B.* **It's the plan.**

Remember, God didn't say 'Adam, IF you eat.' He said 'Adam, WHEN you eat.' And here's Paul saying the same thing: "God LOCKED us in disobedience SO THAT he could show mercy." Adam's fuckup ain't plan B. It is THE plan.

Now watch what Paul does next, and why it's impossible to wiggle out of is "all" really ALL? The Greek "tous pantas" (THE ALL) shows up *twice* in the same sentence. Same word. Same group. Either everyone is bound or everyone gets mercy. Pick one or the other. Either "tous pantas" means ALL in BOTH places, or it means SOME in BOTH places. You can't change the definition mid-sentence. That's like speaking "Spanglish."

Did we humans choose this? No, we're too stingy. And besides we're not that smart. We'd rather put restrictions of the unlimited and very generous covenant God made with Abraham.

Anyway, this verse describes GOD'S strategy. We didn't choose to be locked in the contamination room. Nevertheless we're there. But why? **Because God put us there! Why? So he could cure every last one of us.**

And it gets even better. How can God lock man in disobedience and then damn him for being disobedient? That's a great question isn't it? Have you ever thought about that? The answer is he can't. He doesn't. He won't.

Remember this? In chapter 5, "WHEN you eat…" Not IF. *God needed man to sin.* Oh shitake mushrooms, we better take a long pause here. *God needed man to sin!* Don't take my word for it. Listen to Paul's letter to the Romans that we just read. It confirms this: God didn't just anticipate rebellion. He LOCKED US IN IT. The "WHEN YOU EAT IT" of Genesis and the "LOCKED US IN IT" of Romans are **THE SAME PLAN**. I can hardly believe I'm saying this, but it's in the bible. I gotta take a breather here, I kid you not.

## Trapped in the Marble

A huge block of marble sat in the courtyard of the Florence cathedral for twenty-five years. Other artists had agreed to carve the biblical David but abandoned the project. On September 13, 1501, the 26-year-old sculptor Michelangelo went to work on the slab. He carved out David in such a way that the artist Giorgio Vasari later described as "the bringing back to life of one who was dead."

When asked how he performed such a feat, Michelangelo replied, "The sculpture is already complete within the marble block before I start my work. It is already there. I just have to chisel away the superfluous material."

God's work of restoration is similar. Through death and resurrection, he isn't creating entirely new beings but **upgrading us beyond what Adam ever was.** *We're not just free from corruption. We're literally **UNABLE** to sin.*

*Adam could choose evil if he wanted to. Did he? Yes he did.*

*But you and me...? We won't be able to. **We won't even have the machinery to generate that choice.*** God's ultimate redemption addresses the heart of the matter. Literally. It's not just about forgiveness or escape from punishment. It's this: **God tears out the corrupted heart and replaces it with one that has NOT ONE IOTA OF SIN-GENERATING MACHINERY.**

This transformation isn't partial or limited; it's COMPLETE and UNIVERSAL for all the families of the earth. Just as the consequence of Adam's sin extends to ALL humanity, so the consequence of Christ's redemptive work extends to ALL humanity.

But for now, marvel at the comprehensiveness of God's solution: not just forgiveness of sins, not just escape from punishment, but complete RE-ENGINEERING of human nature. Not back to Adam's vulnerable state, but forward to God's invulnerable nature where sin isn't just wrong—IT'S IMPOSSIBLE! That's a redemption worth celebrating!

I know you've been chomping at the bit with all your "yeah but what about" question. So in the coming chapters, we'll address these objections and examine the passages often used to support eternal conscious torment. But first, we need to understand how Western Christianity got so far off track. Because the shocking truth is that the two most traumatic doctrines in Christianity: infinite torture and inherited guilt both trace back to the same source: *One man's inability to read the original biblical languages.*

## Chapter 15

# The Fraud

One of the most common objections to the doctrine of 'complete restoration for all' is that **it's a modern invention** that flies in the face of what Christians have believed throughout history. "The vast majority of believers," they reckon, "assume that **eternal conscious torment** is the unanimous teaching of the church since the beginning."

It has NOT been unanimous.

But before we dive into the forgotten history of early Christian universalism, we need to understand how Western Christianity went so catastrophically off the rails. The story centers **on one man** whose *inability to read the original biblical languages* gave us not one, but TWO foundational false doctrines that have infiltrated Christianity for over 1,500 years.

### Brilliant. But Blind.

A brilliant foreman builds a skyscraper from translated blueprints. He doesn't speak the architect's language, so he relies entirely on a translator who's made critical errors in the foundation measurements and load-bearing specifications.

*This is precisely what happened with Augustine and Western Christianity.*

Augustine's weak Greek is no secret. Scholars universally acknowledge he relied on Latin translations because he struggled with Greek and knew no Hebrew. His letters to Jerome repeatedly ask for help understanding original texts. Don't take my word for it: Google "Augustine Greek limitations."

Picture the scene: Here's the most influential theologian in Western Christianity. He sits in his study in North Africa, and wrestles with passages that will shape the faith of millions.

Eastern theologians debate nuanced meanings of Greek words. They draw on cultural contexts and linguistic subtleties. Augustine? It flies right over his head.

Meanwhile, *Augustine essentially flies blind.* He erects massive theological frameworks on Latin translations that **he can't verify against the source material**. It's like a pilot who navigates through a storm using instruments that are calibrated wrong, with no way to check his readings against actual conditions.

**This is a catastrophic impact:** *Millions of Christians* for over 1,500 years have built their understanding of eternal destiny on Augustine's Latin-filtered interpretations. The man who gave Western Christianity its understanding of inherited guilt and eternal torment worked from translations he couldn't verify.

It's not Augustine's fault that his Hebrew and Greek was severely limited. *But it is Christianity's fault for not checking his work against the original sources.* I shall repeat the recurring theme, and the foundational premise of this book:

*Nearly all false doctrines taught today by*
*Christians and cultists alike can be traced to*
*the distortion of the meaning of Biblical words*

### Augustine's Language Problem:
### THE FOUNDATION OF FALSE DOCTRINE

Augustine of Hippo (354-430 CE) was undoubtedly one of the most influential theologians in Christian history. Both Catholic and Protestant traditions trace major doctrinal developments back to his writings.

There's just one problem: **Augustine had severely limited Hebrew and insufficient Greek for complex biblical analysis**.

Folks, this wasn't a minor limitation. The Old Testament was written in Hebrew. The New Testament was written in Greek. The early church fathers, but not Augustine, wrote in Greek and Hebrew.

The most sophisticated theological discussions happened in these original languages. *And Augustine worked from Latin translations that were often inaccurate, incomplete, or filtered through philosophical assumptions foreign to the biblical text.*

## Poison for Billions

Picture a brilliant pharmacist who's colorblind and can't read the color-coded medication labels. For years, he's relied on handwritten notes with critical transcription errors he cannot detect. His expertise is extraordinary. But every treatment he prescribes is based on fundamentally incorrect information about the medications.

*This is Augustine's situation with scripture.* His theological brilliance was undeniable, **but his entire system was built on mistranslated source material he couldn't verify**.

## False Doctrine #1: ETERNAL TORMENT

Augustine championed *eternal conscious torture,* **partly based on the MISTRANSLATED Latin texts he read from**. When Jerome translated the Bible into Latin in the 4th century, he consistently translated the Hebrew and Greek word "**aiōnios**" (age-pertaining) as "**aeternum**" (which DOES mean eternal, everlasting, with no end). "Age-pertaining" means it has an expiration date. *That was an epic fail, Jerome!*

The difference is found in Mark 10:30, where Jesus promises his followers will receive blessings "now in this present age (*aiōn*)." He continues, "and in the age (*aiōn*) to come, eternal (*aiōnios*) life." If *aiōn* meant "eternity," you'd have "this eternity" and "the eternity to come." There's not two eternities. Fifth-grade translation: *aiōnios* has an expiration date. Long, but it ends.

Imagine you've spent thirty years of your life: sermons, books, seminary tuition, heated debates. All of it defending a doctrine built on mistranslated words.

Now some actor with a Greek lexicon tells you *aiōnios* has an expiration date. What do you do? The entire doctrine collapses in a pile of debris when *aiōnios* has an expiration date.

Here's the problem with admitting *aiōnios* doesn't mean "forever." Seminaries don't hand out tenure for dismantling the doctrines they've taught for centuries. Publishers don't write fat advances for books that say, "Oops, we've been terrorizing people with bad Greek since Augustine." And megachurch boards don't exactly promote pastors who announce, "Good news, everyone! That eternal torment thing? Yeah, we got that wrong."

Empires don't surrender because someone points out a crack in the foundation. They patch it, paint over it, pretend it's not there. Because once you admit the crack exists, the whole thing comes down.

One Greek word is that crack. *Aiōnios.* And every scholar who's honest with their lexicon knows it. But who wants to be the one to bring down 1,500 years of theology? Admitting *aiōnios* has an expiration date doesn't just correct a translation error. It indicts everything they've ever preached.

That's a helluva thing to confess.

I know what I'm asking is huge. I'm asking pastors to admit they've terrified people with a mistranslation. I'm asking teachers to unlearn what seminary drilled into them. I'm asking you to lose friends, maybe your job, maybe your church. That's not nothing. But the truth isn't nothing either. You inherited this. You didn't create it. But someone did.

This **single mistranslation**, ONE MISTRANSLATION, has altered how Western Christianity understands God's judgment and eternal conscious torment. Augustine couldn't check Jerome's work against the original Hebrew and Greek, and so he **erects an elaborate theological framework on a faulty foundation**.

**But the translation errors go even deeper.** Remember our discovery in Genesis 2:17? When God warns Adam he will die '**b'yom**' (in the day) that he eats the forbidden fruit, theologians assume this means **immediate death**. When Adam doesn't drop dead instantly, **theologians INVENT 'spiritual death'** to explain the discrepancy *even though Genesis never mentions spiritual death. It's nowhere to be found.*

This pattern of mistranslation creates the entire foundation for both infinite torture AND inherited guilt.

This is a big deal! Augustine builds his massive theological empire on Latin translations that **corrupt the most basic biblical concepts** about eternal conscious torment.

If you think the *aiōnios* mistranslation was bad…well then, just you wait until you see what Augustine did with Romans 5:12. His second translation disaster doesn't just create another false doctrine; it fundamentally distorts how Western Christianity understands human nature itself.

**False Doctrine #2: "ORIGINAL SIN" AS INHERITED GUILT**

Augustine's second translation disaster: Romans 5:12, which creates the doctrine that all humans are guilty of Adam's personal sin.

Romans 5:12 in Greek says: "Death came to all people **BECAUSE** all sinned."

Augustine's Latin Bible says: "Death came to all people **IN WHOM** all sinned."

**Big, Huge, Gigantic Difference Between "Because" and "In Whom"**

Augustine reads "IN WHOM." Therefore he concludes we all somehow sinned inside Adam, which makes us guilty of his crime before we're even born. *Like saying a newborn is guilty of eating fruit 6,000 years ago.*

But it gets even worse. Modern scholars confirm: The Greek "eph' ho" means "because." Not "in whom." That's like translating 'I'm full because I ate the pizza' as 'I'm full inside the pizza.' Big difference. And "eph' ho"—pronounced F Ho, is now my retort to Augustine: "F that, Ho!"

The correct Greek says DEATH spreads to all people. It describes what happened. Augustine's Latin says we're guilty of Adam's personal sin: inherited guilt.

One describes a consequence. The other invents a crime. Augustine invents inherited guilt through a mistranslation. *A mistranslation!*

Listen to me, we inherit Adam's **corruption**. Not his **guilt**. You're **infected**. Not **indicted**.

## *You're infected—not indicted*

### The Counterfeit Currency Scam

Imagine counterfeit bills so convincing they fool bank presidents. For decades, major financial institutions build lending policies around fake currency. When they discover the counterfeits, it requires they rebuild entire financial systems that were based on false assumptions.

Augustine's "original sin" doctrine is built on this kind of **COUNTERFEIT TRANSLATION**. And like counterfeit currency, its impact isn't limited to one area. It infects Western Christianity's entire empire of eternal conscious torment.

### What It Actually Says

When we read Romans 5:12 correctly, it snaps into place with everything we've already established: Adam sinned. His blood became corrupted. He died within God's timeframe. That's it! Adam's corrupted blood, not his guilt, passes to all his descendants, so all of us inherit the corruption that leads to death.

And "all sinned"? That refers to everyone's own personal sins, which are inevitable when you're running on corrupted blood. NOT inherited guilt from Adam's sin.

140

See the difference? *The passage isn't about **inheriting Adam's guilt.** It's about INHERITING ADAM'S CORRUPTED BLOOD.* It's this corruption that makes our own death inevitable.

### The Invented Death

Remember our discovery from Chapter 3? When Christians noticed that Adam didn't drop dead the moment he ate the forbidden fruit, *they invented the concept of "spiritual death" to explain the discrepancy* **even though Genesis NEVER mentions spiritual** death. Nowhere. Not anywhere.

*Even so, Augustine's "inherited guilt" doctrine is built on the same faulty foundation.* Just as theologians invented "**spiritual death**" to explain why Adam didn't die right away, even when the Hebrew text actually says he'd die within God's timeframe of 1,000 years, well then Augustine invents "**inherited guilt**" to explain a translation that was **wrong in the first place.**

Both false doctrines pull the same trick: invent fancy theology to fix problems that AREN'T EVEN THERE if you read the Hebrew and Greek. As I've said before (and I'll say it again):

*Nearly all false doctrines taught today can be traced to the distortion of the meaning of Biblical words.*

### Wrong Man Convicted

Picture a detective who builds an entire murder case around a crucial piece of evidence: a fingerprint that appears to prove the suspect's guilt. The detective is thorough, brilliant, and sincere. He constructs an elaborate theory about motive, opportunity, and method based on this fingerprint evidence.

Years later, forensic technology advances and reveals that the "fingerprint" was actually a smudge created by faulty evidence processing. *The entire case is built on a false foundation.*

This is Augustine's situation with both eternal conscious torture and inherited guilt.

**HIS THEOLOGICAL BRILLIANCE CONSTRUCTS ELABORATE THEORIES ON A FOUNDATION THAT WAS FLAWED FROM THE START.** It's "sophisticated error." Theologians have perfected the skill of articulating a flawed position so convincingly it sounds unassailable. It's a brilliant man who can defend the wrong address with perfect directions.

### The Smoking Gun

Here's what's mind-blowing: Augustine's **"original sin"** doctrine is built on *the same foundation as eternal conscious torture*. That is: Latin mistranslations of Hebrew and Greek texts that Augustine couldn't verify.

### What Augustine Couldn't Read

Now that we understand how Augustine's language limitations distorted Western theology, let's examine what the early church actually taught. **Especially those guys who COULD read the New Testament and Old Testament in their original languages**.

In the first five centuries of Christianity, there are three main views on final judgment:

1.  **Complete Restoration (Apokatastasis)**—God restores ALL created beings to harmony with himself after purification. That's the whole enchilada. That's what this book is about. God restores ALL created beings to harmony with himself after ripping the evil out of their hearts. This was *widespread and respected* in the early church, especially in the Greek-speaking East.

2.  **Conditional Immortality (Annihilationism)**—The belief that the souls of the wicked will eventually be destroyed rather than suffer eternally.

3.  **Eternal Conscious Torment**—The belief that the wicked will suffer conscious punishment that never ends. (Notice this one doesn't have a fancy Greek name? That's because it wasn't formalized until Augustine made it dominant.)

## The Pattern

**Eternal conscious torment** was **NOT** the dominant view in the early church. Did you know that? Especially in the East where Christianity first flourished and *where theologians expertly read the original languages.* That's right, those who could read Hebrew and Greek by and large viewed God's word to say "Hell No!" to eternal conscious torment.

For the first 500 years of Christianity *when church leaders could still read the original languages,* complete restoration is taught openly in Christianity's most prestigious theological centers. Alexandria and Caesarea, *where the original languages were studied*, explicitly taught that God ultimately restores all creation.

Many Greek-speaking Eastern fathers from Alexandria and Caesarea, where the original languages were studied most rigorously believed in *complete restoration.*

Here's where shit gets real: The Latin-speaking western fathers who couldn't verify the original texts believed in *ETERNAL CONSCIOUS TORMENT.*

The same is true today. It's a rare human who thoroughly knows both Greek and Hebrew that believes in eternal conscious torment. It's remarkable how many scholars who master the original languages end up questioning eternal conscious torment.

Let me make this crystal clear with names and facts:

**These early church father proficient in original languages taught complete restoration.** Clement of Alexandria. Gregory of Nyssa. Didymus the Blind. And Origen, who also mastered Hebrew and created the first critical Hebrew Bible.

**The early church father who taught eternal conscious torment LACKED PROFICIENCY in the original languages.** Augustine couldn't read Greek. Tertullian had no Hebrew. Minucius Felix had little Greek and no Hebrew.

**The one exception? Jerome. Well, his story exposes the whole scam.**
Jerome initially embraced complete restoration, praised Origen's work, and
studied under Origenist teachers. (Origen, Origenist…these are "universalism"
teachers.) Then around 393 AD, facing excommunication and political ruin,
*Jerome suddenly flipped to save his career.* He never published one linguistic
defense of his reversal. Never addressed the *olam* problem, the *aiōnios* issue,
or any Hebrew/Greek textual questions. His change was pure politics, not
scholarship. (*Olam* and *aiōnios* are Hebrew and Greek words that are
mistranslated by non-original language experts as "forever without end.")

The pattern is absolute: **Know the languages, teach restoration. Trust
translations, teach torture.**

The tom-fuckery happens around the 5th century. As Greek literacy dies in
the West, *infinite conscious torment becomes dominant.* Especially after
Augustine (who admitted he couldn't read Greek) built his theology on
Jerome's Latin **mistranslations.**

When complete restoration is finally "condemned" in 553 CE, it was
Emperor Justinian, a **POLITICIAN,** not a theologian who pushes for it. By
then, most bishops who voted couldn't read a lick of Greek texts they make
pronouncements about. (Typical crooked politicians.) These ass-clowns
condemn an interpretation of scripture they can't even read.

**The bombshell**: Those who CAN read God's actual words see *restoration*.

Those who can't and thus read faulty translations see *torture*.

You do the math.

### The Day the Original Languages Died

Imagine a great library that contains thousands of ancient texts in their
original languages. The library has two wings: one where scholars who can
read the original languages study and teach, and another where scholars who
only read translations work.

Then a fire destroys most of the wing where the original-language scholars work. *The remaining scholarship becomes dominated by the translation-dependent wing.*

Over time, **people forget that there were ever different interpretations**, and the *translation-based views* are now the only "orthodox" positions.

So the guys who read Hebrew and Greek got ignored, and the guy who admitted he couldn't read Greek? He wrote the rulebook. Welcome to Western Christianity.

Fool me once, shame on you; fool me twice, shame on me; fool me for fifteen centuries, and my mind becomes irreparably set in stone, damaged beyond repair, and doomed to a life of adding to God's word in complete disregard to Proverbs 30:6, "Don't ADD to God's word lest he rebuke you, and prove you to be a liar."

*The bullshit stops here. It's time to name names.*

### Origen

Origen of Alexandria (185-254 CE), one of the most brilliant theologians in church history, read Hebrew and Greek fluently.

*Working directly from original texts*, Origen developed a **comprehensive theological system that includes the eventual restoration of ALL CREATED BEINGS.**

For Origen, divine punishment was always **remedial** and **restorative**. Never merely *retributive*. In his work "On First Principles," he writes:

> *When the end has been restored to the beginning... that condition will be REESTABLISHED in which rational nature was placed, when it had no need to eat of the tree of the knowledge of good and evil.*

In plain English, Origen says: God restores EVERYONE to their original pre-sin condition. Back to Eden before the fall, before evil fuses itself into the DNA of Adam. Complete restoration of ALL souls to their original goodness.

Origen understands *what Augustine misses*: **God's fire is meant to PURIFY. Not TORTURE INFINITELY.**

## Who You Gonna Trust?

Picture two scholars who debate a complex legal document. One scholar reads the document in its original language and understands the cultural context, legal terminology, and subtle linguistic nuances. The other scholar works from a translation that contains several key errors and misses important cultural references.

*Pick your side.*

This was the difference between early church fathers like Origen and Gregory of Nyssa (who could read the originals) versus later Western theologians like Augustine (who couldn't).

## Gregory of Nyssa

I just mentioned Gregory of Nyssa (335-395 CE), one of the most brilliant theologians of the fourth century, who was probably the most explicit advocate of **complete restoration** among universally respected church fathers.

Working from Greek texts, Gregory writes in his "Catechetical Orations":

> *Healing is proportioned to the evil in each of us. When evil is purged, good takes its place. There is NO OTHER WAY for evil to be removed except by being TRANSFORMED INTO GOOD. Restoration comes through painful, curative ages.*

Understand that Gregory and I reach the same destination: **complete restoration**. But through different routes. He believes evil is *transformed into good*. But as I've shown, *evil doesn't transform*. **God destroys it. Christ-as-sin** isn't *transformed* on the cross; **Christ-as-sin** is *annihilated on the cross*. God wipes him out. God destroys him. But then…at 3 PM, it's over. "It is finished."

And so evil doesn't get preserved eternally in hell. **Evil gets COMPLETELY DESTROYED. ANNIHILATED.**

*Yes, the corruption dies, but the person lives.* God destroys the evil, and the person rises BETTER than Adam *ever* was. **Incapable of sin**. Not just innocent of it.

This was **not a fringe view** but the teaching of one of the most respected theologians of the fourth century.

*We're not inventing new theology.* ***We're digging up what got buried.***

### How Eternal Torment Became Dominant: The Perfect Storm

If **complete restoration** was so widespread among educated early Christians, ***how did eternal conscious torment become dominant?*** The answer reveals a perfect storm of **translation errors**, **political interference**, and **theological isolation**.

### The Hostile Takeover

Imagine a tech company founded by brilliant engineers who understand the core technology intimately. Over time, the company grows and brings in managers who don't understand the technology but they're skilled at corporate politics.

Eventually, these non-technical managers gain control of the company. They make decisions based on business theories instead of technological reality. The original engineers are marginalized, or they leave. Within a few generations, the company's products are based more on corporate management theories than on the original technological insights.

*This is essentially what happened to Western Christianity.* The Hebrew and Greek-reading theologians were gradually replaced by *Latin-only administrators* whose theological systems were based more on Roman legal and philosophical concepts than on biblical insights.

### The Politician Who Needs to Eat Shit

In 553 CE, Byzantine Emperor Justinian convened the Fifth Ecumenical Council. Justinian, a **political ruler**, not a theologian *wanted Origen's teachings condemned* including **universal restoration**.

Here's the critical point: *The Council's official acts **don't actually contain a condemnation of universal restoration***. No, that'd be an insurmountable task. Instead, here's what that asswipe Justinian did. He added fifteen anathemas against Origen to the Council records AFTER THE FACT. **Without proper ecclesiastical approval.**

It was political bastardization, not theological consensus, that led to the *first official action against complete restoration*.

## The Fake Vote

Picture a company where the board of directors votes on an important policy. After the meeting, the chairman waits until everyone leaves. Then he **adds items to the official minutes that they never actually voted on**. Years later, people refer to these fabricated "decisions" as *official company policy*.

This is precisely what Justinian did with the Fifth Ecumenical Council. *He doctored the records*. That son of a bitch! He DOCTORED THE RECORDS to include *condemnations* that were *never actually approved by the theological experts*. (You beta male Justinian, if God doesn't smear shit on your face, I'll grab a bucketful and dunk your face in it.) Note to the reader, if you don't remember that God smears shit on their faces, look at Malachi 2:3. And we're not talking dry cow patties. These were slaughtered animals. Warm, greasy, runny diarrhea. That's what God promises to smear on the faces of corrupt religious leaders. I'd bitch slap Justinian when I get to heaven, but by that time, God will have ripped the evil out of BOTH are hearts and I'll give him a hug.

## The Three Pillars. Three Lies.

Let's be crystal clear about what we've discovered:

The three most *traumatic* doctrines in Western Christianity: **eternal conscious torment, inherited guilt**, and **spiritual death** all trace back to the same source: *Augustine's kindergarten-level ability to read Hebrew and Greek,* and so are built upon Jerome's earlier *mistranslations*.

## The Triple Fraud

- **Genesis foundation**: Built on mistranslating **"b'yom"** as immediate death instead of within God's timeframe, leading to the invention of "spiritual death."

- **Eternal torment**: Built on mistranslating **"aiōnios"** as endless duration instead of age-pertaining. It has an expiration date.

- **Inherited guilt**: Built on mistranslating **"eph' ho"** as "in whom" instead of "because."

All three errors share the same DNA:

1. Latin mistranslations of Hebrew and Greek texts

2. Augustine's inability to verify the original sources

3. Western Christianity's isolation from original-language scholarship

This isn't coincidence. It's a **systematic pattern**. When you build theology on *bad translations* instead of **original sources**, you get *bad theology* that corrupts **every major aspect** of the faith. And then when you add onto their illiteracy the corruption of that bitch Justinian (whom I'll hug when I see him), and you have the perfect storm that has duped Christians for 1500 years.

*Nearly all false doctrines taught today by Christians and cultists alike can be traced to the distortion of the meaning of Biblical words*

### When Two Lies Turned Out to Be One Liar

Imagine an insurance investigator who discovers that two seemingly unrelated massive claims are both filed by the same person using the same fraudulent documentation. What looks like separate incidents turns out to be part of a systematic pattern of deception.

This is what we've uncovered with Augustine's theological legacy. What appears to be three separate doctrinal developments (**eternal torment,**

**inherited guilt,** and **spiritual death**) turn out to be *products of the same systematic translation problems.*

### Time to Stop Swallowing Augustine's Bullshit

This doesn't mean we dismiss Augustine entirely. His insights on grace and many other topics remain valuable. But we can no longer pretend that his language limitations don't fundamentally compromise his understanding of eternal conscious torment.

I'll say it again: It's not Augustine's fault that he couldn't read Hebrew and Greek, but *it's* **Christianity's fault** *that we failed to check his work against the original sources.*

The solution is simple: **Return to the original sources.**

*Read scripture in its original languages.*

Follow the **hermeneutical principles** that prioritize *earlier sources* over *later traditions.*

**Let the bible interpret the bible** instead of letting Latin *mistranslations* interpret the bible.

When we do this honestly, both eternal conscious torment and inherited guilt COLLAPSE…and God's *ultimate plan for complete restoration* emerges as the coherent, hope-filled vision that sustained the early church's greatest theologians.

This that I present to you is not **theological innovation.**

*It's theological restoration.*

### We Don't Destroy. We Excavate.

Picture an ancient manuscript discovered in a monastery basement. For centuries, monks have been copying copies of copies, each generation adding marginal notes that eventually get incorporated into the main text. Scholars assume the bloated, contradictory document is the original until someone finds the source manuscript hidden behind a wall.

When they compare the texts, the truth is shocking! Half of what they thought was scripture is actually centuries of human additions. The original is cleaner, simpler, and more beautiful than the corrupted version everyone's been reading.

This is what happens when we remove Augustine's translation-based additions from biblical theology. *The original vision of God's ultimate redemption emerges,* not as a modern innovation, but as the **recovery** of Christianity's most staggering teachings.

We don't abandon orthodoxy.

We RESCUE IT from centuries of mistranslation and political manipulation.

The real question is not "Why should we believe in complete restoration?"

The real question is "Why did Western Christianity *abandon the hope that sustained its greatest early theologians?"*

The answer is simple: **They couldn't read the original texts. And we failed to check their work.**

This chapter transforms the debate from "Why abandon 1500 years of teaching?" to *"Why continue defending mistranslations from a smart dude who couldn't read Hebrew and Greek?"*

Good question, huh? I've said it before; I'll say it again...

*Nearly all false doctrines taught today by Christians and cultists alike can be traced to the distortion of the meaning of Biblical words*

FREE RESOURCE FOR READERS

I created something for you.

It's called The Sweet 16, a single printable page with every mistranslated Greek and Hebrew word exposed in this book. The original word, what it actually means, and why it matters. Print it out. Stick it in your bible. Pull it out the next time someone tells you God runs an eternal torture chamber.

Here's how to get it:

1.   Go to ShittyToHappy.com/sweet16

2.   Enter your email address

3.   Hit the button

That's it. No password. No hoops. No bull. You enter your email; the cheat sheet is yours instantly.

I'll also send you updates on The 2030 Prophecy and other projects, but the Sweet 16 is the reason to go there right now.

ShittyToHappy.com/sweet16

# Chapter 16

# The Pruning

Remember I promised to blow your mind and razzle your dazzle?

Buckle up, Buttercup.

Here's the bombshell that nukes traditional theology: The Greek word translated as "**PUNISHMENT**" is **kolasis** (κόλασις), which in classical Greek refers specifically to **CORRECTIVE PUNISHMENT**. NOT retributive punishment. It's the same word used for *pruning a tree to make it healthier.*

Did you get that? I don't think you did. Read it again:

> *The Greek word translated as "**punishment**" is* **CORRECTIVE PUNISHMENT.** *NOT retributive punishment.*

That's like finding out the 'death penalty' on the menu just means spicy wings. Or ordering 'Pollo Diablo' and getting chicken with a sprinkle of paprika.

But listen to me very carefully: If Jesus had meant to say "retributive punishment," he *had another option of words to use.* He could have said **timoria** (τιμωρία), which means **vindictive, payback punishment**. But he didn't say "vindictive, payback punishment."

Instead, he deliberately chooses **kolasis**. The word that emphasizes *correction and restoration* over **vengeance** and **endless suffering**.

Why did Jesus use this specific word if he really means **eternal conscious torment**?

Great question, huh?

Think about it: If Jesus wanted to communicate endless, hopeless punishment, he had the **perfect** Greek word available to say "endless, hopeless punishment." That word is **timoria**. Every educated person in his audience would easily understand **timoria** as *payback punishment...with no hope of restoration.*

But Jesus didn't use **timoria, "payback punishment."**

I REPEAT: *He didn't use **timoria**, payback punishment.*

I'll say it one more time for those in the nosebleed section:

*Jesus did NOT use the word **timoria**...payback punishment*

He could have said "vindictive, payback punishment" if he wanted to say "vindictive, payback punishment."

**But he didn't.**

Instead, Jesus chooses **kolasis**, a word that every Greek speaker associates with *correction, pruning, and restoration.* It's like a doctor choosing the word "surgery" instead of "torture" when he describes a medical procedure. *The word choice reveals the intent.*

It's like a chef choosing 'let it marinate' over 'burn it to hell.' It's like a parent choosing between 'time-out' and 'I'm gonna beat your ass till Tuesday.' Jesus has the vocabulary to use if he means **vengeance**. But he deliberately chooses **restoration**.

This isn't accidental. Jesus was the master teacher who *chose his words with surgical precision.* When he selects **kolasis** (corrective punishment) over **timoria** (payback punishment), he tells us something profound about the nature and purpose of divine discipline.

Jesus chooses RESTORATION over REVENGE. When the Son of God had two words available: one meaning **vindictive payback**, the other meaning **corrective healing**...he deliberately picks *corrective healing*. That's not accidental. That's revelatory of God's heart.

154

Eternal conscious torment fanboys **CANNOT** ignore the fact that Jesus chose **kolasis** (corrective punishment) over **timoria** (payback punishment).

*Jesus' word choice was deliberate and meaningful,*
*not some random selection that traditional theology can gloss over*

I have a question for you: *What do you think this corrective discipline actually looks like?*

Jesus gives us the perfect picture.

Think of a master jeweler who works with precious gold. He doesn't put the gold in fire to destroy it. He uses fire to burn away the impurities so the pure gold can shine.

That's exactly what this "**punishment**" does. *It's the refiner's fire that burns away the evil that fused itself into the human heart when Adam sinned.* This "punishment" (what a shitty translation the interpreters picked) …but anyway, this "punishment" that acts as refiner's fire leaves the person **purified** and **restored**. Brought back whole.

This radically renovates our understanding of '**punishment.**' It's like discovering that what you thought was a wrecking ball is actually a surgeon's scalpel.

The purification fire doesn't destroy **the person**. The fire destroys what **corrupts the person**.

I'll ask the prevailing question again: When God destroys the evil, what's left? Any rebellion? Any at all? No. Any anger at God? No. Any inkling to give God the middle finger? No. It's all gone. None of that. **It's ALL GONE.**

*The fire doesn't destroy the **person**.*
*It destroys what's **corrupting** the person.*

Now watch their prize bull, Matthew 25:46 turn into a dairy cow. The verse preachers use to scare the hell INTO you actually gets the hell OUT.

*And these will go away into **age-long correction***
*(remember: 'age-long' has an end point) but the righteous*
*into **age-long divine life**...also an end point.*

Let me drive this home once more like a boot through a screen door: The Greek word for "punishment" here is **kolasis**, which means *correction*, like *pruning a tree to make it healthier*. And also don't forget: Jesus had another word available, **timoria**, which means revenge punishment. **But he deliberately chooses the pruning / correction word.**

*Why in hell would Jesus choose 'correction' if he means 'endless torture'?* Either Jesus was linguistically incompetent, or traditional theology is full of shit. Guess which?

Oh, by the way, remember Malachi 2:3 where God promised to rub shit in the faces of corrupt priests who twist his words? Traditional theologians might want to check their cheeks, because butchering kolasis as "torture" when Jesus deliberately chooses the "correction" meaning of the word is exactly the kind of language-twisting that makes God reach for a cow paddy.

*Now watch Matthew 25:46 make perfect sense.* Both the correction and the divine life belong to the coming age. Both are about quality. Not duration. The correction is thorough and complete. But it's designed to **restore**. Not **torture forever**.

Now before you think "This sounds like Catholic purgatory," let me show you why this is something completely different, and *infinitely better*.

### Bless Your Heart, This Ain't Catholic Purgatory

Purgatory is about paying *temporal punishment* for sins that *have already been forgiven*. It's based on human merit and the state of your soul when you die. Only certain Catholics in a state of grace go there, and the purpose is to suffer enough to "satisfy" divine justice.

What we're describing is something **radically different**. *We're describing the biblical solution to the universal human condition.*

This isn't about paying for sins (Christ already did that) or satisfying divine justice for venial sins (the penalty for sins was physical death, so if you're reading this, it hasn't been carried out yet, but it will be).

Purgatory is about as different from complete restoration as a speeding ticket is from a heart transplant. Complete restoration where God rips the evil out of your heart…it's about **separating evil from human nature**. *Divine surgery to remove the corruption* that Adam introduced to all humanity.

*Forget "paying for sins." There's not enough money in the Vatican basement to pay for our sins. Jesus already paid.*
**This is surgical extraction of evil!**

What would it cost to extract your evil? Not even Elon's got that kind of money. Well, maybe enough for one guy. Maybe. But look, here's the difference in a nutshell:

Purgatory says: "Some Catholics who died in grace need to suffer a bit more to clean up." Biblical purification says: *"Every human who ever lived gets the evil surgically removed from their heart."*

Purgatory says: "You gotta pay for what you did." Biblical purification says: *"God restores you BETTER than you ever were."*

Purgatory is medieval church tradition that tries to explain the unexplainable. *Biblical purification is what the original Greek and Hebrew actually say. That is, when you read them without Jerome's translation beer goggles.*

Now let's apply everything we've learned. **Aiōnios** (quality not duration). **Kolasis** (correction not revenge). Time to aim these weapons at the verse eternal conscious torment cheerleaders treat as their ultimate weapon.

### Their Best Shot Lands in a Port-a-Potty

For 1,500 years, Matthew 25:46 has terrorized millions. But now that you know aiōnios has an expiration date, let's watch the foundation crumble. Oh wait, I almost forgot. There's a second Greek word in this verse that makes it even worse for Team Torture. "**Punishment**" (kolasis) doesn't mean torture. It means **correction**. Like pruning a tree. Jesus had the perfect word for **revenge punishment** (timoria) available, but he deliberately chose **the correction word** instead. Team Torture huddles up: "Coach, they're saying 'punishment' means 'pruning.' What do we do?" Coach Augustine: "I don't know, I couldn't read the playbook."

So Matthew 25:46 actually says: "These will go away into **correction** (*not punishment*) until the age ends, but the righteous into divine life for that age." Both enter the same age. One group into correction, the other into divine life. How long does correction last? Until the age ends. How long does divine life last? Until the age ends. Same clock. Same finish line. Different lanes.

Now let's see what actually triggers this "*age-long correction.*"

## Sheep and Goats

Matthew 25:31-46 as a "proof of eternal conscious torment" text is going to make every traditional theologian as nervous as the ladies when Captain Hook shows up at the gynecologist convention. Here's Jesus' description of **final judgment**—the ultimate separation—**and he completely forgets to mention the sinner's prayer**. Instead, the son of God divides humanity based on...*giving thirsty people water?*

Watch traditional theologians saw off the branch they're sitting on: "Then the king will say to those on his right, 'Come, you who are blessed by my father, inherit the kingdom prepared for you from the foundation of the world. For I was hungry, and you gave me food. I was thirsty, and you gave me drink.'"

And to those on his left? "Depart from me, you cursed, into the eternal fire prepared for the devil and his angels. For I was **hungry**, and you *gave me no food*. I was **thirsty**, and *you gave me no drink*."

This creates an impossible theological pretzel no evangelical can swallow.

*Either "eternal punishment" means what they claim: endless torment, but it's triggered by **not visiting prisoners** (which* *destroys their entire faith-not-works theology), OR "eternal punishment" doesn't mean endless torment (which proves our linguistic argument about **aiōnios**).*

No Christian who believes in 'salvation by faith alone' would DARE say someone burns forever *for not feeding the hungry*. That's works-based salvation, their ultimate heresy. Yet here's Jesus explicitly connecting "**eternal punishment**" to *failing to clothe the naked*.

Have fun explaining that one.

Oh, and by the way, this isn't the only time Jesus connects judgment to ignoring suffering people. Remember Rich Man and Lazarus?

### Rich Man, Poor Man

Same Jesus.

Same judgment criteria.

The rich man's torment? *Not for wrong theology*. **For stepping over suffering Lazarus**.

Now in Matthew 25, the "goats" face punishment for the identical sin: ignoring "the least of these."

**Two passages.** *Zero mentions of accepting Jesus into your heart.*

*Both judgments based entirely on **concrete compassion for the vulnerable**.*

Traditional theology has to pick its poison: Accept works-based salvation (heresy!) or admit "eternal" doesn't mean forever (proving **aiōnios** means age-pertaining with a definite endpoint).

**They can't have it both ways.** You can't suck and blow at the same time.

*Jesus never teaches hell-avoidance theology.* He teaches kingdom transformation that manifests in feeding the hungry.

The passage doesn't teach "charity saves you." *It reveals that "eternal" never meant what Augustine claimed.* And Jesus' actual message was always about the kingdom breaking into THIS world through concrete acts of love.

Chew on that till your jaw hurts. The most cited verse for eternal conscious torment actually describes God's restorative workshop where God separates evil from human nature. Traditional theology built an entire empire on misunderstanding two Greek words: **aiōnios** (age-pertaining with an endpoint) and **kolasis** (correction).

**The FIRE doesn't *destroy the person.*
It destroys what CORRUPTS the person.**

When we read what Jesus actually says in Greek, **eternal conscious torment disappears.** *And God's restoration of all humanity emerges.*

Yeah, I've said this more than once, and I'll say it again: *Once the evil's ripped out, who in their right mind rejects God?* You'll have no evil left to generate the rejection. It's like expecting someone to choose rotten meat over a steak dinner after you've fixed their taste buds.

*There's no machinery for rebellion.* There's no capacity to flip God the middle finger. *The very impulse to resist God gets incinerated with the corruption.*

And here's what makes the "accept Jesus" crowd choke on their Sunday morning donuts: the patient doesn't have to agree to the surgery.

Remember the executioners at the cross? The ones driving nails through

His wrists, gambling for His clothes, mocking Him while He bled out? They didn't pray a prayer. They didn't accept anything. They cursed Him.

And Jesus said, "Father, forgive them."

Not "Father, forgive them IF they repent." Not "Father, forgive them WHEN they ask nicely." Just... "Forgive them."

That's jubilee. Unilateral. Unconditional. The debtor doesn't get a vote.

Traditional theology has no problem with the operating room. They have a problem with the guest list. They want God checking IDs at the door. But Jesus forgave the men who murdered Him while they were still holding the hammer.

No compliance. No agreement. No prayer. Just grace that doesn't ask permission.

**This isn't just better theology. It's BETTER NEWS.**

God doesn't plan to torture *any* of his children, and certainly not forever.

He plans the ultimate surgical extraction of EVERYTHING that's ever hurt them.

Every addiction that's enslaved them…

Every wound that's broken them…

Every lie that's poisoned them…

Every evil that's corrupted them…

**All of it—GONE.**

And here's the devastating irony that should terrify traditional theologians: The two verses they've pointed to for fifteen centuries as their ultimate proof. Matthew 25:46 and Revelation 21:8 actually prove complete restoration when you read the Greek.

Matthew 25:46 uses aiōnios (age-pertaining, not endless) and kolasis (correction, not revenge). Jesus deliberately chose the corrective word when the revenge word was available.

Revelation 21:8 says "their portion" (the corrupted part, not the whole person) goes into the lake of fire, "which is the second death." And Romans 6:7 promises: "Anyone who has died has been set free from sin."

Their nuclear weapons just became our strongest evidence.

I don't dodge their arguments. I weaponize them.

That's not heresy…*That's the Gospel Jesus actually preached*

## Chapter 17

# The Long Con

We've demolished their "punishment" argument. Now let's finish off their "eternal" argument once and for all. This is where traditional theology trips over its own shoelaces when they confuse two completely different Greek concepts that English translators mashed into one word. This is rich complexity, so take a shot of whiskey and let's get into it. Greek has TWO distinct ways to talk about life.

### Two Words, Two Meanings: The Two Eternals

The first is *zōē aiōnios* (ζωή αἰώνιος), typically translated "eternal life," but more accurately "life of the age" (meaning it has an expiration date). Think "medieval life" or "colonial life." It doesn't mean life that lasts forever. It means life that belongs to a particular era. This phrase emphasizes QUALITY and CHARACTER of life. It's the kind of life you have right now. Birthdays, Christmases, family vacations, kids' school, work, and weekend picnics.

The second is *zōē eis ton aiōna* (ζωή εἰς τὸν αἰῶνα). This one actually means "life forever" (meaning NO expiration date). Think trillions of years. Quadrillions. Then keep going. This phrase emphasizes DURATION. It's about how long you get to have it. Answer: Gazillions of years.

Jesus uses BOTH, and as you can see they mean different things.

### Exhibit A

Watch what Jesus does in John 6:47-51. In verse 47, he says: "Whoever believes has eternal life (*zōēn aiōnion*)." Which one is that? Quality. Expiration date. Then in verse 51: "Whoever eats this bread will live forever (*zēsei eis ton aiōna*)." And that one? Duration. No expiration date. Gazillions of years.

Jesus is making a distinction between QUALITY of life and DURATION of life.

Eternal life (*aiōnios*) is the QUALITY of God's life you experience right here, right now. Live forever (*eis ton aiōna*) is the DURATION that you'll experience it, as in the word "forever and ever" we're acquainted with in English.

Here's the bombshell: Jesus already solved your duration problem. You WILL live forever in the gazillions of years sense of the word. The one that means without end, never-ending, trillions, quadrillions of years (John 6:51). He conquers death. Therefore you get endless existence. Without end.

However, when Jesus talks about "eternal life" (*aiōnios*), he's not talking about quadrillions of years. He's talking about your life with your family this weekend. Comes to an end. Not forever.

## The Inheritance

Imagine a wealthy father who gives his son two graduation gifts.

Gift #1 is a trust fund that provides money forever. That's DURATION.

Gift #2 is master violin training that transforms him from note-player to music-creator. That's QUALITY.

Both gifts are valuable, but they serve different purposes.

Jesus gives us BOTH gifts.

The first gift is Forever Life (*eis ton aiōna*). Duration of life. Jesus' blood conquers death, solves the Genesis penalty, and gives endless existence. Problem SOLVED. Done. "It is finished!"

The second gift is Eternal Life (*aiōnios*). Quality of life. In the here and now. This is knowing God personally (John 17:3), experiencing divine relationship, living in God's character while we're on this earth. This is a solution-in-progress. It's ongoing. Today.

Traditional theology's error? They've been counting YEARS when Jesus was describing BLESSINGS. They confused the gift of endless existence (which Jesus already guaranteed) with the gift of divine relationship which is a work-in-progress, and it's what *aiōnios* actually means. It's like counting the years of your marriage instead of enjoying your wife. It's like getting a Lamborghini and only caring about how many miles are on the odometer. It's like your crush finally texting back and you only care how many characters they used.

## The Final Nail

1 John 5:20 seals it: "This is the true God and eternal life (kai zōē aiōnios)." Eternal life isn't separate from God. It IS God. You don't GET eternal life like a gift card. You step INTO it like walking into sunlight. It's about BEING IN HIM, not about HOW LONG you exist.

Here's what traditional theology missed for 1,500 years: Jesus already gives you gazillions-of-years life. How? He conquers death. That train has left the station. Duration? Handled.

The question Jesus addresses isn't "How long will I exist?" The question is "What QUALITY of existence will I have?" It's the difference between asking "How many years will I be married?" versus "Will my marriage be any good?"

This is the aiōnios kind. The kind of life where you wake up and actually want to be awake.

When Jesus talks about "eternal life" (the one with the expiration date, not the gazillions kind) he's not describing a timeline. He's describing a relationship.

## The Workshop

Here's a crucial distinction that pulls the pin on this grenade: The "**coming age**" (**aiōnios**) could last days, hours, or however long it takes for God to rip the evil out of our hearts. It's the "age of correction" defined by its **character** (*God's purifying work*), **not its duration**.

This corrective age ends when God bitch-slaps the evil out of our hearts. The parasite that Adam let in.

After that comes endless gazillions-of-years life WITHOUT that corruption, **pure** and **uncorrupted** existence in fellowship with God. This is the "forever without end life" that Jesus' blood purchased when He became the concentrated sewage of all human evil… then he conquered that death.

Remember: God made Christ to be SIN: a disease-riddled, cancer-ridden, vile, corrupt ogre who two years earlier was Legion in the Gerasene man. So when Legion screamed, "Have you come to torment us before the appointed time?" …What did he mean? What appointed time was he talking about? The appointed time was on the cross when God turned Christ into that incomprehensible, despicable ogre. LEGION himself.

Legion's time had finally come. As he writhes and struggles for his life, he screams, one last bloodthirsty scream OUT OF THE MOUTH OF CHRIST. A scream that is fully evil from deep within the bowels of the sinless lamb, "My God, my God, why have you forsaken me!" Don't think of that scream as desperation. Think of it as a deep, guttural, horrific monstrous scream… "My God, My God, why have you forsaken me!"

That guttural scream was Legion…whom Christ had become.

When God destroyed the body of Christ, he destroyed Legion. The lamb of God who was foreordained from the foundation of the world became the vile, evil monster that God swore in the garden that he would crush.

And now we await the shedding of this earthly body—death—so that God can welcome us into the operating room, lay us down on the surgeon's table where he once and for all rips the evil, kicking and screaming, out of our hearts.

Matthew 25:46 doesn't describe endless torture. It describes the coming corrective age where God rips out the heart of stone and replaces it with a heart of flesh.

The "**coming age**" (**aiōnios**) is God's workshop.

The **"forever"** (**eis ton aiōna**) is *the finished masterpiece.*

Traditional theology confuses the workshop with the final gallery. They mistake the **temporary corrective age** for the **permanent state**.

So now we understand. "Eternal" (*aiōnios*) means quality, not duration. Jesus already solved duration. We WILL live forever. The "coming age" (*aiōnios*) is God's corrective workshop. And "forever" (*eis ton aiōna*) is the finished masterpiece.

## Chapter 18

# Shooting Blanks

We've demolished their crown jewel, Matthew 25:46. But traditional theology has more ammunition in the bunker. Time to empty it.

'What about the rich man and Lazarus?'

'What about all those hell passages?'

These good people are about to discover that their 'smoking guns' are *shooting blanks*.

It's time to examine these supposed 'proof texts' and discover what they actually say **when we apply the same linguistic precision** that exposes Augustine's errors.

### Case Dismissed

Imagine a courtroom where a prosecutor presents what appears to be a smoking gun. It's a key piece of evidence that seems to prove the defendant's guilt. The defense attorney doesn't panic or ignore the evidence. Instead, he carefully examines it using proper forensic methods.

When analyzed correctly, the "smoking gun" actually exonerates his client.

The prosecutor's face drains of color as the defense attorney holds up the evidence to the light. "You see this residue pattern? You've been reading it backwards. This proves my client was twenty feet away, not holding the weapon."

The courtroom gasps. The prosecutor scrambles through his notes. His entire case just collapsed. *What he'd confidently presented as proof of guilt for six months was actually **proof of innocence.*** He'd read the forensic report

169

through his assumption of guilt, which made the evidence appear to say something it didn't.

"Your Honor," the defense attorney says calmly, "the prosecution's own evidence proves my client couldn't have committed this crime. They've been so convinced of guilt; they never bothered to read what the evidence actually says."

*That's exactly what we're about to do with traditional theology's favorite proof texts.* We'll examine their evidence. We'll **use the same linguistic forensics that exposed Augustine's train wreck**. And we'll watch their case *completely collapse.*

### The Brandon Mayfield FBI Fingerprint Case

In 2004, FBI fingerprint experts confidently identified attorney Brandon Mayfield as a terrorist involved in the Madrid train bombings. Their "smoking gun" was what they believed to be a perfect fingerprint match: 15 points of comparison that seemed to provide ironclad scientific proof of his guilt.

The FBI agents, prosecutors, and fingerprint experts all had noble intentions. They genuinely believed they were protecting national security and bringing a terrorist to justice. *No one was trying to frame an innocent man.* They were using the **best forensic science available** and **following proper procedures**.

But when Spanish authorities examined the same fingerprint evidence **using fresh eyes and different methods,** they discovered something shocking: *the 'perfect match' was actually a false positive*. What seemed like undeniable scientific proof was actually a case of **confirmation bias**. Experts *saw what they expected to see* rather than what was actually there.

This is exactly what's happened with Matthew 25:46, the supposedly perfect fingerprint match for eternal torment. For centuries, sincere theologians with noble intentions have presented it as the *smoking gun* that proves eternal conscious torment. But when we examine it *with proper biblical forensics—* when we use the original Greek and sound hermeneutical principles, *it actually SUPPORTS complete restoration*.

The 'perfect match' for eternal torment turns out to be **theological confirmation bias**. Experts see what 1,500 years of tradition taught them to see instead of what the Greek actually says.

But what about the apparent contradiction this creates? If Matthew 25:46 actually supports restoration, *why does it seem to conflict with this interpretation at first glance?* The answer lies in following the same interpretive rules that have guided biblical scholarship for centuries.

Here's the fundamental principle: When two scriptures seem to conflict, like Matthew 25:46 that appears to support eternal torment while other passages support complete restoration, then proper hermeneutical rules demand that we interpret the unclear passage in light of the clearer ones. We let *scripture interpret scripture* rather than force contradictory meanings.

**And the clearer passages start at the very beginning.** Remember where we began this journey? In Genesis 2:17, God warns Adam: "In the day (**b'yom**) that you eat of it you shall surely die."

The penalty for sin was death within God's timeframe. Not eternal conscious torment. When we understand Matthew 25:46 through this foundational lens, and through the proper meaning of its Greek words, then the apparent contradiction disappears, and **we discover that scripture has been CONSISTENT all along about God's ultimate restoration of all creation.** I've said it before; I'll say it again:

*Nearly all false doctrines taught today by Christians and cultists alike can be traced to the **distortion of the meaning of Biblical words**.*

So who exactly IS going to hell? Glad you asked. Let's talk about who's going to hell, according to whom.

### A Comprehensive List of Everybody That's Going to Hell

The Hindus think the Christians are going to hell. The Christians think the Jews are going to hell. The Jews think the Christians are going to hell. The Muslims think the Christians and Jews are going to hell. The Christians think the Muslims are going to hell. The Buddhists don't believe in hell, which makes the Christians think the Buddhists are going to hell. The Mormons think pretty much everyone except Mormons is going to hell. The Baptists think the Catholics are going to hell. The Catholics used to be sure the Protestants were going to hell. And the atheists think everyone who believes in hell is delusional, which ironically puts them at the top of everyone else's hell list.

Hell's getting crowded. Anybody else smell the bullshit?

But wait! It gets better. Even among the people who say the sinner's prayer, there's a whole subset of people *still going to hell*:

**People who said the prayer but didn't really mean it.** You know, the ones who hedged their bets at summer camp.

**People who said it but still fornicate on the weekends.** Because apparently salvation has a behavioral clause.

**People who said it but afterward had doubts.** One theological question and boom: hell.

**People who said it but never got baptized.** Because the prayer doesn't count without the pool, apparently.

**People who said it but didn't produce enough "fruit."** Not spiritual enough, not serving enough, not Christian enough.

**People who said it but walked away from the faith.** Because free will giveth and free will taketh away your salvation.

**People who said it but said it to the wrong Jesus.** Jehovah's Witnesses, Mormons, Oneness Pentecostals. Wrong Jesus. Away with you! Burn in hell!

So according to the gatekeepers, even the password isn't enough. You can say the magic words and still end up on the wrong side of the velvet rope.

Step back and look at this dumpster fire. Billions of people over thousands of years, all convinced their little club has the VIP pass and everyone else burns forever. That's not theology. That's a Twitter argument with eternal stakes.

**This is God running salvation like the worst DMV in existence.** You wait in line for your whole life, finally get to the window, and they say: "Sorry, you filled out form 10-9 instead of form 9-10. You said the prayer in the wrong denomination. Your baptism wasn't valid because it was a sprinkle instead of a dunk. Your faith didn't produce the minimum required fruit tonnage. Next window, please, the one marked 'ETERNAL CONSCIOUS TORMENT.'"

**Or maybe it's more like a combination lock with 47 moving parts** and God "forgot" to tell anyone the complete combination. So you've got billions of people spinning the dial: "Is it faith? Faith plus works? Faith plus baptism? Which baptism? Sinner's prayer? Which version? Do I need to speak in tongues? How much fruit? What kind of fruit?" And after 50 billion people try, and 49.999 billion fail, two Reformed theologians walk up, spin the dial three times, and announce: "See? We got it! Too bad about literally everyone else who ever lived. Should've read more Calvin."

**Here's the thing: It wouldn't be this confusing if we'd just read what God actually writes.** All this theological chaos, the endless debates about who's in and who's out, the 47-part combination lock, the bureaucratic nightmare…it all traces back to the same problem we've exposed throughout this book:

## The Real Culprit

I'll say it again: *Nearly all false doctrines taught today by Christians and cultists alike can be traced to the **distortion of the meaning of Biblical words**.* THAT'S THE REAL CULPRIT.

Once you see this pattern, it becomes glaringly obvious. The "contradictions" weren't in scripture. They were in **our mistranslations, misinterpretations**, and **theological assumptions** that we've *layered on top of God's actual words* for centuries.

It's like discovering that what you thought was a symphony playing two different songs was actually one beautiful, harmonious piece, but you had some instruments playing from sheet music that had been copied wrong.

Scripture doesn't contradict itself. WE do.

Alrighty, we're almost there. We'll examine Matthew 25:46 in detail, so cool your jets. I know you're jumpier than a virgin at a prison rodeo but trust me. It'll be worth the wait.

So before we dive into Matthew 25:46, let's demolish the other favorite proof texts and watch traditional theology's case completely collapse. Let me show you exactly how this works with the passages traditionalists desperately cling to.

First up in the traditional arsenal:

### Revelation 14:11— "The Smoke of Their Torment"

*And the smoke of their torment goes up forever and ever, and they have no rest, day or night, these worshipers of the beast and its image, and whoever receives the mark of its name.*

Traditional interpretation: People are tormented forever and ever without rest.

First, notice that it's the "**smoke**" that rises forever, *not necessarily the torment itself.* This is **symbolic language** borrowed from the Old Testament, where similar phrases describe *the destruction of cities and nations.*

Remember the law of first mention? When we trace this 'smoke rising forever' language back to its first biblical use, traditional theology gets torched by its own proof text. We discover it describes the *complete destruction of places like Sodom and Edom.* **Not endless burning**. Last I checked, Edom isn't still on fire. The smoke isn't still rising.

For 1500 years, theologians have been squinting through Augustine's beer goggles. They literally can't see what the text actually says. It's because they're trained to see what tradition tells them it says.

## The Symbolic Photograph

Picture a man that stares at an old photograph of smoke rising from the ruins of Dresden after its firebombing in World War II. A child asks him, "Is Dresden still burning today?"

The man replies, "No, child. The city was destroyed decades ago. This photograph captures the aftermath of destruction; a moment frozen in time. The smoke is emblematic of the city's complete destruction, not an indication that it's still burning today."

Similarly, when Revelation speaks of smoke rising "forever and ever," it's using **apocalyptic imagery** to emphasize the **completeness of judgment**, not its *eternal duration*. It's a snapshot of divine judgment *frozen in symbolic time*.

For example, Isaiah 34:10 says about Edom: "Night and day it shall not be quenched; its smoke shall go up forever." Yet Edom isn't still burning today; it was completely destroyed. The "forever" language symbolizes **complete destruction.** NOT eternal ongoing action.

Second, the phrase "forever and ever" is a translation of "eis tous aiónas tón aiónón" (εἰς τοὺς αἰῶνας τῶν αἰώνων), literally "unto the ages of the ages." Again, this doesn't necessarily mean "never-ending" but rather "throughout the ages" or "for a very long time." In other words...THERE'S AN EXPIRATION DATE!

Revelation is apocalyptic literature. It's wall-to-wall symbolism. Taking this passage literally is like watching a political cartoon and thinking donkeys actually run the Democratic Party.

Traditional theology knows Revelation is symbolic when it talks about seven-headed beasts but suddenly **goes literal** when it mentions smoke. That's like reading Harry Potter and saying the magic is obviously made up but Hogwarts is definitely a real school.

How convenient.

### Mark 9:47-48 - "Where the Worm Does Not Die"

Jesus says:

> *And if your eye causes you to stumble, throw it out; it is better*
> *for you to enter the kingdom of God with one eye, than having*
> *two eyes, to be cast into hell, where their worm does not die,*
> *and the fire is not quenched.*

Traditional interpretation: Hell involves eternal conscious torment by
undying worms and unquenchable fire. But here are three problems that
demolish this traditional interpretation:

**First**, look at the very next verse that traditionalists conveniently skip:
Mark 9:49 says '*everyone will be salted with fire.*' **Everyone.** Not just the
wicked. And what does salt do? **It preserves** and **purifies**. It doesn't destroy.

Jesus says everyone will be 'salted with fire.' His fire acts like salt, a
purifying agent that preserves what's valuable while it removes the corruption.

Traditional theology reads **'eternal torture'** while Jesus explicitly says
**'purifying salt.'**

That's not interpretation. That's like ordering a burger and getting a yoga
mat.

**Second**, Jesus quotes Isaiah 66:24 about worms and fire that **consumes
dead bodies,** not torments living souls. Go read it yourself. Isaiah specifically
says "they will look upon the **dead bodies** of those who rebelled." Worms eat
corpses. Not conscious beings. Jesus knows his audience recognizes this
reference to corpse disposal. Not eternal torment.

**Third**, 'unquenchable fire' doesn't mean 'fire that burns forever.' It means
fire that **can't be prematurely extinguished** before it completes its work. Like
a controlled burn that rangers won't let anyone stop until the fire consumes all
the underbrush.

The emphasis is on the **completeness** of the destruction. Not on eternal
conscious torment. The fire consumes completely, leaving nothing of what was
corrupted.

## The Smell That Should Have Given It Away

Imagine a visitor to Jerusalem in Jesus' time who was taken to the Valley of Hinnom (Gehenna) just outside the city walls. He's horrified by what he sees: a smoldering garbage dump where trash continuously burns and worms consume the refuse.

"Does this fire ever go out?" he asks his guide.

"No," he explains. "The fire is unquenchable because we keep adding fuel, the city's garbage. And the worms never die because there's always more waste for them to feed on."

But notice…they're consuming dead things, not living people. *This is a place of disposal and decomposition.* **Not torture.**"

This is what Jesus' audience pictures when he mentions Gehenna. *It's a disposal site for* **CORRUPTION**. **Not a torture chamber for souls.**

*Traditional theology turned a* **garbage dump** *into an* **eternal concentration camp.**

When Jesus mentions "where their worm does not die," every Jew knows he is quoting Isaiah 66:24 about dead bodies being consumed. The Isaiah passage ends with 'they will be loathsome to all mankind.' You know what's loathsome? Rotting corpses. You know what Isaiah never mentions? Living people tormented forever.

Jesus' audience understands he is describing **the final destruction of corruption**. The complete disposal of everything sin has infected. When Jesus speaks of Gehenna, he describes the complete destruction of everything corrupted. Not just the physical body that returns to dust, but more importantly: **THE EVIL THAT HAS CORRUPTED HUMAN NATURE.**

*God destroys the corrupted human nature!* ***The evil.*** *NOT THE MAN.* Remember, Paul said it plain: The fire burns up the garbage, "but yet the man will be saved even though only as one escaping through the flames" (1 Corinthians 3:15). The fire destroys the corruption. The man walks out alive.

177

Traditional theology takes Jesus' reference to corpse disposal and transforms it into *eternal conscious torment*. **That's not interpretation.** THAT'S INVENTION.

*The garbage gets incinerated.*

***The person gets resurrected.***

### Thessalonians 1:9— "Eternal Destruction"

Paul writes:

> *They will suffer the punishment of eternal destruction, away from the presence of the Lord and from the glory of his might.*

Traditional interpretation: "Eternal destruction" means people will exist forever in a state of being destroyed, conscious torment without end.

Wait. Read that again.

They think "destruction" means "existing forever"?

That's not theology. That's Opposite Day.

Destruction means something gets DESTROYED. Gone. Eliminated. Ceased to exist.

If I destroy a building, the building doesn't exist forever in a "destroyed state." It's GONE.

Traditional theology has literally redefined destruction to mean its opposite.

Consider a building scheduled for demolition. The demolition company doesn't preserve the building in a perpetual state of being demolished. They destroy it completely. The result is *absence of the building*. It's permanent, but the process of destruction is **finite**.

Similarly, "eternal destruction" (olethron aiónion) doesn't mean an eternal process of being destroyed. No, it means *destruction with finality*. The emphasis is on the **completeness** of the destruction. **Not its duration.**

Furthermore, the word "**destruction**" (olethros) means exactly that. **Destruction.** *NOT torment.*

**Plot twist:** Paul uses this same word in 1 Corinthians 5:5, where he delivers a man to satan "for the **destruction** of the flesh, *so that his **spirit may be saved** in the day of the Lord.*"

Think about that. The same "**destruction**" Paul mentions in 2 Thessalonians **accomplishes salvation** in 1 Corinthians. Clearly, this destruction is remedial and temporary. It's not eternal vindictive torture.

**And remember: It's THE CORRUPTION God destroys. NOT the person.**

*God's fire doesn't destroy the person. It destroys what corrupts the person.*

*God's fire doesn't destroy the person.*
*It destroys what corrupts the person.*

### Matthew 25:41 - "Eternal Fire"

Jesus speaks of *the eternal fire prepared for the devil and his angels.*

Traditional interpretation: There's a fire that burns people eternally.

Notice what Jesus actually said: **This fire was prepared for "the devil and his angels."** Not for humans. Throughout scripture, these represent the spiritual forces of evil that have corrupted human nature since the Fall. When evil fused itself with human hearts in Eden, it brought along its entire corrupting influence.

*This fire was prepared to destroy the evil that corrupts humanity. **Not humanity itself.***

But here's what demolishes their interpretation: Jude 7 says that Sodom and Gomorrah "serve as an example by undergoing a punishment of **eternal fire**."

You might want to check Google Maps. Are Sodom and Gomorrah still burning today? Of course not. God doesn't even pay the gas bill anymore. They were completely consumed and turned to ash. The **"eternal fire"** completely destroyed them. Past tense. Done. Finished.

So when Jesus uses the exact same phrase "eternal fire," he doesn't describe duration but **completeness**. The fire that was prepared to destroy evil forces will *completely consume all corruption*. It leaves nothing of it behind.

Imagine a forest ranger explaining different types of wildfires to a group of students. "Some fires burn briefly and go out," he says. "Others burn until extinguished. But 'transformative fires' change entire landscapes, burning out underbrush, cracking open seeds that only germinate with heat, creating healthier forests. The fire doesn't burn forever. *But its effects are permanent.*"

Once again, **"eternal fire"** (to pyr to aiónion) is better translated as "**age-pertaining fire**." It describes the fire's purpose. *Complete destruction of evil. Not endless duration.* In other words, there's an expiration date.

The fire destroys the evil that corrupts human hearts. The person gets freed from what possesses them.

*The fire doesn't destroy the person.*
*It destroys what's corrupting the person.*

### Luke 16:19-31 – "The Rich Man and Lazarus"

This account describes a rich man who experiences torment in Hades while Lazarus is comforted in "Abraham's bosom."

Traditional interpretation: This describes the eternal state of the wicked in hell. *Except there's one massive problem traditional theology consistently overlooks.*

But before I show you, I need to confess something.

This story messed with my head because I had a rock-solid, dyed-in-the-wool conviction that this passage was concrete proof of eternal hell torment. **I defended this interpretation for decades.** We're talking about doctrinal concrete that's been setting for centuries, so deeply entrenched a misinterpretation that will require a theological crowbar and some serious dynamite to blast through the assumptions most Christians have about this story. *So let's light the fuse.*

What's particularly notable about this account is that, unlike most of Jesus' parables, it includes the actual names of two figures: Lazarus and Abraham. This has led many to assume it must be a literal historical account rather than a parable. But when we dig deeper, the evidence actually points in the **opposite** direction. *In fact, the names are the dead giveaway that proves it's a parable.*

### The Egyptian Tale

There was a popular Egyptian folk tale that circulated throughout the Mediterranean world during Jesus' time. It was a story about a rich man and poor man whose fortunes reversed in the afterlife. The parallels to Jesus' account are unmistakable, and most biblical scholars now recognize Jesus was adapting this well-known story.

Here's the brilliant part: Jesus named the poor man "Lazarus," which was the most common Jewish male name of the first century, equivalent to "John" or "Michael" today. But it means "God has helped," and that's the whole theological point. In the original Egyptian tale, the poor man was nameless or generic. But Jesus picked the most generic Jewish name possible and loaded it with meaning.

This isn't a historical figure. It's Every Poor Man whom God helps. The rich man represents Every Wealthy Person who ignores suffering. Jesus' audience knew this story structure like we know "It's a Wonderful Life." Nobody thinks George Bailey is real, and nobody thought this Lazarus was real either.

Abraham's presence in this story should make every theologian squirm. Here's the father of faith supposedly holding people in his lap while chatting casually across the cosmic void with souls in torment.

Think about what traditional theology asks you to swallow: Abraham, the man who argues with God to spare Sodom, who begs for mercy for the wicked, is now contentedly cradling saved souls while watching others burn? The same Abraham who negotiates God down from fifty righteous people to ten now shrugs his shoulders at eternal torture?

But here's what destroys the literal reading completely: "Abraham's bosom" was a Jewish idiom everyone understood, like saying someone "went to be with their fathers" or "gathered to their people." It's **allegory**. It's not Abraham's actual physical lap, unless you believe Abraham's lap has room for millions of people. Unless you think the father of faith does cosmic daycare for billions of souls, personally holds every single righteous person who's ever died. Your sweet grandmother, martyred apostles, every saved child…all physically sit on Abraham's lap right now?

And why is Abraham running the afterlife anyway? Since when does God outsource eternal destinies to a human patriarch? Why would Abraham have authority to deny or grant requests about eternal fate?

If this is literal, you have to believe Abraham became heaven's receptionist, hell's negotiator, and paradise's bouncer. All jobs that belong to God alone. The conversation only makes sense as Jesus using familiar cultural imagery to make his point about *indifference to suffering*.

Yet traditional theology builds their entire torture chamber doctrine on what's obviously a parable dressed in Jewish idioms that everyone in Jesus' audience recognizes as symbolic. Traditional theology turned Abraham into middle management of the afterlife, missing that this was obviously a teaching story using familiar Jewish imagery.

Now here's the prophetic twist that'll hit you harder than your mama when she finds your browser history: Jesus tells this parable *knowing he will soon raise an actual man named Lazarus from the dead.* Not a coincidence. Not a recycled name. A deliberate prophetic preview that traditional theology completely misses.

**Watch this divine chess move:** In the parable, the rich man desperately begs Abraham: "Send Lazarus back from the dead to warn my brothers!" Abraham's chilling response? "If they won't listen to Moses and the prophets, they won't be convinced even if someone rises from the dead."

Here's where this gets GOOD: Fast forward to John 11. Jesus stands at a tomb in Bethany, about to raise his friend Lazarus. That's right, LAZARUS...from the dead. The same name. The same miracle the rich man begged for.

And what happens? Jesus raises Lazarus after four days of decomposition, and the religious leaders' response isn't belief. They respond with a plot to kill both Jesus AND Lazarus to *cover up the evidence.*

Think about that for a second. Jesus predicts in his parable that even his raising Lazarus from the dead won't convince the hardhearted. Then he literally raises Lazarus from the dead, and the Pharisees prove him right when they try to murder the evidence, both Jesus and Lazarus.

Jesus fulfills his own parable, demonstrates his own prophecy, and validates his own warning, all while traditional theology sits there insisting the first Lazarus story must be literal history about hell. They miss that Jesus plays theological 4D chess while they play old-man checkers as they scratch their hairy balls. The irony is so thick you could cut it with a communion wafer.

Traditional theology turns Jesus' parable about compassion into a literal map of hell. That's not interpretation. That's missing the entire point.

But we're not done.

The Bonfire Brigade, the Eternal Conscious Torment fanboys have one more card to play. Their trump card. The passage they've been saving for last because they think it's the kill shot.

The Lake of Fire.

Billions screaming forever in an eternal lava pit. Christianity's ultimate horror movie.

Except there's a Greek word hiding in plain sight that demolishes their entire interpretation. A word that doesn't mean what they told you it means. A word that turns their torture chamber back into what it always was.

A hospital.

Buckle up.

**Chapter 19**

# The Lake of Fire

Before we get to the lake of fire, Jesus tells a parable that sets up everything.

A parable about debt. About forgiveness. About what happens when you refuse to pass along the mercy you've been given.

And buried in this parable is a Greek word that traditional theology desperately hopes you never look up.

They translated it "torturers."

It doesn't mean torturers.

Jesus tells a parable about a servant who owed his master ten thousand talents. That's roughly 200,000 years of wages. Unpayable. The master forgives the whole debt. But then this forgiven servant goes out and chokes a fellow servant who owes him a hundred denarii. Maybe four months' wages. Pocket change compared to what he'd been forgiven.

The master finds out. He's furious. And here's where traditional theology starts salivating:

"And his master, being angry, delivered him to the **torturers** until he should pay all that was owed."

Torturers! See? God tortures people! Eternal conscious torment! Case closed!

Not so fast, Sparkle Farts.

The Greek word for "torturers" is βασανισταῖς (basanistais). It comes from the root word βάσανος (basanos).

And here's where Team Torture is about to have a very bad day.

Basanos doesn't mean "torturer."

Basanos means **touchstone**.

A touchstone is a black stone used to test the purity of gold. You rub the gold against it, and the streak it leaves reveals whether the gold is genuine or counterfeit. Pure or corrupted. Real or fake.

The word evolved over time. From "touchstone" to "tester" to "examiner" to "questioner." Eventually, because testing could be uncomfortable and invasive, it took on the meaning of "torturer."

But the root meaning never changed: **someone who tests for purity.**

The master didn't hand the servant over to sadists who enjoy inflicting pain. He handed him over to **refiners**. Testers. Examiners. People who would rub him against the touchstone until the corruption was exposed and removed.

Sound familiar?

Same concept as kolasis (corrective pruning). Hang onto this touchstone idea. You're gonna need it in about two minutes.

God isn't interested in revenge. He's interested in **results**.

But here's what should stop every forever-burn brigade dead in their tracks.

Look at the end of verse 34: "...until he should pay all that was owed."

**Until.**

The Greek word is ἕως (heōs). It means "until." It denotes a limit. An end point. A finish line.

If this were eternal conscious torment, there'd be no "until." The sentence would be forever. No parole. No completion. No goal.

But Jesus says "until."

The testing has a purpose. The refining has an end. The examination leads somewhere.

Traditional theology reads Matthew 18:34 and sees: "God tortures people forever."

The actual Greek says: "God hands people over to refiners until the purification is complete."

One of these is a horror movie. The other is a hospital.

But the brimstone bunch have one more card to play. It's their trump card. It's their ace in the hole. It's their Death Star of doctrine, their ironclad kill shot signed, sealed, and notarized by the Almighty himself. It's time to call their bluff. (And it's too bad they're holding a joker.)

## The Lake of Fire

Traditional theology's favorite horror movie: **the lake of fire**. They've turned it into Christianity's ultimate nightmare. An eternal lava pit where billions scream forever while swimming underwater like Jaws.

But watch what happens when we actually READ Revelation 20:14-15.

The text literally defines this lake: "This is the second death."

**Death.** Not torture. Not torment. No eternal swimming lessons in molten lava.

**DEATH.**

And here's what should make you weep with relief. Throughout scripture, death is how God FREES us from sin's power. *Death is a good thing.* Romans 6:7 promises. Look it up yourself. "Anyone who has died has been set free from evil." Is that the deal? I die to be set free from evil? Sold!

Think about that. The lake of fire is where God uses death itself as liberation. Not damnation. It's where everything poisoned by sin finally DIES so the upgrade...Plan A...the masterpiece...what Adam never had can begin.

187

It's the surgical suite where God performs the ultimate operation. He kills the cancer so as to save the patient.

But this next one demolishes the traditional reading completely. Revelation 21:8 doesn't say "they will be thrown into the lake." It says "their **portion** will be in the lake that burns with fire and sulfur. This is the second death."

Their **portion**. Not them. Their **portion**.

If God meant the whole person burns forever, why use the word "portion"? The Greek word is *meros* meaning "a part," not "the whole." John has plenty of words available to say "they themselves" or "their whole being." Instead, he deliberately chooses "their **portion**."

What **portion** goes into the lake? The evil corrupted **portion** that's destroyed them since Adam. *The evil that fused itself with human nature gets thrown into the lake to die.* And then, when that corrupted **portion** experiences "the second death," Romans 6:7 kicks in: "Anyone who has died has been set free from sin."

The corrupted **portion** dies. The person goes free.

What burns in the lake? The same evil that's tormented humanity since Eden. Whether you call it Satan, the serpent, or the evil that's fused to your heart. It all goes into the fire. It all dies. You walk out unscathed.

But don't take my word for it. Look at what God calls this process.

The Greek word for judgment is *krisis* (Strong's # G2920). This literally means 'separation' or 'distinction.' Not condemnation to endless torture. God judges by separating corruption from purity, dross from gold.

And here's the detail that'll make you want to dive into the lake yourself, and YOU do the backstroke. The Greek word translated "torment" in these passages? It's *basanizó*…and **it doesn't mean torture at all**. *"Whaaat, Steve, 'torment' doesn't mean torture?"* No silly goose, *basanizó* comes from *basanos*, which means "touchstone." It's that black stone jewelers use to test gold purity. You rub gold across it, and the streak tells you if it's real or fake. Pure gold leaves one color. Impure gold leaves another.

The word literally means '**to purify**.' It's the process that burns away dross to reveal pure metal. Not 'to torture.' To PURIFY.

When Revelation describes what happens in the lake of fire, it doesn't describe eternal torture. It describes **purification**. *It describes the final fire* that burns away corruption and **leaves what's pure**. The fire consumes the dross and destroys it. The gold emerges and remains.

Even the word "basalt"—the volcanic rock—comes from this same root. Because basalt was the stone used for testing metals.

**And here's where the imagery gets wild:** The Greek word translated "lake"? It's *limné,* which can mean anything from a large lake to a **small pond**. Context determines size. John could choose words that specifically mean "sea" or "ocean." He doesn't. He chooses a word that ancient readers recognize as describing something small enough to be a **goldsmith's crucible**...*a tiny pool of molten metal.*

The lake of fire isn't a vast ocean. It's a **refiner's workbench tool**.

Revelation 3:18 confirms this: "I counsel you to buy from me gold refined by fire." Christ himself uses refining imagery. Fire + sulfur + gold = purification process. Sulfur was used in ancient metalworking to remove impurities. It reacts with base metals, separating them from pure gold. That's not torture equipment. That's metallurgy.

So when you combine portion (not the whole person) with lake meaning second death (not eternal torture) with basanizó meaning purification (not torment) ...you get God's final quality control system. God purifies everyone. God incinerates the junk. All that remains: PURE GOLD.

The lake of fire isn't where people go to suffer. **It's where evil goes to die.** Every parent who's lost a child to addiction knows this ache. You'd do anything to separate your baby from what destroys them. That's the lake of fire. It's not that God inflicts torture on his children. It's that God finally, completely, permanently DESTROYS the evil that's tortured his kids since Eden.

The fire burns away the parasite. **The person emerges free.**

*Same person, minus the parasite.* Your loved ones aren't fuel for an eternal Bunsen burner. They're patients in God's final hospital where the Great Physician burns away everything that ever hurt them, disappointed them, corrupted them, destroyed them. Traditional theology turned God's emergency room into a torture chamber. They made the Great Physician into a cosmic sadist.

BUT…**the fire doesn't destroy the person.** *It destroys what's been corrupting the person.*

So how did purification become punishment? How did the Great Physician's operating room get rebranded as a torture chamber?

Somebody ran a con. And you bought the ticket.

# Chapter 20

# The Ghost Word

Now that we've established the proper hermeneutical principles for how to interpret difficult passages, let's apply these same methods to another category of texts that traditional theology claims to support eternal conscious torment: that is, Jesus' references to '**hell**.'

Spoiler alert: Jesus never used the word 'hell' as we know it because 'hell' as we use it in English doesn't exist in his language.

That word that terrorizes billions of people, that's driven more folks to church than free donuts, that's scared more sinners straight than a shotgun wedding, that's filled offering plates and emptied sleep schedules, that's been the centerpiece of evangelism for 1,500 years...**Jesus never said it.** Not once. Because it literally doesn't exist in Hebrew or Greek. The most powerful word in Christian history is a ghost. You've been running from a word that ain't even in the book.

So where did this ghost come from? Here's the translation clusterfuck that should have seminary deans practicing "Would you like fries with that?"

Four different words. Four different meanings. One catastrophic blender.

When we examine what Jesus actually says in the original languages and use the cultural and historical context his audience understands, a whole different picture emerges that demolishes 1,500 years of fire-and-brimstone sermons.

Jesus often used the word "**Gehenna**" (γέεννα), which is typically translated as "**hell**" in English Bibles.

For example, in Matthew 10:28:

191

*And do not fear those who kill the body but cannot kill the*
*soul. Rather fear him who can **destroy** both soul and body in*
*hell [Gehenna].*

Traditional interpretation: *God torments souls eternally in hell.*

Except that's not what Jesus says. Look at that word again: **DESTROY**. Fear him who can DESTROY…

**Destroy. Not torment…DESTROY.** The Greek word is "apollumi." It means to destroy, ruin, kill. It's the same word used when Jesus says the wineskins will be "destroyed" (Matthew 9:17). Nobody thinks those wineskins are being tortured forever. They're gone.

To understand what Jesus actually meant, you take a short walk outside Jerusalem's walls.

## The Valley Field Trip

Picture this: Jesus takes his disciples on a field trip to the Valley of Hinnom. Gehenna in Greek. Just outside Jerusalem's walls. They're standing ankle-deep in the city dump. Trash fires smolder. Dead animals rot in the sun. Maggots crawl over yesterday's garbage. The smell hits you in the throat. And Jesus points at this steaming pile of garbage and says: "This is what happens to corruption. Just as this garbage is consumed by fire and worms, leaving nothing behind, so will evil ultimately be eliminated from God's creation. The fire consumes utterly, leaving only what God originally created."

Notice, Gehenna was for disposal of dead things and waste. Not torment of living beings.

Gehenna was a real place. The Valley of Hinnom outside Jerusalem. It was a garbage dump where trash constantly burns, and it had a notorious history as a place where some ancient Israelites sacrificed their children to the pagan god Molech.

By Jesus' time, it had become a symbol of divine judgment. But the emphasis was on **destruction**. *Not eternal torment.* Note Jesus' words: God can 'destroy both soul and body' in Gehenna. Not *torture them eternally*. When

192

Jesus says God can 'destroy both soul and body' in Gehenna, he means the complete annihilation of the evil-infestation of man that swooped in and infused itself with Adam's DNA four thousand years earlier.

Jesus' audience sees garbage being destroyed. Not people being tortured. That shapes every Gehenna reference he made.

### The Bastardized Translation

Here's the translation boondoggle that nobody bothers to fact-check: *The English word 'hell' is used to translate four completely different words:*

1.  Sheol (Hebrew) – simply the grave or the realm of the dead. **Not a torture chamber.**

2.  Hades (Greek) – the Greek equivalent of Sheol. **Not a place of flames.**

3.  Tartarus (Greek) – mentioned only once (2 Peter 2:4) regarding evil forces awaiting destruction. **Not about humans.**

4.  Gehenna (Greek) – the Valley of Hinnom, as discussed above. **Not eternal. Just a garbage dump.**

Traditional theology takes four distinct concepts and mashes them into one word. **'Hell.'** Then adds **torture**. A torture that none of the original words contain. That's not translation. That's making shit up.

### The Translation Time Machine

Let's run a simple test. Travel back in time and talk to the original writers and readers of scripture. You show them a modern Bible with the word "hell" in it, then explain our contemporary understanding of hell as a place of eternal conscious torment.

"Is that what you meant by Sheol?" you ask a Hebrew prophet.

"No," he replies, baffled. "Sheol is just the grave where all the dead go."

"Is that what you meant by Hades?" you ask a Greek-speaking early Christian.

"No," he says, incredulous. "Hades is the unseen realm of the dead, not an eternal torture chamber."

"Is that what you meant by Gehenna?" you ask a first-century Jew.

"No," he says, laughing, pointing toward Jerusalem's walls. "Gehenna is that burning garbage dump in the valley over there. We use it as a symbol of destructive judgment, not eternal torture."

Our modern concept of 'hell' is as foreign to biblical writers as smartphones and Netflix. They'd have no idea what we're talking about.

*It's like spending centuries warning people about the dangers of elbow grease. Sounds official until you realize it's not grease.*

### The Part Where Jerry Sells Out

Here's the single mistranslation that terrorized humanity longer than fruitcake has terrorized Christmas: Jerome, aka 'Jerry,' takes the Greek word "aiōnios" (age-pertaining) and turns it into Latin "aeternum" (eternal). *He literally changes* **'temporary'** *into* **'forever.'** That's like swapping a timeout corner for Alcatraz.

This one-word swap creates centuries of bamboozlement that Jerry can't fix because the dumbass wasn't stupid. He was **wrong on purpose**. *He concocted a load of bullshit that Jesus never preached.* And so billions of people live in fear of eternal torture because Jerry flubbed his Greek homework.

I've said it before; I'll say it again:

*Nearly all false doctrines taught today by Christians and cultists alike can be traced to the distortion of the meaning of Biblical words*

### The Receipts

Now that we've demolished every 'hell' text, here's what scripture actually teaches. These aren't obscure verses. These are clear, universal statements that traditional theology is forced to explain away:

- Romans 5:18: "Therefore, as one trespass led to condemnation for **all** men, so one act of righteousness leads to justification and life for **all** men." **"ALL men"** appears twice. **Same scope.**

- 1 Corinthians 15:22: "For as in Adam **all** die, so also in Christ shall **all** be made alive." **"ALL die"** ... **"ALL made alive." Identical scope.**

- Colossians 1:19-20: "For in him all the fullness of God was pleased to dwell, and through him to reconcile to himself **all** things, whether on earth or in heaven, making peace by the blood of his cross." **"ALL things." No** exceptions listed.

- 1 Timothy 2:3-6: "God our Savior, who desires **all** people to receive liberation from the corruption of this age and to come to the knowledge of the truth. For there is one God, and there is one mediator between God and men, the man Christ Jesus, who gave himself as a ransom for **ALL**." **God desires "ALL." And God gets what he wants.**

- Philippians 2:10-11: "At the name of Jesus **every** knee should bow, in heaven and on earth and under the earth, and **every** tongue confess that Jesus Christ is Lord, to the glory of God the father." **"EVERY knee...EVERY tongue." No holdouts.**

Count how many times 'ALL' and 'EVERY' appear. This isn't ambiguous. *God's plan is universal.*

These passages use universal language ("ALL men," "ALL things," "EVERY knee," "EVERY tongue") to describe the scope of Christ's redemptive work. They align perfectly with our understanding of *God's ultimate plan* to restore **ALL** things.

But forget the Greek for a second. Forget the theology. Let's talk about what you already know in your gut.

Think about what God did. He knocked Abraham out and made an unconditional covenant...a covenant that depends on GOD, not you. He sent his son to BECOME the evil fused to your heart. Not carry it. BECOME it.

And then God killed God to kill sin. He shredded his own son like meat through a grinder while Jesus screamed the death screams evil will scream at the last judgment. God made his son become the vile and wicked evil that's tortured humanity since Adam.

Yes, God made Jesus to be the evil. Not pretend. Not vicariously. HE TURNED HIM INTO THE EVIL MONSTER that has tormented mankind since the garden. And then he designed a divine surgery to rip that same evil out of your chest and throw it into the lake of fire.

All of that...and you burn forever on a technicality? God did all that work just to let you slip through his fingers because you didn't say the magic words before a truck hit you? That's not the way unconditional covenants work.

Think about a mother. She carries her baby for nine months. Holds him. Nurses him. Walks the floor at 3 AM when he won't stop crying. Teaches him to walk. Watches him fall. Picks him up. Kisses his boo boos. Cries as she watches him on his first day of kindergarten. Cheers him on as he plays soccer. Hugs him as he graduates high school. Admires him as he builds a successful company.

And then...he fucks up.

You think she'd throw her son into an endless fire for that? Light the match herself and walk away while he screams for eternity because he tracked mud on the carpet? Because he spilled his milk? Because he forgot to say "I love you" before bed?

The sinner's prayer. Mud on the carpet. And they're telling you God will burn you forever if you don't say it.

What kind of mother would do that? What kind of Father?

He's not a God who loses on technicalities. He's not a bureaucrat with a blowtorch. He's a father who finishes what he starts.

Take a deep breath and...*relax*...are you relaxed?

**Hell** is a *mistranslation*. **Eternal torment** is a *fabrication* and God's **actual plan** is *to restore ALL things*. It's been sitting right there in scripture all along, patiently waiting for a redneck wild man like me, a rebellious actor with no formal seminary training. Rambunctious enough to actually read what God says instead of what theologians claim he says.

STILL WITH ME?

If your brain just detonated, welcome to the club.

Everything you just read about Augustine's translation disasters, the three false doctrines built on bad Latin, and the early church fathers who actually read the originals. I condensed the key Greek and Hebrew evidence onto a single printable page called The Sweet 16.

Sixteen words. Sixteen mistranslations. One page that demolishes 1,500 years of theological error.

Do this right now:

1. Go to ShittyToHappy.com/sweet16

2. Enter your email

3. Hit the button

4. Download the cheat sheet. No password required

Print it. Share it. Hand it to your pastor. Leave it on your mother-in-law's kitchen table.

ShittyToHappy.com/sweet16

## Chapter 21

# The Last Stand

I've presented a biblical case for complete restoration, shown how traditional "eternal torment" texts are misinterpreted, and I've laid out a coherent theological framework. But you might still have some questions and concerns. Let's address them head-on.

### "Why Evangelize?"

This is usually the first objection I hear. "If everyone is eventually restored, what's the point of sharing the gospel?"

Look, if your only motivation for evangelism is to save people from eternal torture, then you've missed the whole point of the gospel. The gospel isn't primarily about avoiding hell. **It's about experiencing the kingdom of God NOW**. *It's about entering into the transformative love of Christ in this life NOW. Not just the next.*

When Jesus sends out his disciples to preach (Matthew 10), does he say, "Go tell everyone they're going to burn forever unless they believe in me"? Hell No! He says, "As you go, proclaim this message: 'The kingdom of heaven has come near.' Heal the sick, raise the dead, cleanse those who have leprosy, drive out demons" (Matthew 10:7-8).

The gospel is good news about God's kingdom that invades diseased bodies and broken hearts in this world NOW. It's that we experience God's peace, joy, and love TODAY. Right now! Not just fire insurance for later.

*Imagine someone discovers a cure for cancer but thinks, "Well, eventually all diseases will be cured in the resurrection, so why bother telling anyone about this cure now?"*

## THAT WOULD BE MONSTROUS!

*People are suffering NOW.*

*The kingdom brings healing NOW. Jesus heals them NOW.* His whole ministry was healing people IN THIS LIFE.

## THAT'S why we evangelize!

### "The License to Sin?"

Another classic objection: "If everyone will eventually be eternally restored back to Adam's perfect state, people will just sin all they want."

This is like asking if antibiotics make you want to get sicker. Or if umbrellas make you hope for hurricanes. Nobody gets rescued from a burning building and thinks, 'You know what? I miss the smoke inhalation.'

Paul addresses this argument in Romans 6:1-2: "Shall we go on sinning so that grace may increase? By no means! We are those who have died to sin; how can we live in it any longer?"

### Wisdom Recognizes Consequences

So can you see why we do not want to sin? *Sure, people will still insist sin is fun, right?* Sure they do, and meth is fun too, right up until your teeth fall out and you're stealing copper wire from your grandma's air conditioner.

Let's get practical for a minute. Even before your heart is fully transformed, simple wisdom teaches you to **avoid sin's destructive consequences**.

*You don't touch a hot stove.* Why? Because it'll burn your hand.

*You don't drink poison.* Why? Because it'll make you sick.

*You don't stick your dick in a meat grinder.* Why? Because it'll ruin your weekend.

When you understand that sin's **earthly** consequences will eat you alive like cancer cells throwing a party in your pancreas, *you avoid sin*. Not from fear of eternal damnation, but from **basic self-preservation**.

Take something as "harmless" as worry. Once you discover worry's devastating consequences, it loses its appeal entirely. What about stress? Stress literally rewrites your DNA, shrinks your brain, and turns your immune system into a wrecking ball that attacks your own body.

Unforgiveness? That's battery acid in your bloodstream. It corrodes your heart, liver, and kidneys from the inside. You're busy massaging your grudge while the other person's off living their life.

When you know the consequences, you avoid unforgiveness the same way you'd avoid touching that hot stove (or the meat grinder). It's because you know what it actually does to you. You fight unforgiveness which, let's be honest, is just your bitchy self that drinks the poison and expects the other person to keel over. (Want to learn the weapons to defeat worry, stress, and unforgiveness like David slew Goliath? Check out my book *Shitty to Happy in 21 Minutes THE SECRET KINGDOM* on Amazon.)

### The Master Artist's Awakening

Okay, here's where it gets real. Once you truly encounter God's grace, avoiding sin becomes like a master artist who's been given the finest canvas and premium paints. He doesn't want to create a sloppy mess. *He wants to create a masterpiece worthy of his materials.*

You avoid sin not just because it blows up your week, but because you want the most beautiful life God paints through you.

*It's no longer about fear or even wisdom.* **It's about mastery of life**. You taste something so magnificent that the cheap counterfeits lose their appeal entirely.

Picture a violinist who's discovered perfect pitch. She doesn't want to play out of tune anymore. Not because the conductor will punish her, but because discord now sounds painful to her ears that have learned true harmony. When your heart encounters knowledge of the devastating consequences of sin, it doesn't just become unwise. *It becomes detestable.*

Furthermore, complete restoration *doesn't mean no consequences for sin.* Go ahead, touch the hot stove, bitch, you gonna dance like you found a snake in your sleeping bag. Sin ain't fun.

### "Free Will?"

"Doesn't complete restoration override human free will?"

Let me ask you something: If your child decides to play in traffic, do you let them because "free will"? Or do you grab him out of the street, even against his will to save him? God's a better father than you are. He won't honor somebody's stupid "free will" and allow them to burn forever in eternal conscious torment so honor their "free will."

Besides, we never chose the corruption in the first place. The Bible tells us that in Adam, all humanity is subject to sin and death. **Not by choice, but by nature.** *Our will is enslaved to sin* (Romans 7:14-25). If our will is universally corrupted **without our choice**…*why couldn't it be universally freed **without our choice**?* That's like catching a disease at birth and being told you need consent for the cure.

### CHECKMATE

You ready? Here's the big kahuna, the question that body-slams every fan of eternal conscious torment: **If God rips the evil out of man's heart, WHERE IS THE DRIVE TO DO EVIL?**

Seriously, where would your love for evil come from?

Picture a patient with a brain tumor that causes violent and irrational behavior. The tumor has been there so long that the patient thinks these violent impulses are just "who he is." He fights the doctors, screams about them removing the tumor because it'll "destroy his free will" and "change his personality."

But once the tumor is removed, does the patient bitch about "Hey, where'd my his violent impulses go? Give them back!"

Does he feel that his "freedom" got violated because he doesn't want to hurt people? **Of course not.** *For the first time in years, he thinks normal.* He's horrified he ever wanted to cause anybody any harm.

His genuine personality…the one that's **kind, rational, loving** *emerges*…**AFTER THE TUMOR IS GONE.**

**The violent impulses weren't part of his true self;** they were *symptoms of the disease.* Get rid of the disease! That doesn't **destroy** his freedom. It **restores** his freedom *to be who God meant him to be.*

> *When God rips the evil out of your heart,*
> *where is your desire to act like an asshole?*

### The Virus That Makes You Do Shit You Hate

Imagine a computer infected with malware that keeps generating pop-up ads, slows down the system, and causes crashes. The computer "chooses" to display these ads and perform these malicious actions, but only because the virus has corrupted its normal operations.

When a technician removes the virus, does the computer lose its "freedom"? Does it miss generating those pop-ups? Does it feel violated because it can no longer crash randomly? (Right, because computers are known for their emotional attachment to malware.) Hell no! The computer now operates according to its original design. Fast, efficient, and helpful.

**The malicious behavior wasn't the computer expressing its true nature.** *It was the computer corrupted by foreign code.* When you remove the virus, it doesn't restrict the computer's function. It liberates the computer to function as it was designed. This is sooo good I gotta say it again:

> *When God rips the evil out of your heart,*
> *what drives do you have left to generate evil?*

## Losing Control

Consider a person addicted to drugs. The addiction rewires their brain chemistry so completely that they "choose" drugs over family, health, and happiness. They lie, steal, and manipulate to get their next fix. Is this their "free will" in action?

The answer is NO. When they get clean, do they grieve the loss of their "freedom" that destroyed their life and the lives of their family? Do they feel that sobriety has somehow violated their autonomy? Never. They're grateful to be free from the compulsion that wrapped its chains around their neck. They can't believe they craved something so destructive.

*The addiction wasn't an expression of their true will.* It was a **corruption** of their will. Recovery doesn't eliminate their freedom. It restores their freedom to choose what they actually want. Health, relationships, purpose.

I'll ask it again and again:

> *When God rips the evil out of your heart,*
> *what drive do you have to do evil?*
> *YOU DON'T*

## Free At Last

At the last judgement, when God strips away the evil out of every man's heart, **he extricates the parasite that controls the man to do evil.**

If God leaves the parasite in, leaving the parasite alone to run roughshod over the man is what robs him of his free will.

You don't have a free will when somebody else is driving the car. But when God extracts the evil from your heart—by the way, when is that extraction? It's at the final judgment on God's operating table. And he doesn't override your will. My God *he gives you the keys back!* He severs the chains of the demoniac puppeteer who's controlled men's evil throughout history. And you think you gotta give God permission?!? When he did all this preparation? Hell no! Suck on that, eternal conscious torment fanboys.

As we are purified at the last judgement, as God separates the fusion of evil from our nature, and our hearts become truly free for the first time ever...*free to live the good, the peace, and the love for which God created us, that rules and reigns supreme*...that's the kind of free will I like!

## When Rebellion Dies

As Philippians 2:10-11 says, "At the name of Jesus *every knee* WILL *bow*, in heaven and on earth and under the earth, and every tongue WILL acknowledge that Jesus Christ is Lord, to the glory of God the father." The only way for EVERY tongue to acknowledge Jesus Christ is Lord is for the father to extricate the manipulative forces of evil that have compelled people to hate God, to hate one another, and to commit despicable acts of evil and violence.

When God finally separates the evil from human nature, people won't *reluctantly* bow to Jesus because they're *forced* to.

*They'll joyfully bow* because they can't help it. THEY FINALLY SEE CLEARLY.

The evil that once whispered lies about God *is gone*.

The corruption that made sin appeal to them *is eradicated*.

If God tears the evil out of man's heart, WHERE IS THE IMPULSE TO DO EVIL? The answer is simple: There's none left. It's gone. God annihilates it. GOD EXTRICATES IT. **GOD DESTOYS IT**...while he saves the man.

That's not 'the violation of free will.' That's 'the LIBERATION of free will.'

*"Okay Steve, but what about that verse where Jesus says 'No one comes to the father except through me'? Doesn't that prove only believers get to go to heaven?"*

I'm so glad you asked.

Eternal conscious torment fanboys love to quote John 14:6: "I am the way, the truth, and the life. No man comes to the father except by me." This verse actually *supports complete restoration* rather than opposes it. Jesus doesn't describe WHO gets access to the father. He describes HOW access to the father works. It's HOW it works. Not WHO gets to come in.

The Greek word 'comes' to the father (*erchomai*) describes *an ongoing process*, not a one-time prayer event. Jesus says that every person who reaches complete restoration with the father does so **only through God's redemptive work**. The pure blood that conquers physical death (we don't have a choice in the matter; therefore we can't choose 'yes' or 'no' … and the divine surgery at the final judgment in God's operating room when he rips evil from the human heart is the HOW. It's for ALL men. Thus he describes HOW. Not WHO.

Since God guarantees "all in all" (1 Corinthians 15:28), EVERYONE eventually gets dragged to the father. Even kicking and screaming. This verse simply GUARANTEES they'll ALL come through Jesus. ALL COME THROUGH THE SHED BLOOD OF JESUS. Not by saying a prayer, not by your acceptance, but through the blood that doesn't ask permission. God doesn't wait for your acceptance speech. He doesn't need your signature on the dotted line. He reaches into the grave, grabs you by the collar, and drags you home.

Jesus isn't the bouncer checking IDs. *He's the 12-lane superhighway that everyone travels to get home…willingly…or unwillingly.*

And so here's what gives traditional eternal conscious torment fanboys diarrhea: God doesn't take "no" for an answer. You want proof? Jesus shows this on the cross when he prays "Father, forgive them." Who's he forgiving? His executioners! You think they agreed to it? Do you think Jesus held back until they came forward, every head bowed, every eye closed? He didn't wait for his killers to say the sinner's prayer; he doesn't even require their consent. Hell, they don't even know the crime they're committing, nor what they're doing, and certainly don't know they need forgiveness.

Even if someone in the mob screams "NO! Fuck you, God!" that doesn't change the fact that Jesus' redemptive work **already accomplishes THEIR** restoration, too. That's why it's not WHO gets in. It's HOW they get in.

206

Their juvenile projectile vomits **HAVE NO POWER TO STOP** God's supersonic power from dragging them home.

And so the eternal conscious torment people arrogantly demand these murderers who are incapable of loving God. You know, his executioners? The asswipes that murdered him? Yeah, you eternal conscious torment people insist these criminals must "accept Jesus into their heart." Are you kidding me? They don't have a clue. How do I know? BECAUSE THEY KILLED HIM.

Remember Abraham? God put him to SLEEP during the covenant ceremony so he couldn't add stupid, arrogant, man-made conditions. God didn't require man's cooperation back then. So then why would God suddenly need man's cooperation today? *God's plan doesn't depend on human cooperation at all.*

**NOT AT ALL!**

People's "no" is just the evil talking, and once God surgically removes that evil in the judgment in operating room, **the "no" disappears. THEIR "NO" CHANGES TO A RESOUNDING "YES!"**

This is theological dynamite that blows up 1,500 years of **"you must mean it from the bottom of your heart"** theology!

*When God rips the evil out of man's heart, the evil gets cast into the pigs like Legion. No more evil. No more impulse to hate God. And just like the Gerasene man, he sits there peacefully after God removes the evil.*

I'll make you a deal. Answer one question, and I'll concede the whole argument. Which comes first: the human agreement BEFORE God rips the evil out, or does God rip the evil out first, and THEN man agrees?

Think carefully. If man has to agree FIRST while the parasite is still fused to his heart, while the corruption still hijacks his will, while the very machinery of rejection is still operational, then you're asking a hostage to negotiate his own release while the kidnapper holds the gun. You're asking the tumor to consent to its own removal. You're asking the drunk to drive himself to rehab.

But if God rips the evil out FIRST…if the Great Physician operates before asking for the patient's signature, then what's left to say no? What machinery lingers to reject the God who spent 6000 years planning the full eradication of evil from your heart? So then, when God rips out the heart of stone and gives you a heart of flesh, WHO WOULD REJECT GOD THEN? And with a brand-new heart of flesh, would you turn around and spit in God's face? If you do then you're dumber than a box of rocks with a head injury.

Would you expect a man who just had his chains cut off to beg for them back?

Would you expect a blind man who just received sight to gouge out his own eyes?

Would you expect a drowning man to dive back under after you pulled him to shore?

The evil IS the rejection mechanism. THE EVIL IS THE REJECTION MECHANISM! Remove it, and rejection becomes anatomically impossible. That's why GOD DOESN'T WAIT FOR YOUR PERMISSION because you are in a corrupted poisonous state of mind; a sick, perverted state of mind. And you think God expects you to make a rational decision when you're crazier than a rat in a coffee can? That's like asking a drowning man to fill out the lifeguard's questionnaire. He saves you first and lets you thank him later.

## Chapter 22

# The Unforgivable Sin

There's one verse that's caused more sleepless nights than "you're test results are in."

Matthew 12:31-32. The blasphemy against the Holy Spirit. The one sin that "will not be forgiven, either in this age or in the age to come."

People read that and panic. *Did I commit it? What if I already did? What if I thought something can't take back?*

Pastors get emails about it weekly. Counselors hear it constantly. It's the theological boogeyman hiding under every believer's bed.

So let's drag it into the light and see what we're actually dealing with.

First, let's see what Jesus actually says. The Pharisees just watched him cast out demons by the spirit's power and they say, "He does it by satan." They didn't doubt or question the miracles. They see God's spirit at work and deliberately call it demonic.

Jesus responds: "This won't be forgiven in this age or the age to come."

Traditional theology reads: "Never, ever, forever...*away to hell with you!*" Look at the Greek. It's "neither in this age nor in the coming one."

**Two specific ages.** Not "throughout all ages forever and ever and ever."

Think of it this way: These Pharisees poisoned themselves so thoroughly they destroyed their own receptors for healing. Like meth addicts who've burned out their ability to even want recovery. Jesus is saying, "This particular brain damage can't be fixed while you're conscious."

The unforgivable sin is unforgivable while you're conscious. Good thing God's got divine chloroform for the ultimate heart surgery where he rips out ALL evil. Even the corruption that couldn't be torched while you were awake.

Remember our tardema pattern? God handles eternal matters while humans are unconscious. These Pharisees couldn't consciously receive forgiveness. They fried their spiritual circuits when they called good evil. But under divine anesthesia at the judgment? That's not "this age" or "the age to come." That's God's surgical suite where he fixes what couldn't be fixed while you fought him like a little bitch.

The passage actually proves my point. Some corruption is so severe it can't be addressed through conscious participation. It requires the unconscious, unilateral divine surgery that only happens in the operating room at the judgment.

Even the unforgivable becomes forgivable when God's the one doing the forgiving while you're knocked out cold on his operating table.

### "Justice for Victims?"

Here's another one: "How is it just for victims and perpetrators to end up in the same place? Doesn't justice demand eternal separation?"

This question assumes that justice means **retribution**…making sure bad people get punished enough to satisfy some cosmic balance sheet. But biblical justice (righteousness) is about **RESTORATION**. Not **retribution**.

The goal of true justice is NOT to ensure that perpetrators suffer. It's to **heal victims, transform perpetrators**, and **restore relationships**.

God's justice doesn't just punish evil. He OVERCOMES evil with good (Romans 12:21).

Consider the parable of the prodigal son (Luke 15). Was justice served when the father welcomed home his wayward son?

*The older brother didn't think so.*

But the father understood that **true justice** is *restored relationship*.

210

God's justice is satisfied *not by eternal punishment* but by the **complete ERADICATION of evil and the RESTORATION of all things to their intended goodness**. God removes the fusion of evil with human nature, and **perpetrators...will no longer...be perpetrators**.

God transforms them into the people God intended them to be.

Notice how eternal conscious torment fanboys play the older brother perfectly. Both Jews and Christians have their exclusive club that excludes really, really bad evil people. They stand outside the celebration, whining like little bitches, insistent that restoration is limited to their guest list.

### "Wishful Thinking?"

"Steve, aren't you just promoting this view because it's more comfortable than traditional teaching?" Are you frickin' kidding me?!? Look, if I wanted **comfort**, *I'd stick with the traditional view*. It's much easier to go with the church tradition of the last 1,500 years, and to embrace the ubiquitous "you gotta ask Jesus into your heart" than it is to buck up against centuries of 'established doctrine' with my "Hell No!" book and have to listen to theologians treat me like I've got leprosy. (Frankly I don't give a shit.)

Maybe it's a helluva lot easier for a man who cares what people think to affirm eternal conscious torment than to challenge it. Teaching complete restoration has cost many theologians their jobs, reputations, and church memberships. That's for sure. But me? I say, "I don't give a Phuket, Nantucket. I seek truth. Not approval."

### "Liberal Theology?"

Here's another favorite of the eternal conscious torment crowd. "Isn't this just watering down the Bible to make it more palatable to modern sensibilities?"

"Watering down," you say? Why do you say that? On the contrary, this view is based on *careful exegesis of scripture*. NOT cultural accommodation.

In fact, it takes the Bible more seriously than Augustine's eternal conscious torment view.

It takes seriously the biblical teaching that **DEATH** *(NOT eternal torment)* is the consequence of sin. Nothing more. Nothing less.

It takes seriously the biblical imagery of **fire as purifying**. *Not punishing*.

It takes seriously the original meanings of key Greek and Hebrew terms rather than later theological impositions.

*This isn't liberal theology.* It's **biblical theology**. The fancy word is *exegesis.* Theology has been mistranslated and buried under centuries of tradition by theologians who thought Greek was a salad dressing option.

The whole theological establishment has been intellectually AWOL for fifteen long centuries. But their diabolical rulership is OVER!

### The Ethical Dilemma

Now then, here's the most damning consequence of "ask Jesus into your heart" theology: it creates *two impossible classes of people* that even its defenders won't address honestly.

Class 1: People who never heard of Jesus. Ask any "sinner's prayer" Christian: "Are they going to hell?" They'll squirm and say, "Well, no, they never had a fair shot."

Perfect! Then why tell anybody about Jesus? Leave them alone! Because according to your theology, if you tell them about Jesus and they reject him, off to hell they go. But if you never tell them, they're safe. *Your evangelism literally increases the number of people going to hell!*

Class 2: The 800-pound gorilla—Jews. Watch prominent Christian theologians in public (not the pulpit where they're safe) …watch them juke and jive when talking to Jews about eternal destiny. They fully believe Jews are going to hell for not accepting Jesus, but do they have the balls to confront them to their face? They'll quote Romans 10:9-10, and dance around the implications. In private they'll say Jews are going to hell, but to Jews face-to face…they become theological cowards.

Here's what their cowardice is hiding from: If eternal conscious torment is correct, then the piles of suitcases and bags of human hair at the Holocaust Museum represent children who escaped Hitler's ovens ONLY TO LAND IN GOD'S OVEN.

*"But Steve, Jesus warned about hell more than he talked about heaven."*

Really, Reverend BackAsswards? What bible are you reading...the one where14 is bigger than 100?

This claim that Jesus talked about hell more than heaven is ridiculously false. Jesus used the word "Gehenna" (translated as "hell") 11 times, and hades (also translated as "hell") 3 times in the Gospels. Total of 14. He spoke about the kingdom of God over 100 times. Total hells: 14. Total Kingdom of Gods: 100. Plus we've seen that 'hell' as we know it isn't even a word in Jesus' vocabulary.

The entire Bible follows this same pattern. Scripture contains roughly 88 references to "hell" concepts (most just meaning "**grave**" or "**death**"), compared to over 1,000 references to life, salvation, kingdom, and restoration themes.

The biblical ratio is approximately 92% LIFE versus 8% death. Even the Old Testament word "**sheol**" simply means "**grave**." You know, like where your grandparents are buried? Jacob, a righteous patriarch, talks about himself going there (hell) when he refuses to let Benjamin go to Egypt. "You will bring down my gray hairs with sorrow to sheol." Not as punishment. Just where the dead go. If someone in 1850 said "I'll be six feet under soon," nobody would assume they meant a torture changer. They meant the grave.

That's the first mention of sheol in the bible. It's morally neutral. It's where EVERYONE goes. No fire. No eternal torment. Just six feet under.

Furthermore, as we've already established, "Gehenna" refers to the Valley of Hinnom outside Jerusalem, which is used as a garbage dump. It symbolized destruction of the evil that plagues man. Destruction of the EVIL. Not eternal conscious torment for the man.

Listen, if God's ultimate plan is to save some while others suffer eternally, then God's love has failed for the majority of humanity. For instance the whole world in Noah's day.

## The Outpouring

But here's what excites me most about this theological restoration: I believe ridding us of 1500 years of 'drawing with crayons on the Mona Lisa' will unleash THE GREATEST OUTPOURING OF GOD'S HEALING POWER THE WORLD HAS EVER SEEN. Just like Jesus promised.

For centuries, we've wondered why we don't see the miraculous works Jesus promised: "Greater works than these shall you do" (John 14:12). Amazing promise, Jesus. But where are the blind eyes opening, the deaf ears hearing, the arms and legs growing out, the dead being raised? Why aren't your people walking in the supernatural power that you promised?

**The answer is found in Jesus' own words: "YOU HAVE MADE THE WORD OF GOD OF NO EFFECT BECAUSE OF YOUR TRADITION." (Matthew 15:6).**

Whaaat?!? Because of OUR tradition?!?

**YES.** Your tradition.

Listen, when we distort God's character through **goofy doctrines**…when we present him as a **cosmic torturer** rather than the Great Physician who **surgically removes evil to restore ALL his children**…*we actively BLOCK God's power.*

When we pray for the sick, we might as well be drooling spittle like a lobotomy patient. God's hands are tied because our traditions make his word "of no effect" (Matthew 15:6). How can his promise—you've heard the promise— "He sends his word and heals them." How can his word effectively work when we pervert his word into cosmic torture chamber theology? We've built a theological Hoover dam against God's healing power because we've bastardized his word.

Sure, there's healing here and there, but it's sporadic. People claim to have seen all of these miracles, and I don't doubt it. But they're nothing on the grand scale like he promised.

But when we understand God's relentless love will not rest until every person is completely restored, and when we grasp that at the final judgment he'll rip the evil out of all men's hearts, then his supernatural power will flow through our hands like never before into a broken and crushed humanity.

It'll flow just like Jesus, who by the way never once said "Accept me into your heart and I'll heal you."

So if Jesus never preached eternal conscious torment, maybe we should emulate him, and then we'll have the same results he did.

And one more thing I want to tell you. In my daily life, I find that I look at people in a completely different light. I see them in their future, fully restored, full of the joy of the Lord. Even though today they're clueless as a blind man in a strip club about what lies ahead for them. Like Jesus' executioners. But if this book is true, then it gives me a renewed love for humanity.

## A More Excellent Way

The doctrine of complete restoration aligns with Paul's assertion that love is the greatest. God's operating room is more powerful than human evil. His scalpel triumphs over wickedness. His redemptive surgery succeeds on every creature.

*God's operating table is more powerful*
*than any man's rebellion...yes, even his executioners*

**Love wins.**

**Rebellion loses.**

END OF STORY.

I'll say it again for those on the back row: ***God's love is more powerful than human rebellion.*** Your rebellion. My rebellion. Your racist uncle's rebellion. That ex who destroyed you. Nobody's rebellion is so strong as to override God's plan to rip the evil out of their heart in the operating room of the last judgement.

But I can hear some of you say, "Steve, those are all fine theological arguments, but what about the bible verses that specifically mention eternal punishment?

What about the passages that seem to clearly teach endless torment?"

I thought you'd never ask.

## Chapter 23

# The Showdown

Remember when I told you to 'cool your jets, pal, you're jumpier than a virgin at a prison rodeo'? Well now's the time to hop onto that buckin' bronco. You've been remarkably patient through several demolition derbies that embarrassed fans of eternal conscious torment in some of their favorite proof texts. *Now let's turn their number one weapon against them.*

So after all that reconstruction work, traditional eternal conscious torment fanboys still have a few other moves. And they're about to play what they think is their number one ace in the hole. I can hear the theological objection choir warming up their voice pipes: 'But what about all those passages that clearly teach eternal punishment? What about the verses that talk about hell, eternal fire, and everlasting torment?"

And here's where traditional theologians get their asses handed back to them. The passages they use to support eternal conscious torment **don't actually teach eternal conscious torment** when we properly understand them.

Let's systematically demolish these one by one.

### Wrong Map

There was a fisherman who got an ancient map from his grandfather showing where to find the best fishing spots. For years, he'd been fishing in one particular cove where the map seemed to indicate a boundless supply of fish. But day after day, he returned home with empty nets.

One day, a marine biologist visits the village and asks to see his map. "This isn't indicating a fishing spot," he scoffs. "These markings actually show a dangerous reef area. No wonder you haven't caught anything. The fish don't hang out there. You've been reading the map wrong all these years."

217

The fisherman has a choice: hang onto his misinterpretation or admit that he's read the map wrong all these years, change locations and start fishing in the right place.

Many Christians are like this fisherman with passages about final judgment. They've inherited a certain way of reading these texts and thus they rigidly cling to their interpretation *even when it doesn't align with scripture.*

As a side note, when interpretations clash with clear biblical scripture, basic hermeneutics says *interpret the **unclear** through the **clear***. If the scripture on complete restoration is as clear as I've shown, **then difficult passages should be understood through that lens**.

However the preponderance of scriptures in this book don't even need to resort to that principle. That's because these supposed 'proof texts' for eternal torment don't actually teach eternal torment. They never did. In fact, they **PROVE EVERY BIT** what I'm saying! Are you ready for a mind-o-gasm?

*Let's take a look at the major passages and see what they really say.*

### Hostile Witness

Here's a big one. This is probably the most commonly cited verse by millions who follow Augustine with his community college Greek, and his linguistic translation skills that are as airtight as a screen door on a submarine.

> *And these will go away into **eternal punishment**, but the **righteous into eternal life**.* (Matthew 25:46)

The traditional interpretation seems ironclad, doesn't it? The punishment must be *eternal in duration*. Just as *eternal life is eternal in duration*. Case closed, right?

But there's a problem with this interpretation. The Greek word translated as "eternal" is **aiōnios** (αἰώνιος), which doesn't necessarily mean "**never-ending**." It's derived from the noun **aión** (αἰών), which means "an age" or "**a period of time**." **Aiōnios—eternal—**describes something that belongs to or is *characteristic of a particular age*. In other words, *it means it doesn't last forever*.

218

Don't just take my word for it. Strong's Concordance #166 gives us the authoritative breakdown. This is a direct quote from Strong's concordance:

> "#166 (**aiŏnios**)—ETERNAL—does not focus on the future per se [read that again: aiŏnios *does not focus on the future*] but rather on *the quality of the age* (165/aiŏn) it relates to.
>
> Not the **future**. The **quality**.
>
> Thus believers live in 'eternal (166 /aiŏnios) life' RIGHT NOW, experiencing this QUALITY of God's life NOW as a *present possession*. (Note the Greek **present tense** of *having eternal life* in John 3:36, 5:24, 6:47; cf. Ro 6:23.)"

Strong's explicitly states that **aiŏnios—eternal—** *"does not focus on the future per se, but rather on THE QUALITY OF THE PRESENT AGE."*

It's about the **CHARACTER** of what belongs to that age. **NOT endless duration**. I repeat: CHARACTER. *Not endless duration.* Must I say that again?

Traditional theology reads eternal is 'age-long' and thinks 'endless.' That's like reading 'fun-size' candy and expecting it to be actually fun.

Think of it this way: If someone says "medieval punishment," you wouldn't assume the punishment lasts from medieval times until now. You'd understand it as punishment *characteristic of the medieval period.*

Similarly, "aiŏnios punishment" is punishment **characteristic** of the coming age. Like "medieval punishment" is characteristic of the medieval ages. Not necessarily punishment that never ends.

But there's more! We're not even close to being through. Just you wait, *just you WAIT* until you hear what **"punishment"** ACTUALLY means in the original Greek. We're talking DEFCON 1 here. It'll rattle your brain like two skeletons wrestling on a tin roof.

### Sleight of Hand

Here's where eternal conscious torment theology trips over its own shoelaces. This linguistic insight about **aiŏnios** (eternal) reveals a massive flaw. If we insist that "**eternal**" means "**never-ending duration**" for the punishment, then we're forced to make salvation primarily about **duration** rather than the **quality-of-life** that Jesus emphasizes. For instance, when Jesus talks about eternal life, he isn't obsessed with how long it lasts. He is talking about **what QUALITY of life it is**. God's life, abundant life, God's quality of life for us RIGHT NOW.

Sure, it never ends, but that's not the meaning of the word. It's like caring more about how many hours a party lasts than whether it's actually fun.

Want proof that God doesn't obsess over duration? Check out Genesis 3:22. It reveals everything about how 'forever' actually works in Hebrew.

Fair warning: this one nearly broke me. I stared at Genesis 3:22 for days, convinced it proved me wrong. The sentence doesn't even finish. God just panics and shoves Adam out of Eden. Why? When it finally clicked in my head, it became the most devastating blow to eternal torment theology I've ever found.

Picture the scene: Adam eats the forbidden fruit. His blood instantly corrupts. Evil instantaneously fuses itself with his DNA like an alien parasite that burrows into his genetic code. The fusion is **immediate**, **molecular**, and **irreversible**. Evil doesn't just influence him. It BECOMES him at the cellular level. Now he has a CORRUPTED OPERATING SYSTEM. God looks at the tree of life, then at Adam, this freshly mutated monster, and suddenly realizes what's about to happen. The Hebrew text literally breaks off mid-sentence—

*Then God bellows— [notice he doesn't even finish his thought] ... 'Lest he reach out and take from the tree of life and live **FOREVER**—'*

BOOM. The sentence stops. Abruptly. No period. God immediately grabs Adam and Eve and shoves them out of Eden like a parent yanks a kid away from a downed power line. The Hebrew DOESN'T EVEN FINISH THE SENTENCE! It's like God's yelling 'EVERYBODY OUT! NOW! MOVE!'

Now here's where you hear it again—CRACK! —that same sound of traditional theology's foundation as it splits under the weight of Hebrew it never examined. Listen to me carefully, folks…if…IF you can wrap your head around this, you've hit the mother lode:

**That English word 'FOREVER is 'olam'—and 'olam' NEVER means endless.**

Take a deep breath and let me prove this beyond any doubt. Hebrew has a specific construction for true eternality: *me-olam ad-olam* (מֵעוֹלָם עַד־עוֹלָם), meaning "from everlasting to everlasting." Search the entire Hebrew bible. This doubled construction appears in Psalms 90, 41, 103, 106, Nehemiah 9, and 1 Chronicles 16 and 29. Every single time, it refers exclusively to **God's eternal nature** or his **divine attributes**. Never once is it applied to human punishment. Not to Gehenna. Not to judgment. Not to anything created. **If the biblical authors believed punishment was truly ETERNAL, they had the vocabulary to say so. But they didn't.**

- Psalm 90:2: "From everlasting to everlasting (*me-olam ad-olam*), You are God" …that's about God

- Psalm 103:17: "The LORD's love is from everlasting to everlasting (*me-olam ad-olam*)" …that's also about God

- 1 Chronicles 16:36: "Blessed be the LORD God of Israel from everlasting to everlasting (*me-olam ad-olam*)" …again, it's about God

But Genesis 3:22 uses a SINGLE 'olam': only ONE 'olam'— 'Lest he reach out and take from the tree of life and live **FOREVER**'—one 'olam' means just 'for the age.' Same as every other supposedly 'eternal-forever' thing that expires:

- Priesthood **'forever'** (olam)—Christ ended it (Hebrews 7:11-12)

- Slaves serve **'forever'** (olam)—until Jubilee (Exodus 21:6)

- Earth's foundations **'forever'** (olam)—getting replaced (2 Peter 3:10)

- Jonah in the fish **'forever'** (olam)—three days (Jonah 2:6)

- Temple standing **'forever'** (olam)—destroyed in 70 (1 Kings 8:13)

221

Each of these uses only ONE 'olam.' Every **'forever'** in scripture that uses only ONE 'olam' EXPIRES. Like the expiration date on a carton of milk.

I must say this again lest you gloss over it, or worse allow cognitive dissonance to take ahold. **Here's the linguistic bombshell that destroys eternal torment theology:** *Every single reference to human punishment, judgment, or "eternal" consequences uses a SINGLE 'olam.' Never the doubled construction. Not once. Not ever.*

- Sodom's "eternal" fire: single 'olam'—and it's not still burning; expiration date

- "Everlasting" punishment (Daniel 12:2): single 'olam'—age-pertaining, doesn't mean never-ending; also has an expiration date

- "Forever" in Gehenna passages: single 'olam'—for that age; again, it has an expiration date

If God means *eternal conscious torment*, he has the linguistic tool available: *me-olam ad-olam.* **But he deliberately chooses NOT to use *me-olam ad-olam* for human judgment.**

That's like having a word for "infinite," but instead you choose "really long time."

A "really long time" is NOT "infinite."

### Code Red!

***So if 'olam' doesn't mean eternal, why does God hit the panic button about Adam living 'olam' (forever)?***

What I'm about to say will make the religious theologians wish my mom had just given head. That word 'olam' means 'for the age.' So then, here comes the razzle for your dazzle: **The tree of life COULD extend life thousands of years beyond God's 1000-year death-penalty limit.**

*"Whoa, Steve, could you repeat that again please?"*

*Yeah, sure.* Remember, Adam lived 930 years, within God's 1000-year timeframe. *But what would the tree of life do to Adam's lifespan?* The tree of life would keep him alive for the entire age until Christ's return, 6,000+ years. The entire AGE. NOT forever.

Remember, God later shortens human lifespan even further, from a thousand years down to one hundred twenty years (Genesis 6:3) precisely because *extended life with corrupted blood* **creates INCOMPREHENSIBLE evil**.

The pre-flood world shows what happens when corrupted humans live 900+ years. *They become so wicked that God regrets* (Hebrew: **comforts himself**) *that he created them.* So he cuts the timeline down to, at most, 120 years.

*But even that was too long.* By King David's time, Psalm 90:10 records an even shorter span: "The years of our life are seventy, or even by reason of strength eighty." Notice this appears in *the same Psalm* that defines God's thousand-year day (Psalm 90:4).

Do you see that? The chapter in the Psalm that establishes God's timeframe while it ALSO documents humanity's progressively shortened lifespan from 1000 years to 120 to 70-80. God keeps reducing human lifespan **as corruption proves more dangerous with extended years**.

Now that you see that God shortens the lifespan of man (from a thousand years down to 70 or 80, some more, some less) but ALL with less than 120.

Here's where you'll have to strap yourself into the rocket ship because we're about to launch. *Now imagine if Adam had eaten from the tree of life and lived 6,000 years with:*

- Corrupted blood with evil molecularly fused to his heart

- Tree of life sustaining that corruption for six millennia

**God springs into action to prevent Adam from becoming a 6,000-year-old demon,** much worse than the 900+ year-old antediluvians. This ogre would've made Hitler look like a choir boy.

This hypothetical scenario completely vindicates God's panic and proves 'olam' (**forever**, written only ONCE—NOT twice in a row) means *there's an end in sight EVEN IF ADAM EATS OF THE TREE OF LIFE.*

Here's where this gets terrifyingly nightmarish. If Adam had eaten from the tree of life after evil fused itself into his heart, he would have lived 'olam'—**forever**—in other words, for the rest of the age. Following biblical chronology, that age spans from the Garden of Eden to Christ's return, approximately 6,000 years. So Adam doesn't live forever without end, but 6000 years is pretty fucking bad.

### The 6000-year-old Monster

Consider this timeline of horror: For the first thousand years, the evil that festers in Adam's heart compounds exponentially. By year 2,000, cruelty is as natural as breathing. By year 3,000, his heart is so thoroughly rotted that compassion is literally impossible. The neural pathways for mercy are completely corroded away.

Then at year 4,000, this monster, wearing Adam's face, stands at Calvary, the evil in his heart resonating with the mob's hatred, leading the screams of "CRUCIFY HIM!" at the Son of God. *But it doesn't end there.*

He continues for another 2,000 years, accumulating evil even after witnessing Christ's resurrection. The corruption so entrenched that even seeing Christ rise doesn't penetrate the darkness.

Only at year 6,000, when Christ returns and "the last enemy to be destroyed is death" (1 Cor 15:26) …that's when the power of the garden's tree of life finally abdicates its power.

This masterfully proves 'olam'—forever—has a definite endpoint. If 'olam' meant never-ending, the tree of life in the garden would grant endless existence, and even Christ's return wouldn't end it. But since it's only ONE 'olam' (for the age), not 'me-olam ad-olam' (infinite duration), *Adam's tree-sustained life ends when the millennial age ends.* At 6000 years.

At that point, the tree of life in Eden becomes obsolete—REPLACED by the trees of life in Revelation 22:2, which appear AFTER evil has been completely eradicated and serve for "the healing of the nations"—*unlike the tree in the garden that **sustains the corruption**.*

But imagine if God had NOT blocked Adam from that tree. Holy shit! Picture what we would have gotten instead: The theological horror is incomprehensible: A 6,000-year-old being with evil so thoroughly fused to his heart that after sixty centuries—SIXTY CENTURIES—Adam becomes humanity's apex predator, stalking the bloodline of David through the ages, hunting for ways to corrupt the bloodline, slamming shut the door between heaven and earth before God steps through, and thus Adam strangles God's plan of redemption in the womb.

Picture this ancient sub-human abomination pulling history's strings from the shadows, orchestrating Herod's massacre, whispering in Judas's ear, his ancient fingers on every trigger that ever aimed at the Messiah. His corruption spreads like gangrene through humanity's veins, poisoning bloodlines, rotting empires from within, doing everything to contaminate the womb that would carry Christ.

For 6,000 years, Adam wages war against heaven's plan, laying siege to every prophetic bloodline, scorching the earth where the Messiah might walk. This monster, wearing Adam's face but with a soul darker than the void, stalks through history with one obsession: find the virgin, corrupt the bloodline, strangle the Christ child in his cradle.

**This is what God saw when he looked at that tree of life.**

This is why he broke into a dead sprint to yank Adam out of the garden.

This perfectly demonstrates the Hebrew distinction: **Even the tree of life COULD NOT grant** *me-olam ad-olam* (מֵעוֹלָם עַד־עוֹלָם)**.** That is true eternality.

Now watch what traditional theology does. It commits linguistic theft.

Traditional theology claims humans burn "forever and ever." **But those are the Hebrew words reserved for God alone.**

Traditional theology literally STOLE God's exclusive eternal language—'*me-olam ad-olam*'—and slapped it onto human punishment like a counterfeit designer slaps a label on a knockoff purse.

And this theft of divine language creates massive confusion about what Jesus actually means by '**eternal life.**'

### The Curtain Call

God blocked a 6,000-year monster.

Traditional theology invented an eternal one.

*Nearly all false doctrines taught today by Christians and cultists alike can be traced to the distortion of the meaning of Biblical words*

Chapter 24

# Radio Silence

Now that we've demolished the "eternal punishment" texts and seen how they actually support the opposite of what preachers say they mean, and that they actually *support* restoration for every man, woman, and child, let's examine the most damning evidence against eternal conscious torment.

*Oh, Steve, this ought to be good. What is it? What is the most damning evidence* **against eternal conscious torment?** *That torment and torture that lasts for gazillions of years?*

Are you ready for this? **JESUS' OWN EVANGELISTIC APPROACH.**

We've established that the biblical penalty for sin was *physical death within God's timeframe.* **NOT eternal torment.**

We've seen that the supposed "hell proofs" actually *describe God's restorative workshop...that operating room where God extricates evil from human nature.*

We've discovered that Augustine's translation problems, ignorant at best, intentional at worst gave us both **eternal torment** AND **inherited guilt** as false doctrines.

But the final nail in traditional theology's coffin is this: **Jesus NEVER ONCE preached what they say he preached.**

*They're writing checks Jesus never signed.*

If eternal conscious torment is real, and if avoiding it requires saying exactly the right prayer with exactly the right theology, then **Jesus Christ was the WORST EVANGELIST IN HISTORY.**

*Kind of like a building inspector who sees the gas leak and talks about the wallpaper.*

If billions of souls hang in the balance based on saying the right prayer, wouldn't the Son of God be crystal clear about this mandate? Wouldn't *every conversation about salvation* include **urgent warnings**, **precise formulas**, and **deadline reminders about ETERNAL FLAMES?**

Wouldn't Jesus say something like: *"Listen carefully, this is **the most** important thing you'll ever hear."* You listen to his words. You brace yourself as you lean into him. You listen intently to his every word: *"Unless you pray this specific prayer and accept me as your personal Savior before you die, you will burn **in conscious torment forever** with no hope of escape."* You listen unabatedly for Jesus to conclude his deadly warning: ***"Nothing else matters compared to this eternal deadline."***

But wait a minute…and folks, this here is going to blow your theological calcified mind: **Jesus never says anything remotely like that.** *Not even close.*

**Not once.**

**Not ever.**

When people came to Jesus to ask him the ultimate questions: *"What must I do to be saved?"* …and… *"What must I do to inherit eternal life?"*— his answers are *radically* alien from modern evangelical formulas.

Let's examine the examples, starting with the most damning ('damning' that is to the eternal conscious torment fanboys).

### The Rich Kid

Matthew 19:16-22, Mark 10 :17-22, Luke 18:18-23

A wealthy young man runs up to Jesus and asks the ultimate question: **"Good teacher, what must I do to inherit eternal life?"**

Well now, if eternal conscious torment is the real issue, this is Jesus' golden opportunity. Here's someone literally asking about eternal destiny.

According to modern evangelism, Jesus should scream with spittle flying and snot flowing, his voice booming through the magnificent sound system:

"ACCEPT ME AS YOUR PERSONAL LORD AND SAVIOR RIGHT NOW OR YOU WILL BURN IN HELL FOREVER! Do you understand what FOREVER means?! A trillion years from now, you won't have even STARTED your suffering! EVERY SECOND for ETERNITY, your flesh will melt off your bones while you scream for mercy that NEVER comes! Your eyeballs will boil in their sockets! Worms will devour your entrails FOREVER! Don't you DARE walk away from me, young man. This is your ONE CHANCE! Pray this prayer with me RIGHT NOW or face ETERNAL CONSCIOUS TORMENT!"

**But that's not what Jesus said.**

Instead, Jesus tells him to keep the commandments, sell his possessions, give to the poor, and follow him.

No mention of hell. No sinner's prayer. No eternal torture chamber. Jesus hammers on present obedience, social justice, and discipleship.

When the young man walks away sad, does Jesus chase after him screaming, *"Wait! You're going to burn forever!"*?

Hell no! Jesus lets him go and uses the moment to teach about *the difficulty of wealth hindering kingdom life.*

**The Devastating Implication**: If eternal conscious torment is real, Jesus just watches someone walk into eternal flames. He never even mentions the supposed danger.

*No hell warning for the rich man.*

If that's not bad enough, now watch Jesus forget to mention it to a Pharisee.

**Night Visit**

John 3:1-21

Nicodemus, a Pharisee and teacher, comes to Jesus at night. This conversation contains the most famous verse in Christianity: John 3:16. *Surely here Jesus explains the eternal torment formula, right?*

**Wrong again, Sparkle Farts.**

When Jesus tells Nicodemus he must be "born again," Nicodemus is confused. But notice Jesus' response in verse 10: *"You are Israel's teacher and do not understand these things?"*

Jesus expects a Hebrew scholar to ALREADY KNOW about being "born again" from the Old Testament. This isn't some new hell-avoidance formula. It's **spiritual renewal** and **covenant restoration** that Jesus expects Hebrew teachers *should recognize.*

The whole conversation is about experiencing God's world, letting the Spirit do his thing, and trusting that God actually loves you. That's it.

What's missing? Apparently Jesus forgets the most important part! No mention of eternal torture. No sinner's prayer formula. No urgent warnings about hell.

Does the son of God seriously just have a late-night theological discussion with a religious leader and forget to mention the eternal BBQ pit?

It's like a firefighter showing up to a burning building and forgetting to mention the fire. Like a doctor examining a patient with stage 4 cancer and only discussing their nice haircut. Like a flight attendant forgetting to mention the plane has no engines.

"Hey Jesus, you forgot the hell part!"

*"The 'what' part?"*

"The eternal conscious torment! The most important thing!"

*"Oh right, that thing I never actually teach. My bad."*

**No mention of any of these.**

## Five Husbands

Jesus encounters a Samaritan woman with a complicated past; five husbands and currently living with a man who isn't her husband. According to traditional evangelism, she's a prime candidate for the "hell avoidance" message.

But Jesus never mentions anything about hell or eternal punishment.

Instead, he offers her "living water." He talks about true worship in spirit and truth, the satisfaction that comes from knowing God, and then drops the bombshell. He's the Messiah.

That's it. No fire. No brimstone. No "you're living in sin and headed for eternal torture." Just a conversation.

The woman becomes an evangelist herself. She brings her whole town to meet Jesus. The result? Many Samaritans believe and declare Jesus "the Savior of the world."

No hell. No eternal torture warnings. No sinner's prayer. Just an invitation to experience God's kingdom now.

## The Tax Man

Luke 19:1-10

Zacchaeus, a corrupt tax collector, encounters Jesus and is transformed. He promises to give half his possessions to the poor and pay back four times what he's stolen.

Jesus' response? *"Today salvation has come to this house."*

That's it? No sinner's prayer? No "asking Jesus into your heart"?

This thieving bastard Zacchaeus, all he did was promise to stop stealing, and then to give away his money.

And Jesus calls THAT salvation?

**What Jesus DIDN'T say:** Jesus didn't lead Zacchaeus in a sinner's prayer.

He doesn't explain a hell-avoidance plan.

He doesn't mention eternal conscious torment.

What Jesus DOES say: Jesus sees *real deliverance* (that's what **"salvation"** actually means: *to deliver from **PRESENT** danger*). Jesus promises this "deliverance from present danger" to Zacchaeus as a result of his transformed behavior. As a result of Zacchaeus' obedience to **make things right**, to **care for the poor**, and to **generously give**.

### Through the Roof

Matthew 9:1-8, Mark 2:1-12, Luke 5:17-26

Friends lower a paralyzed man through a roof to reach Jesus. The man never says a word.

Never asks for anything.

Never prays any prayer.

Jesus heals him. Guess what the Greek word for "heals" is? The Greek word for **"heals"** here is σῴζω (**sozo**), *the exact same word translated as* "saved" everywhere else in the New Testament. (Including Romans 10:9,10. Look it up. I dare you.) See for yourself that your favorite salvation verse uses the exact, same, identical word as *physical healing*.

*The salvation prayer verse literally means 'get your legs fixed.'*

That's right. When Jesus heals this man's legs, the Bible says Jesus **"saves"** him. Quit trying to stick a wet noodle up a wildcat's ass. Hell, every altar call should be throwing away crutches instead of handing out salvation cards.

This is what SALVATION is. **According to the actual biblical meaning of the word**. This is what SALVATION looks like: *A paralyzed man suddenly* *walks*. Not a sinner prays a prayer. Not a person accepts Jesus into their heart. The Greek text literally says Jesus **"saves"** him by *fixing his legs*.

And my goodness, how the religious leaders were outraged! They're thoroughly pissed at Jesus. Just like the endless punishment posse will be when someone points out **"saved"** means physical deliverance. Not tickets to get to go to heaven.

Oh, and here's what else is devastating: This man was **"saved"** (σῴζω) **without praying, without believing a creed, without asking Jesus into his heart.** Nope, Jesus **"saves"** him by *healing his paralysis*.

*Every time you read "saved" in your Bible, remember it's the same word used when Jesus made paralyzed legs work again.*

By the way, when Jesus tells the paralytic, 'Your sins are **forgiven**' (Mark 2:5), he used **aphiemi. JUBILEE.** Remember JUBILEE?

Then he proves JUBILEE by healing the man's legs. The **JUBILEE** wasn't just spiritual. It was **total restoration, body** and **soul**.

We've just established that **"saved"** (**sozo**) means *physical healing*, and now we're adding that **"forgiven"** (**aphiemi**) means **JUBILEE**. This shows that both words describe **total restoration.** Not just **spiritual concepts**.

## The Forgery

Acts 8:26-40

Philip encounters an Ethiopian official reading Isaiah. After explaining the gospel, the eunuch asks, *"What prevents me from being baptized?"*

The eunuch's declaration? *"I believe that Jesus Christ is the Son of God."* (Fun fact: This entire verse was added centuries later. It's not in any early manuscripts. It's in KJV, but not in ESV, NIV, NRSV, NASB, and *most modern translations*. Turns out scribes have been adding salvation formulas since the 6th century. Like theological graffiti artists 'improving' scripture with their doctrinal spray paint. They literally **forged a confession** because Philip apparently didn't get the memo about salvation formulas.)

This is a nuclear bomb that explodes in the face of the hellfire enthusiasts. Their example of an early "confession of faith" was literally *invented by later scribes who couldn't handle a baptism story without a verbal formula.*

Another fun fact: The oldest Greek manuscripts, including the 3rd century Papyrus 45 and the 4th century Codex Sinaiticus and Vaticanus all *omit verse 37 completely,* which means it didn't exist when the early church fathers wrote about baptism. Okay, back to our regularly scheduled programming.

Philip "preached Jesus" from Isaiah, and apparently that gospel had nothing to do with hell avoidance. The conversation was about **kingdom identity**, not *punishment avoidance.* (Remember Nicodemus? Jesus expected him to already know "**born again**" from the Old Testament. Same thing here. **The gospel was already in Isaiah.**)

So if eternal conscious torment is the real issue, why doesn't Philip explain the eternal torture chamber when he "preaches Jesus"? *And why did later scribes feel compelled to* **add a confession that wasn't there**?

Maybe because even they couldn't stomach a gospel without magic words.

### The Jailer

Acts 16:25-34

After an earthquake frees Paul and Silas from prison, the terrified jailer asks the ultimate question: *"What must I do to be saved?"*

(Context: The jailer had just drawn his sword to kill himself because under Roman law, guards who lost prisoners were executed. He's asking "How do I avoid execution?" Not "How do I get to heaven?")

Paul's answer? *"Believe in the Lord Jesus, and you will be saved."* (Remember: *saved* included '**get your legs fixed**.')

The traditional damnation devotees jump on this as proof of their formula, but before you shout "gotcha," notice what actually happens:

Paul doesn't stop with "believe." He speaks the word of the Lord to the whole household. Remember "saved" (σῴζω) means *physical deliverance*. The same word used when Jesus "saved" the disciples from drowning, and don't forget it includes 'get your legs fixed.'

The jailer and his whole household get baptized. No sinner's prayer. No hell warnings. No eternal deadlines. Just present transformation and kingdom allegiance. Remember aphesis? Not "forgiveness" like a judge stamping paperwork. Release. Liberation. Freedom from captivity. The jailer locked people up for a living. Now aphesis unlocks him. The prison guard becomes the freed prisoner. That's not religion. That's a jailbreak.

### Jubilee Through Murder

Luke 23:34

But here's an even more devastating truth that *obliterates every traditional salvation formula.* As the soldiers are literally nailing Jesus to the cross, committing the most despicable crime in human history, Jesus cries out:

*"Father, forgive them, for they know not what they do."*

Jesus prayed for the forgiveness of people who did not ask for forgiveness. That's critical. People who were actively murdering the Son of God. People who were completely unaware they even needed forgiveness. People committing the worst crime in human history.

*And here's what should terrify the "burn forever" theologians:* **Is it true that every single one of Jesus' prayers got answered?** (Hint: YES.)

So then, is it true that when the Son of God prays to the father, "Forgive them" you can bet the whole kit and caboodle the answer is emphatically **"Yes!"**

What does this mean? The Roman soldiers, the Jewish leaders, everyone involved in the crucifixion **receives the forgiveness Jesus requests for them** *without praying a sinner's prayer, without accepting Jesus into their hearts, without even knowing they needed forgiveness.* They didn't ask. He gave anyway.

235

Just like the Abrahamic covenant where God puts Abraham to sleep and takes full responsibility for blessing all families of earth, Jesus takes unilateral action to *forgive without requiring human cooperation*.

*Where's the hell warning?* If eternal conscious torment is the real issue, this is the moment for Jesus to scream to his executioners, *"You're about to face eternal torture unless you repent right now!"* Instead, **he prays for their forgiveness**.

**Where was the salvation formula?** Jesus doesn't say, *"If any of you want to avoid hell, pray this prayer..."* He simply forgives them **UNILATERALLY**. *He takes the initiative himself.* **JUST LIKE GOD'S COVENANT WITH ABRAHAM. Completely one-sided. Zero human requirements**.

This demolishes every traditional evangelistic assumption. Jesus requires no prayer from the recipients. Their awareness of their need is irrelevant. He doesn't discuss "hell avoidance" during the worst crime in human history. Jesus takes the initiative to forgive, with no demand for them to initiate, no requirement that they be willing, not even a need for them to understand what he's doing.

If Jesus is willing to **forgive his own executioners without them asking**, what does that reveal about *his heart toward all humanity?* **If his approach to the WORST SINNERS IN HISTORY is immediate intercession rather than eternal damnation threats**, maybe we've completely misunderstood the gospel he came to preach.

If Jesus forgives those who murder him...**without them asking**...I repeat: WITHOUT THEM ASKING...what makes you think he refuses to forgive those who today **completely ignore him, spit on him, curse him, and flip him the middle finger.** *Ya think he forgives them without them asking?*

Oh, and just you wait a minute...I'm not done with this crucifixion scene. Not by a long shot. There's more, so much more...

Traditional theologians will desperately claim: "Jesus didn't teach 'invite me into your heart' because it wasn't possible until after his resurrection." **Are you kidding me?** If billions of souls would spend forever in agony based on a technicality whether or not they said the right words AFTER his resurrection, then Jesus would have spent **every waking moment** *preparing people* for this cosmic deadline!

Picture this scenario: If you know a nuclear bomb will detonate in three years, and the only way to survive is a specific shelter protocol that won't be available until the bomb goes off, wouldn't you spend those three years obsessively explaining exactly what the protocol will be, why it's absolutely critical, how to recognize when it becomes available, and the eternal consequences of missing it?

**But no sir, Jesus never mentions ANY of this.** No warnings about a coming prayer requirement. No urgent preparations for post-resurrection salvation formulas.

Instead, from the cross, Jesus proclaims something infinitely more powerful: *"Father, forgive them."* And as we discovered that word isn't "forgiveness" but **aphes**, from **aphesis. JUBILEE.**

Think about the magnitude of this moment. With nail-pierced hands, and while his executioners gamble for his clothes, while religious leaders mock his agony, Jesus proclaims their **COMPLETE LIBERATION**.

Not merely a pardon for their guilt while he leaves them corrupted.

**TOTAL JUBILEE.**

What is TOTAL JUBILEE? Every debt cancelled. Every chain broken. *Every corrupted heart marked for complete restoration.*

The Roman soldiers, the Jewish leaders, the mocking crowd ALL receive **JUBILEE** they never asked for, never knew they needed, never participated in securing. Yet Jesus gives it freely, UNCONDITIONALLY. No strings attached.

Just like Abraham sleeps through the covenant ceremony, these murderers are oblivious to the liberation being proclaimed over them. God takes unilateral action. Again.

237

If traditional theology is correct, Jesus is the WORST evangelist in history. He spends his final breath to proclaim JUBILEE instead of stern warnings about prayer requirements.

**The truth?** Jesus uses his last tortured breath to declare what he's always taught. God's unstoppable determination to liberate humanity. ALL of humanity, **independent of their cooperation**.

Jesus declares their JUBILEE while they (and we) still cruelly, viciously murder him. Scream obscenities at him. Curse him.

But Jesus says, "Father forgive them."

No human cooperation required.

No formula necessary. None of the "I accept Jesus" stuff.

Only one thing is on Jesus' mind...

**Aphesis** (JUBILEE)...

...from the cross.

Universal. Unilateral. **Unstoppable.**

We have turned Jesus himself into a witness AGAINST the doctrine we have attributed to him.

And thanks to God, who **FORCES** it upon man with such divine providence that it's impossible for man to fuck it up, even with his own obstinate, stubborn, determined, asinine, idiotic, stupid, obtuse refusal...

...to do what?

To accept **God's JUBILEE**.

It...

...is...

...finished.

# Chapter 25

# The Trial

## A Courtroom Drama

*The courtroom is packed tighter than a megachurch parking lot on Easter Sunday. Theologians clutch their study bibles like security blankets. Seminary professors nervously adjust their bow ties. In the gallery, curious believers lean forward, sensing they're about to witness either the theological trial of the century or the most expensive theology lesson in history.*

**BAILIFF:** *(banging gavel with the enthusiasm of someone who's waited his whole career for this moment)* All rise! The Theological **Court of Ultimate Truth** is now in session, the Honorable Judge Scripture presiding!

*JUDGE SCRIPTURE enters wearing flowing black robes and carrying a bible so massive it probably has its own zip code. He settles into his chair with the gravity of someone about to referee a heavyweight championship bout between God and tradition.*

**JUDGE SCRIPTURE:** Be seated. *(The crowd rustles like moviegoers settling in for the main feature)* We're here for *The People vs. The Doctrine of Complete Restoration.* Today we determine whether **universal restoration** is biblical truth or **theological heresy with better marketing**.

*He surveys both legal teams like a principal about to break up the academic fight of the century.*

Counselor Traditionworth, you represent 1500 years of church tradition and really impressive cathedral architecture. Advocate Truthdigger, you represent whatever linguistic bombshells you've been digging up in those ancient manuscripts.

*He adjusts his reading glasses with judicial authority.*

Counselor Traditionworth, your opening statement.

---

**PROSECUTION'S OPENING STATEMENT**

*COUNSELOR TRADITIONWORTH rises slowly. He adjusts his bow tie with the confidence of a man who's never lost a theological argument at the seminary faculty lounge. He's distinguished, silver-haired, and carries himself like someone whose systematic theology has never been systematically challenged.*

**COUNSELOR TRADITIONWORTH:** Thank you, Your Honor. Ladies and gentlemen of the jury, today I will prove that this so-called "complete restoration" doctrine is more dangerous than a shepherd leading a flock off a cliff.

*He begins pacing with practiced authority.*

For two millennia, the church has understood Jesus Christ's clear teaching about **eternal punishment**. The defendant wants you to throw away this towering monument of orthodox Christianity based on... what? Creative reinterpretations? Linguistic gymnastics?

*He stops dramatically, facing the jury.*

I will show you that **abandoning eternal conscious punishment** is *abandoning the gospel itself.* It removes the urgency from evangelism, the teeth from divine justice, and turns the Almighty into a cosmic teddy bear who can't say no to anybody.

*He gestures toward ADVOCATE TRUTHDIGGER, who sits calmly with stacks of Hebrew and Greek texts.*

Don't be fooled by fancy word studies. The Holy Spirit has preserved truth through his church for fifteen centuries. To suggest otherwise is to suggest God took a 1500-year coffee break while Augustine butchered his word.

*He returns to his seat, straightening his pocket watch like a man who's just delivered the theological equivalent of a mic drop.*

240

## DEFENSE'S OPENING STATEMENT

*ADVOCATE TRUTHDIGGER rises with the easy confidence of someone who's been digging through ancient manuscripts by candlelight and found more translation errors than a medieval monk copying manuscripts after too much communion wine. He moves toward the jury like he's about to share the theological discovery of the millennium.*

**ADVOCATE TRUTHDIGGER:** *(with a slight grin)* Your Honor, what we have here isn't a case *against* biblical truth. It's a case FOR biblical truth against centuries of theological tradition built on Augustine's inability to read the instruction manual.

*He holds up a Greek text.*

My distinguished colleague wants you to trust what humans have said about God's words for 1500 years. I want to show you what God **actually** says before *translation train wrecks*, *political manipulations*, and *theological additions* that would make a seminary dean update his LinkedIn to 'seeking new opportunities.'

*He leans on the jury rail conversationally.*

The question before this court is devastatingly simple: **What did God actually say** in Hebrew and Greek versus what *humans added later* because they can't tell the difference between a vowel and a consonant?

*His voice grows passionate.*

By the end of this trial, you'll see that complete restoration isn't dangerous innovation. It's recovery of the original Christian hope that got mugged by a guy who thought Greek was just a salad dressing option.

*He sits down. Whispers ripple through the courtroom.*

## THE PROSECUTION CASE

**COUNSELOR TRADITIONWORTH:** Your Honor, I call Dr. Pompous McTradition, who's never met a simple doctrine he couldn't complicate.

*An elderly professor approaches the witness stand in a dated suit, carrying an over-highlighted Bible.*

**BAILIFF:** Do you swear to give testimony according to your theological convictions and the Westminster Confession?

**DR. MCTRADITION:** *(placing his hand on the Bible with academic gravity)* I do, so help me God and systematic theology.

**COUNSELOR TRADITIONWORTH:** Doctor, what's your position on universal salvation?

**DR. MCTRADITION:** *(speaking with the authority of someone who's never colored outside the theological lines)* Universal salvation undermines the gospel's very essence. If everyone receives ultimate restoration regardless of their response to Christ, then evangelism becomes pointless, God's justice gets neutered, and we might as well turn churches into community centers with better music.

**COUNSELOR TRADITIONWORTH:** What about Jesus' words in Matthew 25:46?

**DR. MCTRADITION:** *(with supreme confidence)* Jesus couldn't be more clear: "These will go away into eternal punishment, but the righteous into eternal life." Same Greek word "eternal" for both. Basic grammar, really quite elementary.

**COUNSELOR TRADITIONWORTH:** No further questions.

*ADVOCATE TRUTHDIGGER approaches the witness stand, Greek New Testament in hand.*

**ADVOCATE TRUTHDIGGER:** Dr. McTradition, you've built your entire argument on the English word "**eternal**." Are you aware that the Greek word "**aiōnios**" means "**age-pertaining**," not "**endless duration**"?

**DR. MCTRADITION:** *(shifting uncomfortably)* Well, there may be some scholarly nuance, but church tradition consistently interprets it as eternal duration...

**ADVOCATE TRUTHDIGGER:** That "tradition" was primarily developed by Augustine, who couldn't read Greek. If Augustine was working from mistranslations, how reliable is that consensus?

**DR. MCTRADITION:** *(more defensive)* The Holy Spirit guided their interpretations despite linguistic limitations...

**ADVOCATE TRUTHDIGGER:** *(grinning)* So the Holy Spirit helped them reach correct conclusions while reading incorrect words? That's like saying God helped someone bake a perfect cake after they confused salt for sugar.

*He pauses for effect.*

Tell me, Doctor, can you read Greek?

**DR. MCTRADITION:** *(confidently)* Of course I can read Greek.

**ADVOCATE TRUTHDIGGER:** Then how did you miss that "**aiōnios**" means *age-pertaining* and "**kolasis**" means *corrective discipline*?

**DR. MCTRADITION:** *(defensively)* Well, we interpret within the framework of established theological tradition...

**ADVOCATE TRUTHDIGGER:** Ah, so you can read the words, but *tradition tells you what they're supposed to mean* instead of **what they actually say**? That's like being able to read a stop sign but driving through it because that's how your grandfather always did it.

*He turns to walk away, then spins back.*

Oh, one more thing. When Jesus spoke of "**punishment**," he used the Greek word "**kolasis**." *Corrective discipline.* He had another word available, "**timoria**," which means *vindictive punishment.* Why do you think the Son of God chose the word that emphasizes correction over revenge?

243

**DR. MCTRADITION:** *(deflating like a whoopee cushion during a church service)* I... the traditional understanding...

**ADVOCATE TRUTHDIGGER:** Right. The tradition based on *mistranslations by people who couldn't read the original* and then **perpetuated by those who could read Greek** but were influenced by that same tradition. No further questions.

*Dr. McTradition exits looking like a man whose systematic theology just got systematically dismantled.*

---

## THE DEFENSE CASE

**ADVOCATE TRUTHDIGGER:** Your Honor, I call the Apostle Paul to the stand.

*A bearded man in simple robes approaches with quiet authority. There's something unmistakably powerful about him. This is someone who's seen the risen Christ and lived to write about it. Murmurs ripple through the courtroom.*

**BAILIFF:** *(with obvious reverence)* Do you swear your testimony will be faithful to the words you were inspired to write?

**PAUL:** *(placing his hand on a Greek New Testament)* I do, by the grace of God who called me while I was still breathing threats against his people.

**ADVOCATE TRUTHDIGGER:** Paul, in Romans 5:18, what did you write about Christ's redemptive scope?

**PAUL:** *(speaking with conviction)* "As one trespass led to condemnation for all men, so one act of righteousness leads to justification and life for all men."

**ADVOCATE TRUTHDIGGER:** The word "all" in both cases...same Greek word?

**PAUL:** Yes, **"pantes."** I used it deliberately. Adam's reach and Christ's reach are identical in scope.

**ADVOCATE TRUTHDIGGER:** What about 1 Corinthians 15:22?

**PAUL:** *(leaning forward)* "As in Adam **all** die, so in Christ **all** will be made alive." Same word "**all**" in both clauses. The universality is intentional.

**COUNSELOR TRADITIONWORTH:** *(jumping up)* Objection! What about 2 Thessalonians: "eternal destruction"?

**PAUL:** *(turns calmly)* I used "**olethron**." *Destruction.* Not *torment.* **Destruction** has an *endpoint. Completion.* **Not endless duration.**

**ADVOCATE TRUTHDIGGER:** Paul, what's God's ultimate end goal in 1 Corinthians 15:28?

**PAUL:** *(with growing passion)* "That God may be all in all." God's presence permeates everything and everyone. No eternal realm where God is absent, no corner of creation cut off from his love.

*Murmurs ripple through the gallery.*

**ADVOCATE TRUTHDIGGER:** Thank you, Paul. I call Abraham, father of all who believe.

*An elderly man with weathered face and kind eyes approaches with the dignity of someone who's walked with God and argued with him about Sodom.*

**ADVOCATE TRUTHDIGGER:** Abraham, tell us about God's covenant in Genesis 15.

**ABRAHAM:** *(with deep reverence)* God promises that through me all families of earth would be blessed. Not some families. All families.

**ADVOCATE TRUTHDIGGER:** Describe the covenant ceremony.

**ABRAHAM:** *(closing his eyes, remembering)* I prepared the animals, cutting them in half. Normally both parties walk between the pieces, each taking responsibility. But God caused deep sleep to fall on me. While I was in that supernatural sleep, a smoking firepot and blazing torch—God's presence—passes between the pieces **alone.**

*He opens his eyes with wonder still evident.*

245

God takes all responsibility upon himself. *I couldn't mess it up because I was asleep.*

**ADVOCATE TRUTHDIGGER:** Was this covenant dependent on your performance?

**ABRAHAM:** *(shaking his head)* Not at all. God put me to sleep specifically *so I couldn't screw it up.* The covenant's fulfillment depends entirely on God's faithfulness.

**ADVOCATE TRUTHDIGGER:** "All families of earth. "How many is that?

**ABRAHAM:** *(with a knowing smile)* All of them. When God says "all," he means all. Not "all except those who didn't get the memo."

*Abraham exits with quiet dignity, leaving the courtroom with unshakeable hope.*

---

## THE STAR WITNESS

*The courtroom falls into absolute silence as a figure in simple robes approaches the witness stand. There's something unmistakably different about him…an authority that needs no introduction, a love that's almost overwhelming, and a presence that makes everyone aware of their own heartbeat.*

**ADVOCATE TRUTHDIGGER:** *(with deep respect)* Your Honor, I call Jesus Christ, the Word made flesh.

*Even Judge Scripture leans forward as Jesus is sworn in. Several people start crying without knowing why.*

**BAILIFF:** *(with obvious reverence)* Do you swear your testimony will be the truth?

**JESUS:** *(with quiet authority that fills the room)* **I am the Truth.**

*The simple statement sends chills through the courtroom.*

**ADVOCATE TRUTHDIGGER:** Jesus, when people asked about eternal life and salvation, did you ever mention eternal conscious torment as the alternative?

**JESUS:** *(shaking his head gently)* No. When the rich young ruler asked about eternal life, I told him to keep commandments, sell possessions, give to the poor, and follow me.

**COUNSELOR TRADITIONWORTH:** *(standing desperately)* But Jesus, Matthew 25:46— "eternal punishment"!

**JESUS:** *(with careful precision)* I used "**kolasis.**" **Corrective discipline.** Not *vindictive torture.* I had other Greek words available for endless torment, but I chose the word that emphasizes **restoration** over **retribution.**

*He pauses; eyes filled with love.*

And "**aiōnios**" refers to the age to come. The time of correction and healing. I never intended endless duration.

**ADVOCATE TRUTHDIGGER:** *(quietly but urgently)* Lord, here's the question that destroys their position: **If God removes evil from everyone's heart during the age of correction, how can anyone choose what they call "eternal death"?** *They won't even have that capability, will they?*

**JESUS:** *(with a smile that could melt granite)* Exactly. Once evil is separated from human nature…**once Adam's corruption is completely removed…***how can anyone choose evil?* They have no inclination, no capacity, no ability to choose it. It's like expecting someone to be thirsty after all thirst has been eliminated from their body.

*He looks directly at Counselor Traditionworth.*

The traditional position requires people to eternally choose evil *after evil has been removed from their nature*. It's like you expect someone to crave alcohol after all addiction has been purged from their system…or feel anger after all rage has been extracted from their heart.

*The courtroom erupts in whispers.*

**ADVOCATE TRUTHDIGGER:** *(with immense awe)* When you were crucified, you suffered history's worst injustice. What did you pray for your executioners?

**JESUS:** *(tears well up)* "Father, forgive them, for they know not what they do."

**ADVOCATE TRUTHDIGGER:** Did you wait for them to ask first?

**JESUS:** *(shaking his head)* No. I took initiative to forgive even those who committed history's greatest crime. Love always takes the first step. And love never gives up.

*Complete silence except for weeping.*

**ADVOCATE TRUTHDIGGER:** *(with reverence)* No further questions, Lord.

*As Jesus prepares to leave, he looks over the courtroom with infinite love.*

**JESUS:** *(to everyone present)* Don't be afraid. The father loves you more than you can imagine, and his love will never let you go. **Not ever.**

*He stands and begins walking toward the back. Suddenly, brilliant light emanates from him that grows brighter and brighter.*

**RANDOM JUROR:** *(squinting)* Where'd Jesus go?

*The light becomes blinding. When it fades, Jesus is gone.*

**SPECTATOR:** *(looking up)* Did... did he just go through the roof?

*Outside, witnesses report seeing a figure of light ascending through clouds, rising until he disappears into heaven. Thunder rumbles despite clear skies.*

**SOMEONE IN THE BACK:** *(in awe)* He went home.

*The courtroom remains stunned, the witness chair glowing faintly with residual light.*

---

## THE VERDICT

*After recess, Judge Scripture returns. The courtroom overflows, supernatural shimmer still in the air.*

**JUDGE SCRIPTURE:** *(visibly shaken)* This court has heard extraordinary testimony that forever changes theological discourse.

*He opens his massive Bible.*

After witnessing direct testimony from inspired authors themselves, and unprecedented supernatural confirmation, this court makes the following findings:

**FIRST:** The penalty for sin in Genesis was physical death within God's timeframe, not eternal torment. God clearly stated the consequence, and that consequence has been carried out for every human who has ever lived.

**SECOND:** Key Greek words have been systematically mistranslated for centuries. "**Aiōnios**" means *age-pertaining*. There is an expiration date. It's not *endless duration*. "**Kolasis**" means **corrective discipline**, not *vindictive torture*.

**THIRD:** Augustine's inability to read Hebrew and Greek **created multiple false doctrines** that have plagued Western Christianity for fifteen centuries.

**FOURTH:** Jesus Christ never preached hell-avoidance when people directly asked about salvation and eternal life. His focus was always kingdom living. *Not punishment escape.*

**FIFTH:** Most devastating of all, if God removes evil from human nature during the age of correction, **the capacity to eternally choose evil is eliminated**. Traditional theology requires a logical impossibility.

*He pauses dramatically as the courtroom holds its breath.*

**THEREFORE:** Complete restoration is not only CONSISTENT WITH BIBLICAL EVIDENCE. It has been VALIDATED by direct testimony from scripture's own authors.

*He bangs his gavel.*

**COURT RULING:** Complete restoration is DIVINELY VALIDATED. All heresy charges DISMISSED WITH SUPERNATURAL PREJUDICE.

*The courtroom erupts in cheers, tears, and awestruck silence.*

**JUDGE SCRIPTURE:** Court adjourned. **May God help us align our theology with his truth rather than our traditions.**

*As he exits, the witness chair gives one final brilliant flash before returning to normal.*

**BAILIFF:** *(unnecessarily)* All rise!

*The courtroom slowly empties, some still staring where Jesus disappeared, others texting seminary professors, all wondering if Christianity will ever be the same.*

## Chapter 26

# The Finish Line

After demolishing Augustine's translation errors…

…after exposing 1,500 years of *theological comedy*…

…after watching *Jesus' own evangelism* contradict traditional theology…

…let's see where this restoration train is actually headed.

You ready? Spoiler alert: *It's BETTER than your wildest dreams*

### The Receipts

Look at what God did.

He pronounced a penalty in the garden. Death, not torture. Dust to dust.

He stated the penalty plainly. Return to dust. Nothing more. Nothing less.

He chose b'yom (in the day you eat) instead of pith'om (immediately when you eat). A timeline that eliminates the spiritual death escape hatch.

He said WHEN you eat, not IF you eat. God didn't anticipate the Fall. He engineered it.

He fulfilled the death penalty exactly. Adam died at 930. Within a thousand-year day. No spiritual death required.

He knocked Abraham unconscious. Divine chloroform so humans can't add conditions to an unconditional covenant.

He locked ALL in disobedience SO THAT he could show mercy to ALL. Same Greek word, same sentence, no loopholes.

He called forgiveness JUBILEE. Aphesis. Total liberation. Not a judge stamping paperwork.

He made judgment mean RECOVERY. Komizomai. "Recover what was stolen." Not "receive punishment."

He chose kolasis, corrective pruning when timoria—vengeful torture—was right there on the shelf.

He built an expiration date into aiōnios. Age-pertaining, not eternal. Has an expiration date. An ending.

He documented Justinian's forgery. Added condemnations AFTER the council. Politics, not theology.

He never said "hell." Four different words. Four different meanings. One catastrophic blender.

He gave the word "hell" zero Hebrew or Greek existence. Ghost word. Running from vocabulary that ain't in the book.

He used olethros for destruction. Same word in 1 Corinthians 5:5 accomplishes SALVATION.

He designed the lake of fire to burn away meros—the corrupted portion. Not the person.

He installed basanizó—the Greek word translated "torment" that actually means "to test for purity"—to purify gold, not torture souls.

He put an "until" in the unforgiving servant's sentence. A finish line. Not an endless loop.

He said everyone salted with fire. Salt preserves and purifies. Doesn't destroy.

He panicked at the tree of life. Genesis 3:22 breaks off mid-sentence. God sprinting to prevent a 6,000-year-old monster.

He made the evil feel the extraction. The corruption writhes. The parasite screams. YOU feel liberation.

He removed the machinery itself. Not just forgiveness of sins. Elimination of sin-generating equipment.

He made sin anatomically impossible after surgery. Like expecting gills after lungs are perfected for air.

He grabs the child from traffic. Doesn't honor "free will" to let them die.

He expected Nicodemus to already know "born again." From the Old Testament. Not some new escape plan.

He told the Lazarus parable BEFORE raising actual Lazarus. Then Pharisees tried to murder the evidence. Prophecy fulfilled.

He let the rich young ruler walk away. No hell warning. No chase. No "you'll burn forever."

He gave Zacchaeus "salvation" for promising to stop stealing. No prayer. No formula.

He "saved" the paralytic by fixing his legs. Sozo. Same word as Romans 10:9.

Jesus NEVER ONCE preached what they say he preached.

He declared his endgame: ALL in ALL. Not some. Not most. ALL.

This is a God who engineered a cosmic surgical suite. An operating room designed across millennia to extract the evil fused to human hearts since Eden.

Now here's the question that demolishes traditional theology:

### The Absurdity

You think after all that work: the cross, the resurrection, the lake of fire, the meticulous extraction of corruption from every human soul...you think God lets the drunk decide if he wants the operation?

The drug addict gets veto power over the Great Physician?

The cancer gets to vote on whether it stays?

What parent would do that?

Your child is dying of a disease that's destroying their mind, hijacking their decisions, making them reject the very help that would save them, and you stand back and say, "Well, I respect your autonomy"?

You don't ask a drowning man if he'd like to be saved. You grab his collar and pull.

You strap them to the gurney, and you cut the cancer out. Because the resistance IS the disease.

## The Worst Evangelist in History

And if traditional theology were true, Jesus was the worst evangelist who ever lived.

A rich young ruler runs up: "What must I do to inherit eternal life?"

Perfect setup. Guy is ASKING how to escape eternal torture.

Jesus says: Keep the commandments. Sell your stuff. Follow me.

Not a word about hell. Not a whisper about praying a prayer to escape the flames.

But here's the monkey wrench that jams their entire machine:

Jesus told him to DO things. Works. Actions. Obedience.

Traditional theology screams "Salvation by faith alone! Not by works!"

So which is it?

Either Jesus preached works-based salvation, which destroys their "faith alone" doctrine.

Or Jesus wasn't talking about escaping hell at all, which destroys their eternal torment doctrine.

Pick your poison. Both options wreck their theology.

They can't have it both ways. You can't scream "faith alone!" on Sunday and then quote Jesus telling a man to sell everything and follow him on Monday.

Jesus wasn't giving an escape plan. He was describing kingdom living. Present tense. Here and now.

A lawyer tests him: "What shall I do to inherit eternal life?"

Jesus says: Love God. Love your neighbor. Do this and you will live.

That's it. No altar call. No sinner's prayer. No "accept me or burn forever."

If the stakes were eternal torture for billions, don't you think Jesus might have MENTIONED the escape plan?

Either Jesus was the worst communicator in history, fumbling the most important message ever delivered…or eternal conscious torment was never the message.

**So why didn't Jesus evangelize the escape plan?**

Because there's no escape plan. There's a SURGERY plan.

And nobody escapes surgery. Everybody gets it.

The cross wasn't an escape hatch. It was the operating table.

The lake of fire isn't a torture chamber. It's the recovery room where the last of the infection burns away.

The whole thing from Eden to the empty tomb to the final flames is one long surgical procedure to extract the evil that's been fused to humanity since the Fall.

And here's the part traditional theology never asks:

**The Killer Question**

What happens AFTER the surgery?

Who in their right mind would commit another act of evil, including rejecting God AFTER the machinery that generates evil has been stripped from their soul?

Think about it.

The rebellion comes from the corrupted heart. Remove the corruption. What's left to rebel?

The rejection comes from the evil fused to human nature since Eden. Incinerate the evil. What's left to reject?

The fist-shaking comes from the disease. Cure the disease. What's left to shake?

Traditional theology believes people will STILL reject God after the very thing that made them reject God is gone.

That's not theology. That's absurdity.

That's like saying a man will still crave heroin after you've removed every trace of addiction from his brain, rewired his neurons, and eliminated the memory of ever using.

Why would he? The craving WAS the disease.

The rejection of God IS the corruption.

Remove one, you remove the other.

Jesus didn't preach an escape plan because nobody needs to escape the hospital.

You just need to survive the surgery.

And everybody does.

### The Jenga Tower

But wait.

Team Torment didn't pull this out of thin air. There's a REASON the Forever Burn Brigade believes what they believe. Billions of sincere people over sixteen centuries can't ALL be idiots.

So let's give the Brimstone Bunch their day in court. Let's trace the logic. Let's see how the ECT Fan Club built their tower.

Here's how eternal conscious torment works, block by block:

**Block 1:** Adam didn't die physically the day he ate the fruit. He lived 930 years. So "death" must mean SPIRITUAL death.

**Block 2:** Spiritual death means separation from God.

**Block 3:** All humans inherit this spiritual separation from Adam. That's original sin.

**Block 4:** This inherited separation is ETERNAL. It doesn't expire.

**Block 5:** Eternal separation from God means eternal conscious torment. You're cut off from the source of all good—forever.

**Block 6:** The ONLY way to break the chain is to accept Jesus as your personal Lord and Savior. Pray the prayer. Mean it. Get baptized. Produce fruit. (Requirements vary by denomination. Check local listings. And funny thing…Jesus never actually mentioned any of this when people asked him how to be saved. But don't let that bother you.)

**Block 7:** Therefore: Pray the prayer or burn forever. No exceptions. No appeals. No parole.

That's the tower. That's the whole structure. Seven blocks stacked on top of each other, each one depending on the one below it.

Looks sturdy, right?

Now watch what happens when we pull the bottom block.

**Block 1** — the foundation the whole tower stands on says Adam didn't die physically that day, so it MUST mean spiritual death.

257

But remember *pith'om*? God had a Hebrew word for "suddenly." For "immediately." For "drop dead on the spot."

He didn't use it.

He used *b'yom*. "In the day" which allows for God's timeframe. A day to the Lord is as a thousand years.

Adam died at 930. Physical death. Right on schedule. Exactly what God said.

If God had used *pith'om*, Team Torment could claim spiritual death. Yes, then it would be a possibility. But he didn't. He chose *b'yom*. And *b'yom* eliminates the spiritual death escape hatch.

No spiritual death means no inherited eternal separation means no original sin as traditionally defined means no need for an escape plan means no eternal conscious torment.

Pull that bottom block...

And the whole tower crashes.

Block 2 has nothing to stand on. Block 3 collapses into Block 4. Blocks 5, 6, and 7 tumble into a heap of theological rubble.

Sixteen centuries of doctrine are exposed as a Jenga tower built on a block that was never there.

The Eternal Torture Fan Club didn't start with bad intentions. They started with a bad translation. And they've been stacking blocks on quicksand ever since.

### So Who's Going to Hell According to the Burn Brigade?

Remember the list?

The Hindus think the Christians are going to hell. The Christians think the Jews are going to hell. The Jews think the Christians are going to hell. The Muslims think the Christians and Jews are going to hell. The Christians think the Muslims are going to hell. The Buddhists don't believe in hell, which makes the Christians think the Buddhists are going to hell. The Mormons think pretty much everyone except Mormons is going to hell. The Baptists think the Catholics are going to hell. The Catholics used to be sure the Protestants were going to hell. And the atheists think everyone who believes in hell is delusional, which ironically puts them at the top of everyone else's hell list.

Billions of people over thousands of years, all convinced their little club has the VIP pass and everyone else burns forever.

Here's what the evidence says:

They're ALL wrong about who's going to hell.

And they're ALL getting in anyway.

The Hindus finally get off the reincarnation wheel. The Christians discover they were right about Jesus but wrong about the torture chamber. The Jews find out "chosen" meant "first in line to bless everyone else." The Muslims get their paradise. Turns out it's bigger than they thought. The Buddhists who didn't believe in hell get the last laugh. The Mormons discover there's only one heaven, and everybody's in it. The Baptists get dunked in grace instead of judgment. The Catholics find out there's no purgatory because God skips the waiting room. The Protestants finally have nothing left to protest.

And the atheists? They get the biggest surprise of all…they still get in.

Not because truth doesn't matter. Not because doctrine is irrelevant. Not because "all roads lead to God." I repeat, not because all roads lead to God!

Because God's stated goal is to be ALL in ALL.

Because the machinery that generates rejection gets incinerated in the lake of fire.

Because no one in their right mind rejects God after the rejection machinery is gone.

### The Verdict

This isn't wishful thinking.

This isn't "love wins" New Age sentimentality.

This is what happens when you ask one simple question:

Why would anyone reject God after the thing that made them reject God has been surgically removed?

They wouldn't.

They couldn't.

The resistance WAS the disease.

The fire doesn't destroy the person.

It destroys what's corrupting the person.

And when the corruption is gone…when the surgery is complete…when the dross has burned away and only gold remains…

God will be all in all.

Not some. Not most.

ALL.

### Future Brothers

Don't read this like academic theology. Grasp what this means for your actual life:

That family member who drives you crazy? Completely restored to who God created them to be. **Whether they want it or not.**

That person who hurt you deeply? The evil that motivated their actions is surgically removed, leaving the person God originally designed **even if they fight it with their last breath.**

Your ex-husband who destroyed your family? Your mother who never said "I love you"? Your childhood friend who now posts anti-Christian memes? Your teenager who rolls their eyes at prayer? Your father who died before you could reconcile? Your best friend who says religion is for weak minds? Their resistance is irrelevant. God doesn't ask permission to remove cancer.

That atheist who mocks everything you believe? That cult leader who destroyed families? That dictator who slaughtered millions? **Their resistance is irrelevant.** *God doesn't ask permission to remove cancer.*

Your own struggles with sin, addiction, and brokenness? All of it—GONE. Not managed, not forgiven and forgotten, but completely extracted like a perfectly successful surgery. **Even the parts of you that perversely cling to the disease.**

Every tragedy, every injustice, every broken heart? Not just comforted or explained away but *completely reversed and restored* to something more beautiful *than if it had never been broken.*

This isn't "pie in the sky when you die" theology. This is God's actual plot that he planned since before the foundation of the world. **And no human obstinance can derail it.**

### The Victory Parade

When God becomes "all in all," it's not just a nice way to end the story. It's the point of the ENTIRE story.

Everything broken gets fixed. **No consent required.** Every wrong gets righted. **No prayer necessary.** Every tear gets wiped away. **No acceptance form to sign.** Every enemy gets destroyed. **No cooperation requested.** Every person gets restored. **No exceptions, no opt-outs, no human veto power.** Every promise gets fulfilled **whether humanity likes it or not.**

This isn't too good to be true. It's so good it MUST be true. Because anything less would mean God's love, power, or plan ultimately fails.

*And the God revealed in Jesus Christ doesn't fail.*

The vision that emerges from careful biblical study isn't just hopeful. It's the most glorious outcome imaginable. *More beautiful than any human dream,* more just than any human court, *more loving than any human heart.*

Augustine couldn't read Hebrew, but God's plan doesn't depend on human translation skills.

Traditional theology gets stuck on eternal torture. *God never did.*

And you. Yes, YOU who yelled at your kids this morning, lied on your taxes, and still haven't called your mother back, and besides, you're a grumpy old man with a smelly butt—YOU get to be part of the greatest restoration project in the history of the universe.

So when you read what God actually says, the truth is better than any lie ever told.

Remember:

*Nearly all false doctrines taught today can be traced to the distortion of biblical words...*

*AND*

*The fire doesn't destroy the person.*
*It destroys what's corrupting the person.*

## Chapter 27

# The Trudge

FADE IN:

EXT. GARDEN OF EDEN—DAY

Sunlight filters through perfect trees. A serpent coils around a branch near the Tree of Knowledge. Eve approaches, curious.

SERPENT: (whispering) *Hath God said you shall not eat...?*

With those words, he tricks the hottest woman ever created... to *add* to God's command.

EVE: (innocently) God said we must not eat it, *neither touch it.*

FREEZE FRAME on Eve's face.

NARRATOR (V.O.): *The bitch added "neither touch it."* **God never said that.**

SMASH CUT TO:

INT. LIBRARY—NIGHT

Ancient theology books line the walls. A man, the author of the book *Hell No! The Great Heist* hunches over Greek and Hebrew texts, candlelight flickering across mistranslations and margin notes.

NARRATOR (V.O.): *Centuries later, we discover that theologians do the same bullshit additions as Eve.*

CLOSE-UP: God's words in Genesis: "You shall surely die."

PULL BACK: Centuries of theological commentary piled on top, obscuring the original text.

NARRATOR (V.O.): *God says, 'you shall surely die.' These boy-bitches added 'spiritual death' and 'eternal torment.'* **Words God never said.**

MONTAGE—THE IRONY:

Eve's hand reaching for the fruit. Theologians' hands writing "eternal conscious torment" in margins. Billions of souls terrified by sermons about hell.

NARRATOR (V.O.): *The irony is almost too perfect.*

> *Eve adds to God's command and brings monstrous corruption to billions of people.*

> *Theologians add to God's death penalty and infect those same billions with a torture chamber God never built.*

> *Both started with God's actual words. Both couldn't leave well enough alone.*

> *So what's a guy supposed to do?*

NARRATOR (V.O.): *The author of this book "Hell No! The Great Heist" puts on his Sherlock Holmes detective hat and goes to work.*

CUT TO: PRESENT DAY

*The author steps out of the ancient texts, brushes the dust off his overalls, and speaks directly to camera.*

After thirty years of study, my journey to understand God's ultimate redemption isn't primarily emotional…but existential. It began with questions I couldn't escape. And I got answers I didn't expect.

Listen, I have no problem worshiping a God who constructs an eternal torture chamber for most of humanity…if that's his plan. I don't like the idea, but I figure he's God, he's smarter than me, and I trust him. So I never allowed my bleeding-heart compassion to influence me. I accepted eternal damnation because… "God said it. I believe it. That settles it."

My questions didn't come from soft feelings. They came from hermeneutical studies that led to a discovery of Augustine's translation errors. Holy Schlitz! It was like finding out I've been reading a map upside-down.

Think about this. You sit across the table from your wife. Same room. Same language. Married thirty years. And you still completely misunderstand what she's trying to say. Same room. Same language. Same century. And we STILL botch it. Now multiply that by three languages, thirty centuries, and a dozen cultures you've never lived in. The surprise isn't that we got it wrong. The surprise would be if we got it right.

## The Question

Like Eve in the Garden, I found myself face-to-face with the question 'Hath God said?' But unlike Eve, I refused to add to God's commands. Instead, I ERASED the bullshit that theologians added.

And it was a battle! Everything in me screamed, ***"This can't be true!"*** I believed my whole life in hell, fire, and brimstone. My preacher father taught me. So did his father. That's why my trek through cognitive dissonance was a major feat of mental transformation.

My trudge reveals the difference between me, Eve, and theologians:

Eve ADDED to God's words.

Theologians ADDED to God's words.

I SUBTRACTED those vagrant violations.

My search sent me on a spiritual excavation through scripture. What did I find? Lo and behold, I discovered the early church's hope **before theologians buried it** under tons of theological debris from *mistranslations*.

The serpent's whisper to Eve: "Question what God says."

The Spirit's whisper to me: "Question what theologians *added* to what God says."

Eve bastardized God's word when she ADDED to God's command.

Augustine bastardized God's word when he ADDED to God's penalty.

Both additions bastardized the word of God. Eve's (and Adam's) bastardization *corrupted life* for billions. Augustine's *terrorized* billions.

This monumental discovery hasn't weakened my faith or made me complacent about sin. It gives me compassion *for every person that crosses my path*. I now look at others with hope rather than disdain because I know that the person whom I dismiss or look down upon is predestined to be conformed to the image of God at the final judgment. My cynical heart is transformed into one that sees people in their future glory.

Whatever questions remain (and many do) I am confident that God's plan is **more persistent than any man's stubborn resistance** to fight AGAINST God's JUBILEE.

God's JUBILEE is *more determined than any human's rejection of God.*

God's JUBILEE is **more TENACIOUS than THE HARDEST OF HEARTS.** Remember Jesus' words as he hung on the cross: "Father, forgive them….." Jesus proclaimed JUBILEE to men holding hammers, not asking permission, not even wanting forgiveness—JUBILEE—to fulfil the covenant God made with Abraham that assured God will rip the murderous evil out of his executioners' hearts, too.

From the first garden to the final frontier, from corruption to restoration, God's JUBILEE has always been the same: to reconcile all things to himself.

"I hate you, God!" scream the demoniac drug infested, evil, corrupt human beings that commit the most atrocious evil. Doesn't matter! He slams their rotten ass onto the operating table at the final judgment, and rips that shit out of their heart. They have no say in the matter. "Pipe down, asswipes!" says God with a twinkle in his eye. Just like he bitch-slapped Abraham out cold. He **deprived** him of his power to rebel.

The God revealed in Jesus Christ will never rest until he becomes **"all in all,"** until *every tear is wiped away*, **until everything broken is mended**, *until all creation sings in harmony with its Creator.*

That's a vision worth living for.

### You Can't Unknow This

Here's the thing. You've read this book. You can't unread it.

You've seen the Greek. You've seen kolasis. You've seen aiōnios. You've seen the touchstone. You've seen Augustine's confession that he couldn't read the original languages. You've watched their proof texts collapse like a house of cards in a hurricane.

You can't claim ignorance anymore.

This isn't some off-the-wall doctrine cooked up by an actor with a concordance and too much time on his hands. This is the foundation of Christianity itself. This is what the early church believed before Augustine's Latin illiteracy and Justinian's political thuggery buried it under 1,500 years of terror.

You now stand at a crossroads. And you must deal with God about what you do next.

Choose wisely.

Because here's what's at stake...

### The Power Problem

Jesus said the Pharisees made "the word of God of no effect" through their traditions. You know what that means? It means God's power got BLOCKED. Clogged pipes. Static on the line. The Pharisees had access to the same God, the same scriptures, the same promises, but their man-made additions shut down the flow.

You want to know why the American church is anemic? Why we see so little of the miraculous? Why the "power that raised Christ from the dead" seems like ancient history instead of Tuesday afternoon?

When you finally see the Father as he truly is, the power starts to flow. When you know the Healer isn't a torturer, your hands become his hands. When you believe in JUBILEE, you become a conduit for it.

The power of God is limited…BLOCKED…in direct proportion to how badly you've misrepresented his character. You want his healing to flow through your hands in these last days? You want to see the blind see and the lame walk and the captives set free?

Then STOP worshiping a deity who runs an eternal Auschwitz.

You've been handed the truth. You've seen the evidence. And now you have a choice: Cling to a doctrine erected on mistranslations, corrupt councils, and fifteen centuries of fear-based crowd control…or let it go.

One option keeps the pipes clogged.

The other one opens the floodgates.

### Now What?

If God's going to fix everybody instead of roasting them forever like s'mores, we can chill out, stop terrorizing people into heaven, and enjoy the ride. *I used to get impatient and annoyed with people.* Now I see future masterpieces that await their restoration at the final judgment.

And it's not just how I see others. It's how I see myself. We can face our own failures and the brokenness around us not with despair but with confident hope, knowing that God's surgical love removes every trace of corruption from our hearts.

We can eagerly and readily worship a God whose love never fails, whose plan makes our theologies look like crayon drawings, and whose final word over every life is not **"depart from me"** … it's **"welcome home."** The same words spoken by the father to his prodigal son after his rebellious wild days of wine, women, and pissing away daddy's money.

But it's not just for the prodigal son. It's for every person that traditional theology damns to hell.

Same rebellion.

Same father.

Same "welcome home."

Forget Augustine's nightmare theology. It's just a bad translation of a beautiful dream. The real God doesn't run a torture chamber—

He runs a restoration project.

# EPILOGUE:
# Your Move

I didn't set out to become a theological troublemaker. Well…maybe a little.

All my life I accepted what I was taught about eternal conscious torment, inherited guilt, and the narrow scope of salvation. I figured if billions of Christians across two millennia believed these doctrines, who was I to question them? And besides, it's easier to nod along with established theology than to spend years digging through Hebrew and Greek texts only to discover that some of Christianity's most foundational teachings are built on shifting sands of scriptural mistranslations.

But here I am.

After decades of careful study, difficult questions, and relentless digs through dusty books, I've reached conclusions that will undoubtedly make scholars, pastors, and the entire body of Christ melt their collective brain cells like a botched lobotomy. I discovered a pattern of **systematic mistranslation** that has shaped Western Christianity for over 1,500 years. **The implications are staggering**. Not just for academic theology, but for millions of believers and how they understand God's character, human nature, and the ultimate destiny of creation.

I hope I'm right about God's plan to restore all humanity. The alternative—*that most of God's children will suffer conscious torment forever*—is horrific to contemplate.

Paradoxically, it's much easier for me not to rock the boat. It's easier to be wrong. It's more comfortable to retreat into traditional interpretations, to apologize for causing waves, and to let sleeping theological dogs lie...but *Hell*

271

*No! The Great Heist* is the path I choose: *To challenge doctrines that have been settled for centuries.*

**That's why I offer this invitation to challenge me!**

I welcome all takers. Nothing would make me happier than for superior scholarship to demolish me. I'll update my book title to *Hell YES! I Was Wrong!* and spend the rest of my days teaching Sunday School using only the King James Version.

If I've made errors in my linguistic analysis, if I've misunderstood historical contexts, if I've drawn faulty conclusions from biblical texts, then please…SHOW ME WHERE I'VE GONE WRONG.

But I have one NON-NEGOTIABLE requirement:

*Prove me wrong using the same rigorous methodology I have employed throughout this book.*

Here's what this means:

Work from the original Hebrew and Greek texts. Not English translations. Don't quote the King James Version or the NIV and assume this settles the matter. Show me what the Hebrew and Greek *actually* say. Not what centuries of translators *think* they say.

Examine the historical development of these doctrines honestly. *Don't just appeal to tradition or church authority.*

Trace these teachings back to their sources.

Acknowledge when and how they developed.

Be willing to admit when political factors or philosophical assumptions influenced theological conclusions.

LET SCRIPTURE INTERPRET SCRIPTURE. Don't force difficult passages to conform to systematic theology. If clear texts seem to contradict traditional interpretations, follow the clear texts rather than protect theological constructs.

Address the specific arguments I've raised. *Don't dismiss my conclusions with general appeals to orthodoxy or accusations of liberalism.*

Engage with my linguistic evidence.

Refute my historical research.

*Show me where my biblical exegesis fails.*

*Abandon preconceived theological notions.* Approach these texts as if you're reading them for the first time. Don't let what you've always believed determine what you allow the bible to say.

I'm NOT asking you to outright agree with me. I'll kick your ass if you do. In fact, I'm BEGGING you to prove me wrong, but do so with the *intellectual rigor* that these eternal questions deserve. The stakes are too high for theological laziness.

Listen:

If eternal conscious torment is true...

...if most of humanity *suffers forever*...

...if God's love ultimately *fails for the majority of his children*...

...then you must support these doctrines with the **solid defense**. Not appeals to tradition and accusations of heresy.

But you'd better damn well be able to prove your position, lest I adorn you in the shameful cloak of Proverbs 30:6: "Do not ADD to his words, or he will rebuke you and prove you a liar."

Therefore, it's not a matter of "well, it's better to be safe than sorry, and besides, what could it hurt to say a sinner's prayer..."

You'd better make sure you're right. Just like I'd better make sure I'm right.

It's simple: Either I'm wrong and a liar, or you're wrong and YOU are the liar.

There's no in-between!

*Whee, ain't this fun?!?*

But seriously: this is a solemn invitation, and at the same time, a challenge.

This invitation extends to every scholar, pastor, theologian, seminary professor, and bible teacher who reads this book. It also extends to every thoughtful believer in the body of Christ who cares deeply about the truth, the whole truth, and nothing but the truth. I've spent years in the original languages. I've wrestled with these texts. I've followed the evidence wherever it leads, *even when it leads to conclusions I never expected to reach.*

Now it's your turn.

If I'm wrong, show me. Prove me wrong. I'll be the first to shout it from the mountaintops, "I WAS WRONG!"

*But show me with Hebrew and Greek. Not with mistranslations.*

Show me with careful historical analysis. Not with appeals to what "the church has always taught."

Show me with biblical exegesis, not with systematic theology that's built on faulty foundations.

*People deserve better than unexamined assumptions.*

God's people deserve to know what scripture actually teaches about his ultimate plan for creation. And if that plan is more hopeful, more comprehensive, and more glorious than we've been told…well, wouldn't that be good news worth examination?

I await your response.

Not your outrage.

Not your accusations.

Not your appeals to authority…

…but your scholarship.

*Prove me wrong* with the same care I've used to reach these conclusions, and I'll be the first to thank you for it.

The invitation stands open.

Your move.


## YOU MADE IT. NOW ARM YOURSELF.

You just read 280 pages of original-language evidence that dismantles eternal conscious torment. You've seen the Greek. You've seen the Hebrew. You've watched their proof texts collapse.

But you can't carry this whole book into every conversation. So I built you a weapon.

The Sweet 16—every critical Greek and Hebrew word from this book on one printable page. The English mistranslation, the original word, what it actually means, and why it blows up their argument.

Here's what you do:

1. Go to ShittyToHappy.com/sweet16

2. Enter your email address

3. Hit the button

4. The Sweet 16 downloads instantly. No password, no nonsense

That's all I need from you—your email. In return you get the single most dangerous page in biblical scholarship sitting in your Bible, ready to deploy.

I'll also keep you in the loop on The 2030 Prophecy, upcoming podcast appearances, and new content I don't post on social media.

ShittyToHappy.com/sweet16

Your move.

# About The Author

This book is the most daunting undertaking of my life, more than any other of my endeavors including acting in television and film, public speaking on stages around the United States and Canada, music performance in Florida State University night clubs, bars, and fraternities, to music and acting performances in a 10,000-member mega church in Los Angeles...more so than the beautiful marriage God gave me as a gift that I destroyed because of my wild dick, more so than raising two beautiful successful Godly kids...more than anything.

Over the last forty-five years my acting roles include starring in a television series with Michelle Pfeiffer called *B.A.D. Cats,* I played Daisy Duke's boyfriend on *Dukes of Hazzard,* and I appeared in the hit film *Jesus Revolution.* I've spoken on stages all over the United States and spent decades in the seminar business where I learned the art of Socratic questioning—the same method I use throughout this book to dismantle 1,500 years of theological tradition one Greek word at a time.

But the real journey started over thirty years ago when I began studying Hebrew and Greek under Dr. Roy Blizzard, one of the foremost scholars of biblical languages in the United States. What I discovered in those original texts made my jaw hit the floor. The God I'd been taught to fear as a cosmic torturer turned out to be a divine surgeon. And the "eternal torment" I'd swallowed my whole life turned out to be built on the linguistic equivalent of a house of cards.

I'm not a seminary graduate. I'm a SAG actor with a Greek lexicon, a Hebrew concordance, and over 1,000 hours of original language research who refuses to let theologians tell me what God said when I can read what God said for myself.

If that makes the religious establishment nervous, good. It should.

You can visit me at ShittyToHappy.com

To contact the author, send an email to: info@ShittyToHappy.com

# Also by Steve Hanks

If *Hell No! The Great Heist* ripped the evil out of your theology, wait until you see what happens when you rip the evil out of your Monday morning.

My book *Shitty to Happy in 21 Minutes: THE SECRET KINGDOM* reveals an accidental discovery that smacked me hard in the face back in 1983—a ridiculously simple method to force-feed peace and happiness into your heart. This method is so powerfully overwhelming that even if for some strange reason you didn't want to be happy, it matters not. When you employ it, your body and heart have no other choice but to follow you on the path to happiness.

Also available: *Shitty to Happy in 21 Minutes: THE EVIL QUEEN* (volume two) and *Shitty to Happy in 21 Minutes: THE GREAT INVASION* (volume three)—the greatest climax of love, joy, and peace you could ever imagine. It is the infestation of God's kingdom on this earth.

Grab a brown bag lunch, a change of clothes, and a bottle of wine. We're going on an adventure.

We ride at dawn.

You can find all my books on Amazon.

### info@ShittyToHappy.com

www.ingramcontent.com/pod-product-compliance
Lightning Source LLC
Chambersburg PA
CBHW070025100426
42740CB00013B/2595